BURT FRANKLIN: RESEARCH & SOURCE WORKS SERIES 595
American Classics in History & Social Science 157

THE CORRESPONDENCE AND PUBLIC PAPERS

OF

JOHN JAY

VOL. III.

1782–1793

THE CORRESPONDENCE AND PUBLIC PAPERS

OF

JOHN JAY

FIRST CHIEF-JUSTICE OF THE UNITED STATES, MEMBER AND PRESIDENT OF THE
CONTINENTAL CONGRESS, MINISTER TO SPAIN, MEMBER OF COMMISSION
TO NEGOTIATE TREATY OF INDEPENDENCE, ENVOY TO GREAT
BRITAIN, GOVERNOR OF NEW YORK, ETC.

1782-1793

EDITED BY

HENRY P. JOHNSTON, A.M.

VOL. III

BURT FRANKLIN
NEW YORK

Published by LENOX HILL Pub. & Dist. Co. (Burt Franklin)
235 East 44th St., New York, N.Y. 10017
Originally Published: 1890
Reprinted: 1970
Printed in the U.S.A.

S.B.N.: 8337-18479
Library of Congress Card Catalog No.: 73-140983
Burt Franklin: Research and Source Works Series 595
American Classics in History and Social Science 157

Reprinted from the original edition in the University of Illinois
Library at Urbana.

CONTENTS OF VOLUME III.

CORRESPONDENCE AND PUBLIC PAPERS

OF

JOHN JAY.

LADY JULIANA PENN[1] TO JAY.

SPRING GARDEN, LONDON,
Nov. 23, 1782.

SIR:

You will be surprised that I take the liberty of addressing
you on my affairs ; but the general character of your benevolence, still more confirm'd to me by a friend of mine now
in the house with me, encourages me to claim your protection and assistance in recovering my rights and those of an
unfortunate family. They never had or could have done
any thing to offend the State which has hitherto treated
them with rigor. But that rigor I trust may cease through
your kind interposition. I therefore conjure you, Sir, in
the present Settlement of Affairs to interest yourself with
that goodness and philanthrophy which you are known to
possess in so eminent a degree, in the restoring us to our
just dues, and to that happiness and prosperity, which the
descendants of William Penn have reason to expect, and
cannot fail to experience if you will undertake their cause.
Certain that you will not refuse me your protection, I
already subscribe myself, Sir,

> Your Excellency's
> Much obliged and Obedient humble Servant,
> > JULIANA PENN.

---

[1] William Penn's daughter-in-law. The greater part of the proprietary estates
of the family had been confiscated during the Revolution by the State of Pennsylvania, and the descendants were now seeking to recover them.

ROBERT R. LIVINGSTON TO JAY.

PHILADELPHIA, November 23d, 1782.

DEAR SIR:

I have before me your letters of the 25th and 28th of June. I congratulate you on your safe arrival at Paris, where I venture to hope your residence will on many accounts be more agreeable than it was at Madrid. Nothing can be more pleasing to us than your determination to write very frequently, since I am sorry to say, that we have not yet been favored with such minute information on many points of importance, as we have reason to expect. Both Dr. Franklin and yourself dwell so much in generals in your last letters, that had it not been for a private letter of the Marquis to me, Congress would have remained ignorant of points, which they have thought sufficiently important to make them the foundation of those resolutions, which are herewith transmitted to you.

You need be under no apprehensions, that Commissioners from the Court of Great Britain will be allowed to negotiate with Congress; their sentiments on this subject are sufficiently manifested in the resolutions, that are sent to you and Dr. Franklin with this. And the case of Mr. Burgess, which you will find in one of the papers of last week, and in my letter to Dr. Franklin, will afford you some evidence of the extreme caution of particular States on this head.

That in the mass of our people, there is a great number, who though resolved on independence, prefer an alliance with England to one with France, must be a mere speculative opinion, which can be reduced to no kind of certainty. If we form our judgment from acts of government, we would suppose that no such sentiment prevailed; they all speak a different language. If from the declarations of individuals, we must entertain the same opinion, since independence and the alliance with France, connect themselves so closely together, that we never speak of them separately. The mass of the people here are not so ignorant of the common principles of policy as to prefer an alliance with a nation whose recent pretensions, and whose vicinity renders them mutual enemies, to that of a Prince who has no claims upon them, and no territory in their neighborhood, at least till the principles of his government shall be changed, and he gives evident proofs of the want of justice and moderation.

I think it unnecessary to repeat to you what I have already written to Dr. Franklin, presuming that you communicate with freedom to each other. Mr. Jefferson will afford, I dare say, a very acceptable aid to your commission ; I have not yet learned from him whether he will take the duties upon him.

Mr. Barlow, a poet of New England, has requested me to transmit you his proposals for printing, by subscription, a poem of which he is the author. I can give no character of the work, but what you will get from the specimen enclosed, which is all I have seen of it. The enclosed resolution informs you of Mr. Boudinot's advancement to the Presidentship. For other intelligence I refer you to my letter to Dr. Franklin, and the papers that accompany this.

I am, Dear Sir, &c.

ROBERT R. LIVINGSTON.

JAY TO LADY JULIANA PENN.

PARIS, 4th December, 1782.

I shall always be exceedingly happy, my Lady, in every opportunity of confirming the favourable opinion with which your Ladyship and the amiable friend to whom I believe you allude, have been impressed. The misfortunes incident to war are always to be regretted, and humanity will not cease to sympathize with those, on either side, who, without deserving, have experienced its rigors. It gives me pleasure to inform your Ladyship that, according to the preliminaries agreed to between Great Britain and America, Congress will recommend in a very benevolent manner to the reconsideration of the different States the measures they have taken against certain individuals. The nature of our government rendered every other mode of revising those cases improper, and as some persons might have much, others little, and many no reason to complain, it was the most eligible and obvious method of ascertaining the merits of each. There is also reason to expect that whatever undue degrees of severity may have been infused into our laws, by a merciless war and a strong sense of injuries, will yield to the influence of those gentler emotions which the mild and cheerful season of peace and tranquillity must naturally excite.

Your Ladyship will therefore see the necessity, as well as propriety, of applying after the war to the Legislature of Pennsylvania, for a reconsideration of the act respecting your family. For my part I believe that justice will be done to all, and I hope that clemency and reconciliation will be refused only to the faithless and the cruel. The same magnanimity which has distinguished the conduct of America in times of danger and distress will doubtless enable her to receive prosperity with dignity and gratitude, and to use it with moderation and philanthropy.

I have the honour to be, with perfect respect,

Your Ladyship's most obedient and most humble servant,   JOHN JAY.

STEPHEN SAYRE TO JAY.

BORDEAUX, 10th Dec^{r.}, 1782.

. SIR:

I did myself the honor of writing to your Excellency by the last post, requesting the favor of bearing the Preliminaries of Peace to Congress, since which we have assurances that they are absolutely signed. If so it is my duty to inform you that the ship *Minerva*, Cap^{n.} Hallet, now in this port, will be ready to sail for Philadelphia before my despatches can arrive ; but as she is freighted by Mr. Brush and myself, she waits your Excellency's orders.

If, however, she carries no public papers, we hope you will not delay to furnish us such certificates, relative to Peace, as may enable her to depart instantly under the advantages of peace. I should presume you will find it a good opportunity of sending duplicates. Please to address your answer under cover to Messrs. V. P. French & Nephew here. I should have wrote to Mr. Franklin also, but suppose he would not immediately reply. Our particular circumstances require an answer, and I hope you will suppose it of some consequence, and do us that favor.

I am most respectfully your Excellency's
Most obedient and humble servant,
STEPHEN SAYRE.

JAY TO ROBERT R. LIVINGSTON.

PARIS, December 12, 1782.

DEAR SIR :

I have already written a long letter to you by this vessel, and should have continued the details of our subsequent proceedings, had my health admitted of the necessary application.

You will receive from us a joint letter with a copy

of the preliminaries.   I shall therefore omit making any remarks on them.

Before I left Spain, and by letters since my arrival here, I desired Mr. Carmichael to make out and transmit the public accounts.   Our negotiations with that Court are at a stand.   The Count d'Aranda either has not, or does not choose to show me a commission to treat.   He is exceedingly civil and frequent visits pass between us.

It gives me pleasure to inform you that perfect unanimity has hitherto prevailed among your Commissioners here ; and I do not recollect that since we began to negotiate with Mr. Oswald there has been the least division or opposition between us.   Mr. Adams was particularly useful respecting the eastern boundary, and Dr. Franklin's firmness and exertions on the subject of the tories did us much service.   I enclose herewith a copy of a letter he wrote about that matter to Mr. Oswald.   It had much weight and is written with a degree of acuteness and spirit seldom to be met with in persons of his age.

I have the honour to be, with great regard and esteem, dear sir, etc.

JOHN JAY.

JAY TO ROBERT R. LIVINGSTON.

PARIS, 14th December, 1782.

DEAR SIR :

From our preliminaries and the King's speech, the present disposition and system of the British Court may, in my opinion, be collected.   Although particular circumstances constrained them to yield us more than perhaps they wished, I still think they meant to make (what they thought would really be) a satisfactory peace with us. In the continuance of this disposition and system too much confidence ought not to be placed, for disappointed violence and mortified ambition are certainly dangerous foundations to build implicit confidence upon ; but I cannot forbear thinking that we ought not, in the common phrase, to throw cold water upon it by improper exultation, extravagant demands, or illiberal publications ; should such a temper appear, it would be wise to discountenance it. It is our policy to be independent in the most extensive sense, and to observe a proper distance towards all nations, minding our own business, and not interfering with, or being influenced by, the views of any, further than they may respect us.

Some of my colleagues flatter themselves with the probability of obtaining compensation for damages. I have no objections to a further trial, but I confess I doubt its success, for Britain has no money to spare, and will think the confiscations should settle that account, for they do not expect that retribution will be made to all.

Our affairs have a very promising aspect, and a little prudence will secure us all that we can reasonably expect. The boundaries between the States should be immediately settled, and all causes of discord between them removed. It would be imprudent to disband the army while a foreign one remains in the country ; and it would be equally unwise to permit

Americans to spill the blood of our friends, in the islands, for in all of them there are many who wish us well. The sale of the continental lands would, if properly regulated and appropriated to that purpose, form a fund on which we might borrow money, especially if foreigners could see good reason to rely on our good faith, which, by being in certain instances violated, has lost much of its credit. I allude particularly to the interest on loan-office certificates, and the publications in our papers on that subject, which do us harm in Europe. Adieu.

I am, dear Robert, your friend,

JOHN JAY.

JAY TO STEPHEN SAYRE.

PARIS, 15th December, 1782.

SIR :

I have been favoured with your letter of the 10th inst., and also with the one mentioned in it.

Preliminary articles for a peace are agreed upon between Britain and America, but at present the two countries are as much at war as ever ; for America neither ought nor is disposed to make a separate peace.

It is not possible therefore to send you the certificates you desire, nor is it necessary for you to detain your vessels for our despatches, more early opportunities having offered and been embraced. We are nevertheless much obliged to you for this mark of attention.

I am, sir,

Your most humble and obedient servant,

JOHN JAY.

EXTRACT FROM JAY'S DIARY.[1]

22d December, 1782.—Between 7 and 8 o'clock this morning I visited Mr. Oswald. After some general conversation he took occasion to say that Lord Mount Stuart, the son of Lord Bute, had dined with him to-day, and that he had also seen his brother Col. Stuart, who had served the whole war in America. He spoke of the Colonel's aversion to the American war, and the account he gave of the want of discipline and the disorder which prevailed in the British army there. He passed several encomiums on the Colonel's character; sometimes of the father and then of the son's, observing how unlike they were to what the father was supposed to be; though for his part he believed that more sins were laid on his back than he had ever committed. He said that Lord Mount Stuart execrated the American war, and had shown him to-day several letters written by him at Turin (where he was Ambassador) to Lord Hillsborough on that subject. Mr. Oswald asked me if I remembered what he had told me of Mr. Pultney's information about the propositions of Count Vergennes, to divide America with Britain. I told him I did. "Well," says he, "the same kind of proposition was made to Lord Mount Stuart. His lordship brought with him here to dinner his letter-book, which he did not choose to leave with his *charge d'affaires*, and in which he showed me his letters written with his own hand, (for he would not confide it to his secretary) to Lord Hillsborough; and the first letter was dated in the

---

[1] See Extracts under date June 23 and October 21, 1782.

month of September, 1780; from which it appears
that a Mr. Malley, who had formerly travelled with
Lord Mount Stuart, and is an honorary professor at
Geneva, and is employed to write the history of Hesse,
etc., for which he receives annuities ; a man, in short,
well known among men of letters, was employed by
Mr. Neckar to make overtures to Lord Mount Stuart,
about putting an end to the war, by dividing America between Britain and France, the latter to have the
eastern part.

Mr. Oswald also says that Lord Mount Stuart went
to Geneva on the occasion, where he conversed with
Mr. Malley, and that his lordship read to him out of his
letter-book French letters from this Mr. Malley to his
lordship on the subject, after his return to Turin ; that
this correspondence contains a very curious and particular account of French intrigues, particularly that
Neckar wished for peace, because his system could
only raise money enough to provide for old arrears
and for current expenses ; and were he obliged to
sustain the expenses of the war, he must break in
upon it, and perhaps be disgraced ; it also mentioned
the intrigues to get De Sartine out of the marine
department ; and Mr. Oswald says that the overtures
about America were conducted with a variety of precautions for secrecy, and with a stipulation or condition that both parties, in case they did not agree,
should be at liberty to deny all that passed. He told
me that my lord wrote strongly to Lord Hillsborough
against the American war, and that the latter in
answer told him it was a subject out of his line, and

with which it was not proper for him to interfere. Lord Mount Stuart was offended with the minister for this, and he brought his letter-book with him to Mr. Oswald to show him the full state of the matter. Mr. Oswald said, that as he had told me the affair of Mr. Pultney, he could not forbear mentioning this also, for it was a little strange that so extraordinary a matter should come so circumstantial and correspondent from such different and unconnected quarters. He desired me to consider this communication as very confidential, adding that he could say more, but that it would not be proper for him at present to enter into a detail of further particulars.

MARQUIS DE LAFAYETTE TO JAY.

CADIZ, December the 26th, 1782.

DEAR SIR:

My letters to Dr. Franklin have hitherto acquainted you with every thing that related to me. I have been with the army as far as Cape St. Mary, and then I came in a frigate to this port. On my way I have despatched a vessel to General Washington, and have communicated particulars of our situation as well as proposals for Military Operations.

The convoy I came with is coming in. A good number of French and Spanish ships are getting ready. The French division at Gibraltar is going to embark, so that we intend to sail with a powerful reinforcement.

On my arrival at this place, I have been told that our American preliminaries are agreed upon for which I heartily rejoice with you . . . but it becomes necessary to go on with Military Operations. I very much hope they will be successful.

In the first moments I saw Count d'Estaing. He asked for my opinion upon the present political situation of our affairs. It appears that the Spanish Court, and Count de Montmorin himself wanted him to take those —— [?] My answer was that America had made treaties and would stand by them ; that her Steadiness was equal to her Spirit, but that unless they give Money, no efforts could be expected. Upon this Money affair I was very urging. Count d'Estaing has wrote a private letter which is to be laid before the Spanish Court. I have wrote one to Carmichael by post which is to be opened by Count de Florida Blanca. I have so far Conquered my hatred to Count O'Reilly as to speak freely with him upon this matter. I do not expect much from the Attempt, but as no American plenipotentiary was committed, as limits and every political idea was out of the way, I have thought there was nothing improper in seizing the present Opportunity to tempt them into an offer to send us Money from the Havanna. I do not believe it will succeed but there is no harm in the trial.

You will greatly oblige me, my dear Sir, to keep me Acquainted with every thing that is interesting to America. My heart is in it you know, and your Communications will be very welcome. I live with Mr. Hamilton and am very happy in his Acquaintance, but your letters had better be sent to M^de. de Lafayette with a particular recommendation.

Be pleased to remember me most Affectionately to Mr. Franklin, Mr. Adams, and Mr. Laurens, and let them know any thing in this letter that appears worth Communicating. My Best Compliments wait upon Doctor Bancroft. I request, my dear Sir, you will be so kind as to present my best respects to Mrs. Jay and to receive the hearty assurance of the high and affectionate regard I have the Honor to be with,

Dear Sir, your obedient humble servant,

LAFAYETTE.

ROBERT MORRIS TO JAY.

PHILADELPHIA, January 3rd, 1783.

DEAR SIR:

You have not heard from me so often as you had a right to expect. I lament, but cannot help it. Constant employment puts it out of my power to do many things I wish to do, and that of writing to my friends is among the number. My private letters, however, cannot be of much consequence, and you must accept the will for the deed.

I cannot take time at present to enter on any political discussions, but you must allow me to declare my perfect satisfaction in and approbation of your conduct in Europe. All who have had the opportunity of knowing what it has been are struck with admiration at your patience under difficulties, and your firmness in rising superior to them. Go on, my friend; you deserve and will receive the gratitude of your country. History will hand down your plaudits to posterity. The men of the present day, who are generally least grateful to their contemporaries esteem it an honour to be of your acquaintance.

I am sorry to hear that M^rs. Jay and yourself have been indisposed, but I hope you are recovered, and partaking the enjoyments of this season with the gay, sprightly inhabitants of Versailles and Paris. My best wishes ever attend you.

Your friend Gouverneur writes you political letters, but as he tells you nothing of himself, it is just that I tell you how industrious, how useful he is; his talents and abilities, you know; they are all faithfully and disinterestedly applied to the service of his country. I could do nothing without him, and our quiet labours do but just keep the wheels in motion.

With sincere attachment, I am, my dear sir,

Your friend and humble servant,

ROBERT MORRIS.

ROBERT R. LIVINGSTON TO JAY.

PHILADELPHIA, January 4th, 1783.

DEAR SIR :

I have before me your despatches of the 4th and 18th of September last, and the 13th of October. It gives me much uneasiness to find by them, that your health is not yet confirmed, particularly as the extreme shortness of your letters, compared with the importance of the matter, gives me reason to fear, that it has suffered more than you would have us believe.

I am under some anxiety relative to the fate of your letter of the 18th September, as only the duplicate copy has arrived, and I find by that you have risked it without a cypher. Should it get to improper hands, it might be attended with disagreeable consequences.

It is of so much importance, that both you and we should judge rightly of the designs of the Court, to whom we have intrusted such extensive powers, that I most earnestly wish you had enlarged on the reasons which have induced you to form the opinion you intimate ; an opinion, which, if well founded, must render your negotiations extremely painful, and the issue of them very uncertain. If on the other hand, it should have been taken up too hastily, it is to be feared, that in defiance of all that prudence and self-possession, for which you are happily distinguished, it will discover itself in a reserve and want of confidence, which may afford hopes to our artful antagonist of exciting jealousies between us and our friends. I so sincerely wish that your conjectures on this head may not be well founded, that I am led to hope you carry your suspicions too far, and the more so as Dr. Franklin, to whom I dare say you have communicated them freely, does not (as you say) agree in sentiment with you. But I pretend not to judge, since I have not the advantage of seeing from the same ground. Perhaps some light may be thrown upon the subject by such facts as I have been able to collect here, and with which it is impossible you should be acquainted.

The policy you suppose to influence the measures of France, can only be founded in a distrust, which I persuade myself she can hardly entertain of those who have put their dearest interest into her hands. She is too well informed of the state of this country, to believe there is the least reason to suppose, that we could have the most distant idea of a separate peace. If such distrust really exists, it would, in my opinion, dictate to them, to let Great Britain acknowledge our independence at once, rather than make it the subject of subsequent negotiation. When satisfied on that point, we can with more advantage contend for those our allies have at heart. Whereas by withholding it, and making it the price of concessions on the part of France, which she may not choose to make, an opportunity would be afforded to embroil and incline us to listen to separate proposals. Upon this principle, France seems to have acted in all the answers, which she has hitherto given, as well to the direct proposals of great Britain as to those made by the imperial Courts. When Mr. Grenville proposed to treat of the independence of the United States with his Most Christian Majesty, an opportunity was afforded to take the lead in the negotiation, and to suspend that part of it; yet we find the reply of the Court of Versailles led to a direct negotiation between Great Britain and us, and ended in the offer of unconditional independence. The reply of the Court of France to that of London, communicated to Mr. Grenville on the 21st of June, speaks the same language.

From these and the following facts you will, when you have compared them with those within your own knowledge, draw your inferences with more judgment than I can pretend to do without those you possess.

Before your letters were received, the Chevalier de la

Luzerne showed me a letter from the Count de Vergennes of the 14th of August, in which he speaks of Mr. Grenville's commission, and the ground it gave him to hope, that negotiations would open an express and unconditional acknowledgment of independence. He mentions the change in the British administration; their assurances, that it should occasion no alteration in the plan of their negotiation, and concludes, by expressing his surprise at the alteration, which afterwards took place in this essential article in the propositions offered by Mr. Fitzherbert, and infers from thence, that Lord Shelburne had no other design than to divide and deceive. In a letter of the 7th of September, he mentions Mr. Oswald's commission, your objections to it, and his doubts of the manner in which these objections will be received. " If," says he, " Mr. Oswald is right in his conjecture, that they will be favorably received and removed, then everything *is said*. If they reject them, because they will not begin where they propose to end, I conceive the negotiations should still go on. We may judge of the intentions of the Court of London by their first propositions. If they have independence for their basis, we may proceed; *if not, we must break off*." In his letter of the 14th of October, he mentions with great apparent satisfaction, the alterations in Mr. Oswald's commission. From the general tenor of these letters, I can discover nothing but an anxious desire for peace, which might very naturally lead him to wish that objections, which he did not conceive essential in the first instance, after having declared to Great Britain that no peace could be made till our independence was acknowledged, should not break off a negotiation which must end in the attainment of an object, which they have as much at heart as we.

Whatever the sentiments of the Count de Vergennes may be, as to the claim of Spain, in a letter which I have seen, he treats them as well as ours, as chimerical and extravagant, and declares, that he does not mean to interfere in them. You can best judge of the sincerity of this declaration. If insincere, I cannot conceive for what purpose it was made, or the subject treated so lightly, or why this should be confided to me. For my own part, I believe their situation with respect to Spain is very delicate, and that they are embarrassed by her demands. I mention these things, that you may, by comparing them with facts within your reach, draw useful inferences from them, and I wish to give you everything that may *possibly* be of use to you.

As to the letter of Marbois, I am by no means surprised at it, since he always endeavored to persuade us that our claim to the fisheries was not well founded. Yet one thing is very remarkable, and I hope evinces the determination of France to serve us on this point. The advice given to discourage the hope is certainly judicious, and yet we find no steps taken in consequence of it. On the contrary, we have been repeatedly told in formal communications since that period, "that the King would do every thing for us that circumstances will admit, and that nothing but dire necessity shall induce him to relinquish any of the objects we have at heart, and that he does not imagine that such necessity will exist." This communication was made on the 21st of last November, from letters of the 7th of September, *previous to our* success at Yorktown, and has been renewed at different periods since. You will undoubtedly avail yourself of this engagement if necessary. Congress relying upon it, have made no alteration in their instructions since the change in their affairs, by the blow the enemy received at Yorktown.

This letter of Marbois, and the conduct of the Court of France, evince the difference between a great politician and a little one. France can, by prohibiting the importation of fish, supply herself; she cannot do more. Our exclusion from the fishery, would only be beneficial to England. The enmity it would excite, the disputes it would give rise to, would, in the course of a few years, obliterate the memory of the favors we have received. England, by sacrificing a part of her fisheries, and protecting us in the enjoyment of them, would render herself necessary to us, our friendship would be transferred to her, and France would in the end be considered as a natural enemy. I am persuaded, she has wisdom enough to see it in its true light.

I know not how far the Marquis may deserve your confidence; you are the best judge of his conduct. I ought, however, in justice to him to mention, that he has steadily, in all his letters, recommended an adherence to our claims, and assured us that both might be obtained if insisted upon.

You see, Sir, I have purposely leaned to the opposite side from that which you appear in some measure to have taken; not because I think you *are* wrong in the opinion you have adopted, but because you *may possibly* be so. Such essential injuries may flow from the slightest jealousies, that I wish you to examine yours with all the coolness you are master of. I am persuaded, the last hope of Britain is founded on the distrusts they may sow among their enemies. I wish you had in a private letter in cypher informed me how you got at the letter of Marbois, and why it was copied in English. I more particularly wish to know whether it passed through the hands of either of the British Commissioners. If it has, it will be of some consequence to see the original, not that I doubt its authenticity, but it may possibly have undergone some alterations. That which follows what is said of the great bank is nonsense, or if it conveys any meaning, I think it is not such as a man of common sense would speak.

Count de Vergennes, in his letters dated a day later than yours, gives no account of your propositions. I should conclude from the circumstance, that they had not been communicated. If I were not convinced, that acting under the instructions you do, you would not withhold them, except for the most weighty reasons, and that if such reasons existed you would have assigned them in your letters, and presuming, therefore, that you had communicated them, I have made no secret of them to the Count de la Luzerne, who appeared much pleased with them, though a little surprised at the article, which relates to commerce, which I cannot suppose perfectly agreeable to them in all its extent ; since it will render a revolution necessary in the commercial system of France, if they wish to have an extensive trade with us. I am extremely pleased, that in freeing ourselves, we have a prospect of unfettering the consciences and the commerce of the world.

We are far from regretting that the Marquis d'Aranda has no powers to treat. We think, with you, that it is time to adopt the Spanish system. We may treat at any time with more advantage than at present. You have received your instructions on this subject before you wrote your last letters. By your saying nothing of them, I suppose you had not decyphered them. Mr. Jefferson being the bearer of this, it is unnecessary to enlarge. News and general politics will be contained in my letter to Dr. Franklin, to whom I also send an instruction on the subject of your commercial proposition. I enclose you a new cypher, which I pray you to make use of. You will find it very easy on a little practice. I must again entreat you to write more fully to us. I have received *from the Count de Vergennes' letters*, the whole progress of the negotiation. Information of this kind it would give me more pleasure to receive through another channel.

I have the honor to be, Dear Sir, with great respect and esteem, &c.

ROBERT R. LIVINGSTON.

JAY TO MRS. JAY.

My Dear Sally :   Rouen, 9th January, 1783.

It is pleasant to observe the goodness of Providence in having made our duty and our happiness consist in the same acts. My attentions to you are stimulated by both these motives, and receive an additional inducement from the reflection that they are never uninteresting.

We arrived here last evening. The country between this and Paris appears to be fertile and well cultivated, and afforded us some agreeable views, notwithstanding the dull drizzling weather which accompanied us almost the whole of the way. Notwithstanding that unfavourable circumstance, I find myself rather better than when I left you ; for I have more appetite and less pain in the breast than usual : as to sleep I still continue a stranger to it ; though were it not necessary to health, I should not regret the loss of it.

As my principal object in this excursion is exercise, we shall set out for Havre on Saturday morning, where I shall stay only a day or two, and then return here. I am told there will probably be much commerce between that port and America. For that reason, I wish to take this opportunity of acquiring some further information respecting it than I now have. In case I should be soon wanted (which I don't think very probable), let me instantly know it. A letter under cover to Mr. Holker, at this place, will be carefully delivered. Remember me to our friends ; kiss our dear little girl for me, and believe me to be,

Your affectionate,   John Jay.

MRS. JAY TO JAY.

PARIS, 11th Jany. 1783.

MY DEAR MR. JAY:

A Mr. Johnston from Virginia who has business to transact with you will be the bearer of this letter.   You 'll readily believe that I am happy in having an opportunity of
informing you of the health and welfare of the family.   The
little girl is in charming spirits, the servants conduct themselves with propriety, and nothing seems wanting to com-
pleat my felicity but a line from you assuring me that my
predictions have already been verified by the advantages
you have derived from your journey.

On Wednesday evening Lady Juliana Penn, her daughter, and grandaughter, her son, Mr. R. Penn, and Mr. Baker
arrived in Paris, and yesterday they were so polite as to call
upon me.

Lady Juliana and Mr. R. Penn were so obliging as to
regret with warmth your absence, and expressed a great
desire of seeing you.   I think their company will be an
agreeable addition to our society.

Mrs. Ridley and her family drank tea with me last Thursday evening.   I have sent her a card to let her know of this
opportunity.   Please present my compliments to Mr. Ridley.

Miss Kitty Walpole desires me to assure you that if you
don't return soon, she shall be in despair : all your friends
express their impatience for your return.   I alone am content to endure your absence until you find a real change in
your health and I flatter myself length of time will not be
necessary for that.

This morning Mr. Laurens and his son set out for London ; the gout increases so much upon the old gentleman
that he is desirous of making another experiment upon the
waters of Bath.

I have not seen Peter since your departure, but expect
that pleasure to-morrow : the things that were sent from
Nantz I 've received.

Mr. R. Penn tells me that Charleston is certainly evacuated.   Intelligence is received at court (as 't is said) that the French troops were embarked for the Islands, and it is generally believed that that measure was taken in consequence of the British troops having first left the continent. I believe there are no late arrivals from America; but if any thing new does occur, you may be assured it will give me pleasure to communicate it to you.

May you my dearest Mr. Jay be ever encircled with blessings and may you never cease to think that one, which entitles me to subscribe myself

Your ever affectionate wife,

SARAH JAY.

MRS. JAY TO JAY.

PARIS, 17ᵗʰ Janʸ·, 1783.

MY DEAR MR. JAY,

I had just sent for paper and etc. to write to you when your letter of the 13ᵗʰ Janʸ· was handed me.   I hope before this you have received mine by Mr. Johnston, who persisted in his resolution of following you, tho' I told him that you would probably have left Rouen before he would arrive there.   You have my thanks, my dear, for both your kind letters.   I am sorry that your health has received so little benefit as yet from your journey : my hopes of service was so very sanguine that that consideration almost banished the dread of separation.   My disappointment will even exceed my former hopes if your absence is not compensated for by additional health.   I believe your sleep and mine have fled together, perhaps to drown the cares of some less happy persons, for my waking hours are not painful ones.

Mrs. Ridley, her cousin and son drank tea with me last evening.   She is not well, but as the cause of her illness is a natural one there is less reason to regret it.

Yesterday at 3 o'clock Mr. Whitfield waited upon me to desire me to inform you that a fine bay horse of Lord

Mount Stuart's which you have seen (but not the unsound one) is to be disposed of at present for 40 Guineas with saddle and bridle, and for 36 Guineas without. Mr. Whitfield wishes to know as soon as possible whether you would choose to make the purchase. Did I tell you Mr. Oswald was going to England? He went last Wednesday afternoon calling upon me for my commands and requesting to be remembered to you. I've received a letter for you from the Marquis de la Fayette, who is at Cadiz, but am ignorant whether you would wish to have it forwarded. The expectations of a peace seem to be again revived but on what grounds I can't tell. I suppose you have heard that Captn Hill has brought some prizes into L'Orient and left a few American Privateers amidst a fleet of Merchantmen consisting of twenty sail and without a convoy, so that it is supposed that they will have their choice. The family are all very well and the servants conduct themselves to a *charm.* Our neighbours are very friendly and we pass our time very sociably *ensemble.*

Maria runs about in a kind of go-cart and continues as fond of me as ever. Adieu my dear Mr. Jay, believe me to be most affectionately yours,

SARAH JAY.

JAY TO MRS. JAY.

ROUEN, 18th January, 1783.

MY DEAR SALLY:

A little letter I wrote you this morning contained a promise of another by to-morrow's post, and to perform it I am now retired to my room. I fear your expectations respecting the speedy recovery of my health are too sanguine. As I lost it by almost imperceptible degrees the restoration of it will doubtless be gradual, and I shall think myself happy if I regain it on these terms. If my endeavours succeed, I shall be grateful ; if not, I shall be resigned. I hope you will always consider these matters in their true points of view, and not permit vain hopes or causeless fears to distress either you or me. The more easy and happy you are the more I shall be so also, and consequently the better prospects we shall both have of future health. I am better than when I left you, though not much. The weather has been and still is very unfavourable, but it must change soon, and, thank God, it cannot change for the worse.

If the letter from the Marquis came by the post— that is, if there are post-marks on the cover, send it to me ; if not, keep it till I return ; and observe the same rule as to all other letters you may receive for me.

This town is daily amused with contradictory reports respecting peace ; they are anxious about it, and with reason, for the uncertainty of its taking place holds commerce suspended and injures the mercantile interest greatly. I am pleased with this city and the people of it ; they are industrious and hospitable. Their manufactures are very considerable and very proper for our country, with whom they will certainly have a great trade, unless it be fettered and embarrassed with superfluous regulations and ill-judged restrictions. I suspect the trade of this country stands in need of revision very generally. Kiss our little girl for me, and believe me to be, my dear Sally,

Your very affectionate husband,

JOHN JAY.

JAY TO THE MARQUIS DE LAFAYETTE.

ROUEN, 19th January, 1783.

DEAR SIR :

Accept my thanks for your obliging letter of the 26th December last, which the Marchioness was so kind as to send me yesterday. I congratulate you on your safe arrival at Cadiz, and you have my best wishes that the same good-fortune you have hitherto experienced may continue to attend you.

The state of my health making a change of air and exercise advisable, I left Paris ten days ago on an excursion into Normandy. Hence, I suppose, it has happened that I have neither heard of nor seen your letters to Dr. Franklin.

If I am not mistaken, a copy of the American preliminaries has been sent to Spain ; and I flatter myself that Count de Montmorin will think them perfectly consistent with our engagements to our allies. It appears to me singular that any doubts should be entertained of American good faith; for as it has been tried, and remains inviolate, they cannot easily be explained on principles honourable to those who entertain them. America has so often repeated and reiterated her professions and assurances of regard to the treaty alluded to, that I hope she will not impair her dignity by making any more of them ; but leave the continued uprightness of her conduct to inspire that confidence which it seems she does not yet possess, although she has always merited.

Our warmest acknowledgments are due to you for the zeal you manifest to serve America at all times and in all places ; but, sir, I have little expectation that your plan of a Spanish loan will succeed. I confess that I am far from being anxious about it. In my opinion, America can with no propriety accept favours from Spain.

My absence from Paris has deprived me of the means of information, and therefore I cannot at present gratify either your wishes or my own on that head. God knows whether or not we shall have peace. A variety of contradictory reports daily reach me, but they deserve little credit. It is again said that Charleston is evacuated—that may be. It is also said the enemy have left New York ; but I adhere to my former opinion, and do not believe a word of it. Mrs. Jay writes me that Mr. Oswald is gone to London, but for what purpose I am ignorant. Thus, my dear sir, are we held in a state of suspense, which nothing but time can remove. I purpose to return next week to Paris, and shall then write to you again. Adieu.

I am, with perfect respect and esteem, Dear sir,
Your most obedient servant,
JOHN JAY.

MRS. JAY TO JAY.

PARIS, 21st Jan^y., 1783.

MY DEAR MR. JAY :

Immediately upon the receipt of your letter of the 18th, I sent to request the favor of Mr. Whitford's company a few minutes and communicated to him your sentiments of the horse. He promised to mount him and give me his opinion after the trial, but as the signing the preliminary articles yesterday was an interesting event, he seemed himself too much agitated to execute his intention. This instant Mr. Whitford has left me, he called upon me booted and spurred for the experiment, but as it is already past twelve I fear I shall not have an answer for you before the post leaves Paris.

My spirits are quite exhausted, for tho' I have in some measure been prepared to expect the welcome tidings, I never was so overcome with joy. At first my spirits were only elevated as upon ordinary pleasing occasions but that was succeeded by such lively emotions of gratitude and wonder that my sensations would have been too painful to support had I not been releived by a very plentiful effusion of tears. I long my dear to embrace you now as well as a deliverer of our Country as an affectionate and tender husband.

Mrs. Ridley has been so good as to send me word that she will spend the day with me and as I expect her every minute I hope you will excuse this scrawl. My compliments to Mr. Ridley and congratulations to you both.

I am, my dear,

Yours affectionately,

SARAH JAY.

THE MARQUIS DE LAFAYETTE TO JAY.

MADRID, February the 15th, 1783.

DEAR SIR :

I am happy in this private Opportunity to write to you, and have long wanted safe means to do it confidentialy ; the same reason, I suppose, has prevented my hearing from you to this moment. But as I am just Arrived in Madrid, and the gentleman who carries this is just setting out I shall only write a few lines.

My feelings on the occasion of a general peace are better known to you than I could express them. They are Consistent with my zeal for our Cause and my love to America, and more I cannot say.

On my leaving Paris I had hopes of our plans. On my arriving at Cadiz, I found they had succeeded beyond my expectations. Nay, besides the more Advantageous Coöperation with America, particulars of which I will relate, I had some Hopes that [more] might be got for [from?] that people. Upon this I wrote to M^r. Carmichael. I had the honor to give you an Account of my Conduct and ideas on the Occasion, but your answer has not come to Hand.

Upon the prospect of a peace, I had a letter from M^r. Carmichael wherein he entreats my Advice upon his future conduct. He had no letters from Paris. My advice being asked for, I gave it in a letter, a Copy of which I enclose, and send it by post for the perusal of the Court of Spain and probably of the Court of Versailles with Spanish Corrections upon it.

I am told Del Campo on his journey to Paris is instructed to settle Matters with you, and I wish it may be upon a popular footing.

I had determined upon going to America, but had a letter from M^r. Carmichael wherein he entreats My coming to Madrid, and says I may be useful in reasoning with this Ministry. I gave up my favourite plan, and contenting myself with sending a letter to Congress, I have posted off to Madrid where now I am, and had only a short Conference with the French Ambassador, and another with M^r. Carmichael whose ideas I am happy to find coincide with mine on the line we ought to follow. In the few days I remain here I would wish 1st to induce this Ministry to give Del Campo liberal instructions ; 2dly to see that the American Charge d'Affaires be officially received ; 3dly to advise their proposing to you a loan of Money. My expectations are very small, but I have been invited here. The little I can do I must exert to the utmost. Whatever disposition I find them in, I will hasten to Paris, and give you every intelligence I can collect. I look upon Myself as your political Aide de Camp; if I may any how serve America, I am Happy and satisfied.

At all events, when my advice is asked for, No Court, no Country, no Consideration can induce me to advise a thing that is not consistent with the dignity of the United States.

By the Month of June I intend taking up again my plan of a voyage to America. Untill that time I have nothing to do, and towards the first of March, I will offer myself to you with Spanish intelligences, and a great zeal to do any thing that may serve the public.

I beg my best respects to be presented to your Colleagues. I do not write to them, and in this letter they may see what you think worth Communicating. My Most respectful compliments wait upon M^rs. Jay. I have hardly time enough left to write a line to M^de. de Lafayette, and in great haste inscribe Myself

    Most Respectfully and Affectionately Yours,

         LAFAYETTE.

M^r. Littlepage having been pleased to come into my family for the expedition I have advised him to go with me on My journey to Paris. His voyage to America is but little [longer] ; and it may prove Agreeable to him to know the best part of France.

JAY TO SILAS DEANE.

         PARIS, 22d February, 1783.

SIR:

Your letter of the 10th inst. was delivered to me a few days ago.

The reason to which you ascribe my not having answered the other you wrote me was the true one, viz., that it was unnecessary.

The time has been, when my writing to you would not have depended on such a circumstance, for you are not mistaken in supposing that I was once your friend. I really was, and should still have been so, had you not advised Americans to desert that independence which they had pledged to each other their lives, their fortunes, and their *sacred honour* to support.

The charges against you of peculation undoubtedly called for strict and speedy inquiry ; but I expected that you would make a satisfactory defence against them. I hope so still.

I will write to Congress about your accounts as you desire. Justice certainly demands that they should be liquidated and settled.

Dr. Bancroft, some time ago, asked my opinion as to your going to England. I told him it would be imprudent, but not that " it would be taken ill." To my knowledge, you were and are suspected of being in the British interest. Such a step would have strengthened that suspicion, and at that interesting period would have countenanced harsh conjectures as to the motives and objects of your journey, which, for my part, I could not divine. Perhaps the suspicion I mention is new to you ; if so, the information is important.

Before this will come to your hands, and you could afterward get to London, the above-mentioned objections will be weakened ; and as circumstances press your going it is probable you will venture. Let me advise you to be prudent, and to be cautious what company you keep and what conversation you hold in that country.

I write thus plainly and fully, because I still indulge an idea that your head may have been more to blame than your heart, and that in some melancholy desponding hour, the disorder of your nerves infected your opinions and your pen.   God grant that this may prove to have been the case, and that I may yet have reason to resume my former opinion, that you were a valuable, a virtuous, and a patriotic man.   Whenever this may happen, I will, with great and sincere satisfaction, again become

Your friend,

JOHN JAY.

PHILIP V. B. LIVINGSTON TO JAY.

NICE, 22d February, 1783.

MY DEAR SIR,

I most heartily congratulate you on the Preliminary Articles of a General Peace being signed, and I hope that the public concerns of your Country will not in future require so much of your attention and application to business as to be prejudicial to your health, which I am convinced was the case when I was at Paris, and that you will have sufficient leizure to make little excursions into the Country to take the advantage of air & exercise, and perfectly re-establish your own health and that of Mrs. Jay.

By the printed Articles of the Preliminaries I observe that Great Britain has stipulated with America for the free navigation of the River Mississippi, and I suppose both Britain and America have done the same with Spain; but our American territory which begins at the 31st. degree of North Latitude is so high up that River, that it will be almost impracticable for any Sea Vessels to get there against the strong Current of the Mississippi. If America could extend her line from the 31st. degree of lattitude to the Southward thro' the middle of the River Mississippi to its confluence with the Bay of Mexico, and obtain from Spain a strip of Land if only 20 or 30 miles to the Eastward of the River, together with the Island of New Orleans, it would be an invaluable acquisition ; but without such an extension or some landing place on the Island of Orleans upon the Banks of the River, (provided it was only two miles square for a port to establish a Custom House, and build Ware Houses upon) all our valuable possessions, if the States establish Settlements in that Western Country, will experience the greatest difficulties in receiving their Supplies and exporting their Commerce. I beg your pardon for mentioning what you are undoubtedly well acquainted with but I am so strong an advocate for that Country that I could not refrain from making this observation.

After I left you at Paris M^r· Curzon and myself determined to go first to Geneva, where we staid a few days, and then came thro Lyons, down to Marseilles, at which place I remained untill the beginning of this month, when I came here.— My purpose in coming has been fully answered with respect to the fine, temperate Climate which I have found to the Southward ; but nevertheless I have not enjoyed so much health as I expected for it has been interrupted by frequent Colds, and these brought on some returns of an old complaint in my Stomach.

I am not determined whether I shall go on from hence farther into Italy, or whether I shall return in the spring to Paris, but I hope that I shall have the pleasure of meeting with you and Mrs. Jay in perfect health somewhere in the course of the Summer. Give my affectionate Love to her. I have taken the liberty to inclose a letter for my father which I shall be much obliged to you to forward by the first opportunity. I am with great regard & esteem

Your obliged and obedient Servt·

PH: LIVINGSTON.

JAY TO GOVERNOR WILLIAM GREENE.

SIR :
                                    PARIS, 4th March, 1783.

The letter which your Excellency did me the honour to write on the 26th December last was lately delivered to me by President Wheelock.

It has long been my opinion that virtue, knowledge, and arms were the great objects on which the attention of America should be constantly fixed. The two first are essential to the preservation of our liberty and union, and without the latter the duration of peace with other nations will be always precarious. I esteem it therefore to be a duty, particularly incumbent on Americans, to promote the interest of learning throughout the whole Confederacy; and I shall be happy to render service to any of the seminaries whenever it may be in my power.

But independent of these considerations, your Excellency's recommendation would have insured my attention and good offices to Mr. Wheelock; for on this and every other occasion it will give me pleasure to manifest the sentiments of respect and esteem with which I have the honour to be, your Excellency's most obedient and very humble servant,

JOHN JAY.

JAY TO ROBERT MORRIS.

DEAR SIR :
                                    PARIS, 10th March, 1783.

You will receive this letter from the hand of Mr. Penn, whom I take the liberty of recommending to your friendly offices and attention. Lady Juliana has for some time past been with her family in the city, and we have reason to wish they may stay here at least as long as we do. Mr. R. Penn and Mr. Baker came over at the same time, but returned soon afterwards ; the former has thought of paying you a visit.

The manner in which Mr. Penn's family has been affected by the American Revolution need not be explained to you. I am not a Pennsylvanian, and therefore forbear discussing that subject. I will only observe that I have no reason to believe that the family have done us injury, and that I wish the ultimate decision of your Commonwealth may leave them no just cause to complain.

As this young gentleman is going among strangers, and under circumstances which demand much discretion and circumspection, it gives me pleasure to recommend him to a gentleman who possesses both, and whose advice is always dictated by prudence and integrity.

Be pleased to present my best compliments to Mrs. Morris, and believe me to be, with sincere regard and esteem, dear sir, your obedient and very humble servant,   JOHN JAY.

JAY TO BENJAMIN VAUGHAN.

DEAR SIR :   PARIS, 28th March, 1783.

Whence came the idea, that the moment a minister loses a question in Parliament he must be displaced ? That kings should adopt such a maxim is not very unnatural, but that a free Parliament should think an influential dictator over *them* necessary to the government of the kingdom, seems rather a new opinion. Perhaps it arose gradually from the practices of the Court and the decay of public virtue during the last hundred years.

So far as the peace respects France and America, I am persuaded it was wise in Britain to conclude it. The cessions to France are not, in my opinion, extravagant; and the terms settled with America, by removing all causes of future variance, certainly lead to conciliation and friendship.

It appears to me that the discussion of this subject might have been more ample and satisfactory. Why was not Parliament told of our offers as to commerce, and the mutual navigation of the American waters? The word *reciprocity* would not then have been deemed so nugatory.

We have received particular instructions on the business of commerce, and Mr. Fitzherbert has been informed of our readiness to add to the provisional treaty an article for opening and regulating the trade between us on principles as liberal and reciprocal as you please. What more can be said or done? Mr. Pitt's bill was a good one, a wise one, and one that will forever do honour to the extent and policy of his views, and to those of the administration under whose auspices it was formed. For my own part, however, I think that America need not be exceedingly anxious about the matter; for it will be in our power to derive, from a navigation act of our own, full as many advantages as we should lose by the restrictions of your laws.

The objections drawn from your treaties with Russia, etc., appear to me weak, and have been answered ; but why not give them similar terms, on similar conditions ? They furnish you with raw materials chiefly, and you them with manufactures only. The gain, therefore, must be yours. With respect to carriage and navigation, they stand in a very different predicament from us.

As to the tories who have received damage from us, why so much noise about *them*, and so little said or thought of whigs, who have suffered ten times as much from these same tories, not to mention the desolations of an unjust and licentious war.

We forget our sufferings, and even agree to recommend to favour a set of men of whom very few would consider the having their deserts in the light of a blessing. How does reciprocity stand in this account ?

Some, it seems, think that New York should be retained as a rod to drive us on in this business of the tories. Strange that the idea of driving us should still be entertained. I pledge myself to you that, should such a design be adopted and become apparent, the refugees will get nothing, and the progress of reconciliation will be as slow as the warmest Gallican could wish.

I hear there is to be a Congress here ; that is, that Britain and France have requested the two imperial Courts to send mediatorial ambassadors here for the purpose of being witnesses to the execution of the definitive treaties,—a very important errand, no doubt, and very complimentary to those sovereigns. Is it probable that a Congress should be called for that poor, single, simple purpose? Why your Court agreed to it is hard to conceive.

I have written to my countrymen, that Lord Shelburne's system respecting them appeared to me to be liberal and conciliatory, but that his hesitations about *avowing* the acknowledgment of our independence, discouraged extensive confidence without further facts. I always think it best to be candid and explicit. I hope we shall soon be in the full possession of our country and of peace, and as we expect to have no further cause of quarrel with Great Britain, we can have no inducement to wish or to do her injury ; on the contrary, we may become as sensible to her future good offices as we have been to her former evil ones. A little good-natured wisdom often does more in politics than much slippery craft. By the former, the French acquired the esteem and gratitude of America, and by the latter, their minister is impairing it.

Thus I have written you a hasty letter. Since the receipt of yours until this moment I have been promising myself the pleasure of paying you a visit. I now find it probable that I shall be detained here some time longer.

Mrs. Jay charges me to say civil things to you. You are a favourite of hers, and deserve to be so of everybody. Our little girl is well, and when able to speak shall be taught to send you her compliments. I shall reply to certain parts of your letter in my next; at present I am pressed for time. I must not, however, forget my worthy friend, Mr. Oswald. He deserves well of his country, and posterity will not only approve, but commend his conduct. Assure him of my esteem and attachment, and believe me to be, with the best wishes for the health and happiness of Mrs. Vaughan and your little daughter, Dear sir,

Your sincere and affectionate friend,

JOHN JAY.

JAY TO ROBERT R. LIVINGSTON.

DEAR SIR :   PARIS, April 7, 1783.

After the preliminaries had been settled and ratified, the Spanish Ambassador informed me that his Court was ready to receive me, not only in form, but " très honnêtement." He *then* expected full instructions relative to the proposed treaty.

The Marquis de Lafayette, in his journey through Madrid, manifested great zeal to serve us there. A copy of a letter from him to the Minister will be sent you by another opportunity, though I imagine he has already forwarded it.

On the 29th ult. the Spanish Ambassador communicated to me the desire of his Court that I would return to Madrid and there complete the treaty, for that, in their opinion, it ought to be concluded either at *Madrid* or Philadelphia.

You will have this communication at large in another letter.

No Ministry yet in England, nor any news of Barney, nor from you, since the 3d of January.

The definitive treaties must be concluded and the heats of summer abated, before either my business here or the very delicate state of my health will admit of a journey to Spain. Be assured of my esteem and regard. I am, dear sir, etc.,

JOHN JAY.

JAY TO ROBERT MORRIS.

DEAR SIR: PARIS, 8th April, 1783.

Permit me to introduce to you a gentleman who is going to help you to pay taxes, and to participate in the liberties which render them necessary, viz., Mr. Joshua Grigley. Mr. B. Vaughan writes me that this gentleman has considerable property, which you know will qualify him for the first, and that he has also much virtue and merit, which will enable him to sustain, as well as to enjoy, the latter. Thus you see he will be an addition to our collective property and respectability, and consequently comes naturally within your two departments of financier and patriot. But you have also another department to which I must take the liberty of recommending this gentleman. He is a friend of Mr. Vaughan—he is a gentleman—he is a stranger—he is young. I know you too well to enlarge, or to add any thing except an assurance with which I could, with as little hesitation, conclude my days as my letter, viz., that I am, with great esteem and affectionate regard,

Dear sir, your friend and servant,

JOHN JAY.

THOMAS JEFFERSON TO JAY.

DEAR SIR :   PHILADELPHIA, April 11th, 1783.

In a letter which I did myself the honour of writing you
by the Chevalier De Chastellux I informed you of my being
at this place with an intention of joining you in Paris; but
the uncommon vigilance of the enemy's cruisers, immediately after the departure of the French fleet, deterred every
vessel from attempting to go out. The arrival of the preliminaries soon after showed the impropriety of my proceeding, and I am just now setting out on my return to
Virginia. I cannot, however, take my departure without
paying to yourself and your worthy colleagues my homage
for the good work you have completed for us, and congratu-
lating you on the singular happiness of having borne so
distinguished a part both in the earliest and latest transactions of this revolution. The terms obtained for us are
indeed great, and are so deemed by your countrymen, a few
ill-designing debtors excepted. I am in hopes you will
continue at some one of the European courts most agreeable
to yourself, that we may still have the benefits of your talents.[1] Accept my warmest wishes for your happiness, and be
assured of the sincerity with which I have the honour to be,

Dear sir,

Your most obedient and humble servant,

TH. JEFFERSON,

---

[1] "The hope expressed in this letter, that Mr. Jay would continue at one of
the European Courts, was likewise entertained by Congress, who on the 1st of
May appointed him, in conjunction with Mr. Adams and Dr. Franklin, a
commissioner to negotiate a treaty of commerce with Great Britain.

"He had, however, already formed the determination to return as soon as duty
would permit to his native country. The court of Spain, probably regretting
the opportunity she had lost of forming a connection with the new States before
the acknowledgment of their independence, was now desirous to repair the
error she had committed, and accordingly invited Mr. Jay to Madrid, to renew
his negotiations. This invitation he did not feel himself at liberty to decline,
and on the 22d April he expressed his intentions to that effect to the Secretary
of Foreign Affairs.

JAY TO ROBERT R. LIVINGSTON.

PARIS, April 11, 1783.

DEAR SIR :

I wrote you a short letter on the seventh instant. Certain intelligence has since arrived from England, that the Duke of Portland is First Lord of the Treasury, Mr. Fox and Lord North Secretaries of State, and Lord John Cavendish Chancellor of the Exchequer. It is also said, that Lord Stormont is President of the Council, and the Duke of Manchester Ambassador to Versailles. I hear that Mr. David Hartley is appointed to conclude a definitive treaty with us.

The Emperor and Russia have been requested in their mediatorial capacity, to send plenipotentiaries to assist at the definitive treaties. The true motives to this measure can as yet be only conjectured. The ostensible one is a mark of respect to their offered, but not accepted, mediation. The proposition originated here. Their answer is expected daily. It is whispered that Russia consents. Safe opportunities of sending important letters from hence to Madrid are so very rare, that I think yours for that place had better be always conveyed directly to Cadiz or other ports in Spain where some American of confidence may be settled.

" It having been rumored that he was to be appointed, after the peace, Minister to England, he addressed the Secretary of Foreign Affairs, May 30, declining in favor of Mr. Adams.

" The delicate state of his health induced him to abandon his design of returning to Spain, and especially as he foresaw that the delays attending the negotiation of the definitive treaty would necessarily detain him in France till the ensuing year."—Jay's " Life of Jay," vol. I., pp. 171–72.

Numberless applications for consulships continue to be made, and some will probably reach you. In my opinion Americans only should be employed to serve America. I early entertained this opinion, and it has been almost daily gathering strength since my arrival in Europe.

I have the honour to be, etc.

JOHN JAY.

JAY TO ROBERT R. LIVINGSTON.

DEAR SIR: PARIS, April 22, 1783.

I wrote to you so lately by Mr. Mason, and there is such a dearth of news, that I now write less to give you information than as a mark of attention.

There are several of your letters which, on account of their length, the importance of their subjects, and the manner in which those subjects were treated, demanded of me more minute answers than my situation admitted of. Mr. Hartley is not yet arrived, but is daily expected. I am told by Mr. Laurens that he will propose that the people of the two countries shall have all the rights of citizens in each. The instruction of Congress on this important point is much to be desired. For my part I think a temporary stipulation of that sort might be expedient. They mean to court us, and in my opinion we should avoid being either too forward or too coy. I have no faith in any Court in Europe, but it would be improper to discover that sentiment. There are circumstances which induce me to believe that Spain is turning her eyes to England for a more intimate connection. They are the only two European powers which have continental possessions on our side of the water, and Spain I think wishes for a league between them for mutual security against us. Perhaps this consideration should lead us to regard the present fervour of the British advances with the less indifference.

On looking over one of my former letters, containing my propositions to Spain, I find that I had omitted to explain the reason of the one for a guaranty of our possessions in North America. That we should *so* guarantee the Spanish possessions as to *fight* for them was as distant from my design as it could be from that of Congress. A common guaranty means nothing more than a *quit claim*, to which we certainly could have had no objection. When more is intended, provisional and express stipulations become necessary. To any such I never would have consented. A confidant of the Minister (and I believe by his directions) had assured me that unless a guaranty was offered any other propositions would not induce the Minister to negotiate for a treaty. To meet that objection I made the offer in the general terms you have seen. I had no doubt but that the Minister was acquainted with my instructions ; and I considered this objection as a pretext for delay. My opinion as to a certain proposed cession was known, and uses not advantageous to us or to me had been made of it. It appeared to me advisable that the intention of Spain with respect to us should have a full trial, and such a one as would convince Congress that I was entirely guided by their views and wishes.

I therefore endeavoured so to frame those propositions as that they should not afford the Minister any pretence for refusing to commence the negotiation. The issue you are acquainted with.

I hope nothing will be done by the States for the tories until the British forces shall be withdrawn, and then I confess it would be for our honour to forgive all except the perfidious and cruel.

After the definitive treaties are finished, I hope I shall be excused in trying the waters of Spa and Bath (which are recommended to me) before I proceed to Spain. Whatever may be their effect, I shall not loiter at either place. After my business at Madrid shall be finished, I wish to devote my care to the recovery of my health and the concerns of my family, which must greatly interfere with the duties of my commission. Besides, as my country has obtained her object, my motives for entering into public life are at an end.

The same principles which drew me from the private station I formerly occupied, bid me to return to it. Actions are the only sure proofs of professions, and if I live mine shall not want that evidence.

I am, dear sir, etc.

JOHN JAY.

P. S.—I am told that a vessel, which went last year from our country, on the Ohio, down that river and through the Mississippi to the Havana, took passports from the Count de la Luzerne. This, if a fact, appears to me a singular one. I mention it merely as a matter of information.   J. J.

JAY TO FRANCIS CHILD.[1]

PARIS, 11th May, 1783.

DEAR FRANK :

Your letter of the 1st of January last was delivered to me yesterday, and gives me pleasure. You do well to look forward to the means of exercising your profession to advantage. You shall continue to have my aid and protection, in such measure and season as circumstances may render proper and expedient.

You belong to a large and helpless family, and I wish to see you as able, as I hope you would be willing, to provide for them.

I think with you that, on the evacuation of New York, you may set up a press there with a good prospect of success. On speaking to Dr. Franklin yesterday about it, he told me that when the enemy left Philadelphia they carried from thence to New York a printing-press of his, and that it is now in the possession of one Robinson, a printer, at New York. As by the provisional treaty the British forces are not to carry away any effects of the inhabitants, this press may perhaps be recovered. The Dr. has desired me to prepare a letter of attorney for the purpose to some person in New York, and, in case it should be restored, will lend it to you. I shall immediately think of furnishing you with some types, and Dr. Franklin has promised his assistance, so that you may soon expect to hear from me again about these

---

[1] Mr. Francis Child was an indigent boy, who had been educated at Mr. Jay's expense. The press mentioned in this letter was obtained, and on it Mr. Child printed the first daily newspaper published in the city of New York after the Revolution.—Jay's " Life of Jay," vol. i., p. 117.

matters.   In the meantime, write a letter of thanks to the Dr. for his kind attention.

I must remind you that you should extend your application beyond the mere mechanical part of your business.   You will have to compose as well as to print, and you should take pains not only to store your mind with useful knowledge, but also to acquire the talent of writing in a clear, concise, and accurate style.   Remember, too, that an acquaintance with accounts, and the method of keeping them, is not to be neglected.   It is important to all men, and particularly to those who cannot afford to be careless.   If you are industrious, prudent, and punctual in the conduct of your business, you will most certainly succeed ; and my desire of helping you, instead of abating, will be increased by your endeavours to help yourself.

I am, with sincere regard, dear Frank,

Your friend and servant,

JOHN JAY.

WILLIAM LIVINGSTON TO JAY.

DEAR SIR :   BURLINGTON, 21 May, 1783.

I embrace the opportunity of Doctor Wearing's going to France (a young Gentleman belonging to South Carolina & strongly recommended to me by President Boudinot) to send you a line which I hope you will never receive provided the non-reception of it is owing to your having left Paris for America, when it arrives in France.

The Treaty is universally applauded ; & the American Commissioners who were concerned in making it, have rendered themselves very popular by it.   The Whigs in this State are however extremely opposed to admitting the refugees amongst us, & I am apprehensive of some difficulty on that account. There is still a greater difficulty that we have to struggle with. For many strong professional Whigs now openly show what I have long suspected them of, that they love their money better than their liberty by their scandalous aversion to pay the necessary taxes. If this reaches you in Europe, I hope I shall hear from you as soon as possible. I am, Sir,

Your most humble servant,
WIL: LIVINGSTON.

JAY TO ELIAS BOUDINOT.

PARIS, 22d May, 1783.

DEAR SIR:

My letter to Mr. Livingston in November last renders it necessary for me to apologize for the liberty I now take in recommending to you the father and family of Mr. B. Vaughan, who go to America with design to become citizens of it.

I consider every such family removal from England to our country as a valuable acquisition ; even if they carry with them much fewer claims to our esteem and regard than Mr. Vaughan's have justly acquired.

I hope the reception they will meet with on your side of the water will compensate in some measure for the pain of separating from their friends and connections on this ; and as you are no less capable of feeling than of seeing the force of this remark, I forbear adding any thing except an assurance of the respect and regard with which I have the honour to be, dear sir, your most obedient and very humble servant,

JOHN JAY.

JAY TO ROBERT R. LIVINGSTON.

PARIS, May 30, 1783.

DEAR SIR:

It cannot in my opinion be long before Congress will think it expedient to name a Minister to the Court of London. Perhaps my friends may wish to add me to the number of candidates for that office. If that should be the case, I request the favour of you to declare, in the most explicit terms, that I view the expectations of Mr. Adams on that head as founded in equity and reason, and that I will not by any means stand in his way. Were I in Congress I should vote for him. He deserves well of his country, and is very able to serve her. It appears to me to be but fair that the disagreeable conclusions, which may be drawn from the abrupt repeal of his former commission, should be obviated by its being restored to him. I do therefore in the most unequivocal manner decline and refuse to be a competitor with that faithful servant of the public for the place in question.

As Mr. Barclay has power to settle our accounts in Europe, I wish that orders may be sent to Mr. Carmichael to come here with the books and documents necessary to enable Mr. Barclay to examine and settle the public accounts in my department. I cannot learn that my repeated requests to him to send a state of those accounts to Philadelphia have as yet been complied with.

I am, dear sir, etc.

JOHN JAY.

JAY TO ROBERT R. LIVINGSTON.

DEAR SIR :   PARIS, June 1st 1783.

I have had the honour of receiving your favour of
the 4th of January last. The cipher you mention to
have enclosed is missing. My letter by Captain
Barney affords an answer to the greater part of your
inquiries. Business here goes on heavily. The Dutch
and English are not yet agreed, and some points
remain still to be adjusted between the latter and the
French and Spaniards. Mr. Hartley has an ample
and proper commission to conclude with us. We are
discussing the terms of a temporary commercial regulation, but as he is waiting for more full instructions,
it may be a week or a fortnight before we shall be
able to inform you of the real intentions of Britain on
that subject.

Before I left Spain, and often since by letters, I
desired Mr. Carmichael to make out and transmit to
Philadelphia a clear and full state of the public accounts ; and also, agreeably to Dr. Franklin's request,
to send him an account of the bills remaining to be
paid. The Doctor has not received his account ;
and I have no reason to suppose that you or Mr.
Morris have received the other. I am not easy about
this matter, for in case of the death or recall of Mr.
Carmichael (by whom all these accounts were kept,
and through whom I managed these transactions),
I might experience difficulties respecting the accounts,
which may now be avoided.

I understand from Mr. Barclay that he is authorized to examine and settle these accounts, and as Mr.

Carmichael has not much to do at Madrid, I am very desirous that he should be ordered to bring here all the books and papers relative to these accounts, and with me to attend their settlement by Mr. Barclay. Be so good as to lay this matter before Congress without delay.

I have the honour to be, etc.

JOHN JAY.

JAY TO GENERAL WASHINGTON.

MY DEAR SIR :   PASSY, 13th June, 1783.

I have, within these few days past, read and admired your address to the army, and their proceedings in consequence of it. Such instances of patriotism are rare, and America must find it difficult to express, in adequate terms, the gratitude she owes to both. Such a degree of glory, so virtuously acquired, and so decently sustained, is as new as our political constellation, and will for ever give lustre to it. May every blessing be yours.

Mr. Hartley has just informed me that orders have been sent to the British commander-in-chief to evacuate the United States. Our attention will then, I hope, be turned to the preservation and improvement of what we have gained ; and a sense of the importance of that task leads me to wish that the execution of it may be facilitated by your counsels and application.

With perfect esteem and affection,

I am, dear sir,

Your most obedient servant,

JOHN JAY.

JAY TO EGBERT BENSON.

PASSY, 10 July, 1783.

DEAR BENSON :

I have received and thank you for your letter of the 25th April last. You did well in not writing in it any thing that might not be read by anybody. I receive no letters by the post (unless under cover to a third person) but what are previously inspected. Jealousy and suspicion never sleep in governments of a certain denomination.

The satisfaction you express respecting the peace gave me pleasure. I would tell you more about it than you know, and much that would increase your content with the terms of it; but those matters must be reserved for a future happy day when we shall meet, and which, if God pleases, will be next summer. I am determined to realize my professions, and will now hasten to become a private citizen and attend to the welfare of my family. Peter and Nancy will be particularly pleased with the information; they are ever in my thoughts and hearts, and one of the greatest pleasures I promise myself is that of contributing to their happiness. I think Peter should immediately have the farm at Rye valued and take it at the valuation; but in my opinion he should not move the family there until after New York shall be evacuated. Indeed it appears to me to be advisable to delay moving until next spring; he will then have the summer before him to begin the work of reparation, and be better prepared to pass a comfortable winter than if he moved in the fall.

I desired Mr. Livingston in a former letter to furnish Peter and Fady with money on my account; if this has been omitted and they should want, Fady may draw upon me for three hundred pounds, York money, at thirty days' sight, of which he must pay one hundred to Peter, one hundred to Nancy, and retain the other hundred for his own disposition.

As soon as public business will permit me, I intend to make a trip to England to receive the money left me by Mr. Peloquin, and to try if the waters at Bath will remove a pain in my breast with which I have been troubled for near a year past.

You say my son is *in health.* I wish you may have had no particular reason for omitting the word *good.* The necessity of attending to his education makes a strong impression upon me, and leads me to regret my long absence from him.

When you see Dr. Van Wyck and his brother assure them of my regard, and that I gratefully remember their kind attention to my family. Present my compliments also to my other friends. You know who they are.

Yours affectionately,

JOHN JAY.

JAY TO MRS. M. LIVINGSTON.

DEAR MADAM :   PASSY, 12th July, 1783.

I have long been accustomed to hear, and I might add read, so much in which the heart has no concern, that the few letters like yours which reach me are particularly welcome.

The peace appears to me, as it does to you, to be seasonable as well as advantageous; and I sincerely join with you in ascribing that and every other of our blessings to the Supreme Author of all the good that ever was and ever will be in the world.

As your letter is of the 12th April, and as I have received others dated late in May, which mention nothing of my sister, I indulge some little hope that she is still alive; if so, I shall be very thankful; if not, God's will be done. To her, this world has not been a paradise. Her leaving it will be a misfortune to the few who knew her worth, and to whom she was attached. She will have reason to rejoice in the change. I feel most sensibly for the effect it would have on my brother; it would double the pressure of all his afflictions. God grant him resignation, and permit me to return soon to comfort him. He has every right to expect it from me, and if my life be spared he shall not be disappointed. I cannot proceed. God bless you, my dear madam.

I am your affectionate and humble servant,

JOHN JAY.

JAY TO GOUVERNEUR MORRIS.

DEAR MORRIS :　　　　PASSY, 17th July, 1783.

By this time I suppose there is much canvassing for foreign appointments. I thank you for thinking of me, but as I mean to return in the spring, your arrangements, so far as respects me, must be altered. Upon this point I am decided, and beg of you to tell my friends so.

Orders are gone to evacuate New York. The present British Ministry are duped, I believe, by an opinion of our not having decision and energy sufficient to regulate our trade so as to retaliate their restrictions. Our ports were opened too soon. Let us, however, be temperate as well as firm.

Our friend Morris, I suspect, is not a favourite of this Court. They say he treats them as his cashier. They refuse absolutely to supply more money. Marbois writes tittle-tattle, and I believe does mischief. Congress certainly should remove to some remote interior town, and they should send a Minister forthwith to England. The French Ambassador at Petersburg has thrown cold water on Dana's being received before a peace.

The Ministers of this Court are qualified to act the part of Proteus. The nation, I think, is with us, and the King seems to be well disposed. Adieu.

Yours, sincerely,

JOHN JAY.

JAY TO GOVERNOR LIVINGSTON.

PASSY, 19th July, 1783.

DEAR SIR :

On the 1st instant I had the pleasure of receiving your favour of the 21st May last.

I am happy to hear that the provisional articles meet with general approbation. The tories will doubtless cause some difficulty, but that they have always done, and as this will probably be the last time, we must make the best of it. A universal indiscriminate condemnation and expulsion of those people would not redound to our honour, because so harsh a measure would partake more of vengeance than of justice. For my part, I wish that all except the *faithless and the cruel* may be forgiven. That exception would indeed extend to very few; but even if it applied to the case of one only, that one ought, in my opinion, to be saved.

The reluctance with which the States in general pay the necessary taxes is much to be regretted; it injures both their reputation and interest abroad, as well as at home, and tends to cherish the hopes and speculations of those who wish we may become and remain an unimportant, divided people. The rising power of America is a serious object of apprehension to more than one nation, and every event that may retard it will be agreeable to them. A continental, national spirit should therefore pervade our country, and Congress should be enabled, by a grant of the necessary powers, to regulate the commerce and general concerns of the confederacy; and we should remember that to be constantly prepared for war is the only way to have peace. The Swiss on the one hand, and the Dutch on the other, bear testimony to the truth of this remark.

The general and the army have, by their late moderation, done themselves infinite honour; and it is to be hoped that the States will not only be just, but generous, to those brave and virtuous citizens. America is at present held in a very respectable point of view, but as the eyes of the world are upon her, the continuance of that consideration will depend on the dignity and wisdom of her conduct.

I mean to return next spring. My health is somewhat better.

I am, dear sir,

Your affectionate and humble servant,

JOHN JAY.

JAY TO ROBERT R. LIVINGSTON.

[Private.]

DEAR ROBERT :   PASSY, 19th July, 1783.

Our despatches by Barney must be ready the day after to-morrow. The many letters I have written and have still to write by him, together with conferences, company, etc., keep me fully employed. You will therefore excuse my not descending so much to particulars as both of us indeed might wish. As little that passes in Congress is kept entirely secret, we think it prudent at least to postpone giving you a more minute detail than you have already received, of the reasons which induced us to sign the provisional articles without previously communicating them to the French Minister. For your private satisfaction, however, I will make a few remarks on that subject.

Your doubts respecting the propriety of our conduct in that instance appear to have arisen from the following circumstances, viz. :

1st. That we entertained and were influenced by distrusts and suspicions which do not seem to you to have been altogether well founded.

2d. That we signed the articles without previously communicating them to this Court.

With respect to the first. In our negotiation with the British commissioner, it was essential to insist on, and, if possible, obtain, his consent to four important concessions.

1st. That Britain should treat with us as being what we were, viz., an independent people. The French Minister thought this demand premature, and that it ought to arise from, and not precede, the treaty.

2d. That Britain should agree to the extent of boundary we claimed. The French Minister thought our demands on that head extravagant in themselves, and as militating against certain views of Spain which he was disposed to favour.

3d. That Britain should admit our right in common to the fishery. The French Minister thought this demand too extensive.

4th. That Britain should not insist on our reinstating the tories. The French Minister argued that they ought to be reinstated.

Was it unnatural for us to conclude from these facts that the French Minister was opposed to our succeeding on these four great points, in the extent we wished? It appeared evident that his plan of a treaty for America was far from being such as America would have preferred; and as we disapproved of his model, we thought it imprudent to give him an opportunity of moulding our treaty by it. Whether the minister was influenced by what he really thought best for us, or by what he really thought would be best for France, is a question which, however easy or difficult to decide, is not very important to the point under consideration. Whatever his motives may have been, certain it is that they were such as opposed our system ; and as in private life it is deemed imprudent to admit opponents to full confidence, especially respecting the very matters in competition, so in public affairs the like caution seems equally proper.

Secondly. But admitting the force of this reasoning, why, when the articles were completed, did we not communicate them to the French minister before we proceeded to sign them ? For the following reasons :

The expectations excited in England by Lord Shelburne's friends, that he would put a speedy period to the war, made it necessary for him either to realize those expectations or prepare to quit his place. The Parliament being to meet before his negotiations with us were concluded, he found it expedient to adjourn it for a short term, in hopes of then meeting it with all the advantages that might be expected from a favourable issue of the negotiation. Hence it was his interest to draw it to a close before that adjournment should expire ; and to obtain that end, both he and his commissioner became less tenacious on certain points than they would otherwise have been. Nay, we have, and then had, good reason to believe that the latitude allowed by the British Cabinet for the exercise of discretion was exceeded on that occasion.

I must now remind you that the King of Great Britain had pledged himself, in Mr. Oswald's commission, to confirm and ratify, *not* what Mr. Oswald should *verbally agree to*, but what he should *formally sign his name and affix his seal to.*

Had we communicated the articles, when ready for signing, to the French Minister, he doubtless would have complimented us on the terms of them ; but, at the same time, he would have insisted on our postponing the signature until the articles then preparing between France, Spain, and Britain should also be ready for signing—he having often intimated to us that we should all sign at the same time and place.

This would have exposed us to a disagreeable dilemma. Had we agreed to postpone signing the articles, the British Cabinet might, and probably would, have taken advantage of it. They might, if better prospects had offered, have insisted that the articles were still *res infectæ*—that Mr. Oswald had exceeded the limits of his instructions—and, for both these reasons, that they conceived themselves still at liberty to depart from his opinions, and to forbid his executing, as their commissioner, a set of articles which they could not approve of.

It is true that this might not have happened, but it is equally true that it might ; and therefore it was a risk of too great importance to be run. The whole business would, in that case, have been set afloat again ; and the Minister of France would have had an opportunity, at least, of approving the objections of the British Court, and of advising us to recede from demands which in his opinion were immoderate, and too inconsistent with the claims of Spain to meet with his concurrence.

If, on the other hand, we had, contrary to his advice and request, refused to postpone the signing, it is natural to suppose that such refusal would have given more offence to the French Minister than our doing it without consulting him at all about the matter.

Our withholding from him the knowledge of these articles until after they were signed was no violation of our treaty with France, and therefore she has no room for complaint, on that principle, against the United States.

Congress had indeed made and published a resolution not to make peace but in confidence and in concurrence with France.

So far as this resolution declares against a separate peace, it has been incontestably observed; and, admitting that the words " in confidence and in concurrence with France" mean that we should mention to the French Minister and consult with him about every step of our proceedings, yet it is most certain that it was founded on a mutual understanding that France would patronize our demands, and assist us in obtaining the objects of them. France, therefore, by discouraging our claims, ceased to be entitled to the degree of confidence respecting them which was specified in the resolution.

It may be said that France must admit the reasonableness of our claims before we could properly expect that she should promote them. She knew what were our claims before the negotiation commenced, though she could only conjecture what reception they would meet with from Britain. If she thought our claims extravagant, she may be excusable for not countenancing them in their full extent ; but then we ought also to be excused for not giving her the full confidence on those subjects, which was promised on the implied condition of her supporting them.

But Congress positively instructed us to do nothing without the advice and consent of the French Minister, and we have departed from that line of conduct. This is also true ; but then I apprehend that Congress marked out that line of conduct for their own sake, and not for the sake of France. The object of that instruction was the supposed interest of America, and not of France ; and we were directed to ask the advice of the French Minister because it was thought advantageous to our country that we should receive and be governed by it. Congress only, therefore, have a right to complain of our departure from the line of that instruction.

If it be urged that confidence ought to subsist between allies, I have only to remark that, as the French Minister did not consult us about his articles, nor make us any communication about them, our giving him as little trouble about ours did not violate any principle of reciprocity.

Our joint letter to you by Captain Barney contains an explanation of our conduct respecting the separate article.

I proceed now to your obliging letter of the 1st May, for which I sincerely thank you.

This will probably find you at Claremont. I consider your resignation as more reconcilable to your plan and views of happiness than to the public good. The war may be ended, but other difficulties of a serious nature remain, and require all the address and wisdom of our best men to manage.

As Benson informed you that my family had no present occasion for supplies from me, I am more easy on that head than I have been. I have some fear, however, that they may rather have been influenced to decline my offers by delicacy with respect to me, than by the ease of their circumstances. I wish you would take an opportunity of talking freely with my brother Peter on this subject. Assure him that it would distress me greatly were he, or indeed any of the family, to experience embarrassments in my power to obviate. He may share with me to the last shilling; and so may Nancy, about whom, until within a day or two, I had been very uneasy. Tell them and Frederick that I mean, if God pleases, to return next spring; and that one of the greatest blessings of my life will be that of rendering it subservient to their ease and welfare. I write to Frederick by this opportunity, and authorize him to draw upon me for £150, New York money, to be divided between the three. If, on conversing with Peter, you should find it to be more convenient to him, be pleased to supply it, and draw upon me for the amount at thirty days' sight.

I have lately heard of Mr. Kissam's death. It affected me much. He was a virtuous and agreeable man, and I owed him many obligations.

Thinking of Mr. Kissam's family calls to my mind the fate of the tories. As far as I can learn, the general opinion in Europe is that they have reason to complain, and that our country ought to manifest magnanimity with respect to them. Europe neither knows nor can be made to believe what inhuman, barbarous wretches the greater part of them have been, and therefore is disposed to pity them more than they deserve. I hope, for my part, that the States will adopt some principle of deciding on their cases, and that it will be such a one as, by being perfectly consistent with justice and humanity, may meet with the approbation, not only of dispassionate nations at present, but also of dispassionate posterity hereafter. My opinion would be to pardon all except the faithless and the cruel, and publicly to declare that by this rule they should be judged and treated. Indiscriminate severity would be wrong as well as unbecoming; nor ought any man to be marked out for vengeance merely because, as King James said, he would make a *bonnie traitor.* In short, I think the faithless and cruel should be banished for ever, and their estates confiscated ; it is just and reasonable. As to the residue, who have either upon principle openly and fairly opposed us, or who, from timidity, have fled from the storm and remained inoffensive, let us not punish the first for behaving like men, nor be extremely severe to the latter because nature had made them like women.

I send you a box of plaster copies of medals. If Mrs. Livingston will permit you to keep so many mistresses, reserve the ladies for yourself, and give the philosophers and poets to Edward.

Now for our girls; I congratulate you on the health of the first, the birth of the second, and the promising appearance of both. I will cheerfully be godfather to the latter ; what is her name ?

Our little one is doing well. If people in heaven see what is going on here below, my ancestors must derive much pleasure from comparing the circumstances attending the expulsion of some of them from this country, with those under which my family has been increased in it.

Since my removal to this place, where the air is remarkably good, the pain in my breast has abated, and I have now no fever. Mrs. Jay is tolerably well. Assure Mrs. Livingston and our other friends with you of our regard.

I am, your affectionate friend,

JOHN JAY.

JAY TO ROBERT MORRIS.

PASSY, 20th July, 1783.

DEAR SIR :

By Captain Barney I was favoured with yours of the 31st May. By this time I hope you will have received several letters from me, which were then on the way. Want of health has long made much writing painful to me, so that my letters in general are short.

My jaunt to Normandy did me some service, but less than I expected. The pure air of this place has been useful to me. The pain in my breast has abated, and I have had no fever since I came here, which was about six weeks ago.

Gouverneur is happy in your esteem; it adds to mine for him. I have long been attached to him, and sincerely wish that our friendship, instead of being diminished, may continue to gain strength with time.

Your intended resignation alarmed me, and would have been followed with ill consequences to our affairs. I rejoice that you continue in office, and by no means regret that it will be less in your power than inclination to retire soon. I am well aware of the difficulties you will continue to experience. Every man so circumstanced must expect them. Your office is neither an easy nor a pleasant one to execute, but it is elevated and important, and therefore envy, with her inseparable companion injustice, will not cease to plague you. Remember, however, that triumphs do not precede victory, and that victory is seldom found in the smooth paths of peace and tranquillity. Your enemies would be happy to drive you to resign, and in my opinion both your interest and that of your country oppose your gratifying them. You have health, fortune, talents, and fortitude, and you have children too. Each of these circumstances recommends perseverance.

As to money, this Court will afford you no further supplies. The Minister has said it was easy to be a financier and draw bills when others provided the funds to pay them. At another time, he intimated that his court was not treated with a proper degree of delicacy on that subject, and said "that you treated them as cashiers." A French officer from America, who is a friend of yours, told me that La Luzerne and Marbois were not pleased with the manner of your applications to them about money matters. I mention these facts, because it may be useful for you to know them.

The loan in Holland goes on, and from that quarter your bills must be saved, if at all. Mr. Adams set out for Amsterdam the day before yesterday, and will push on that business. If the Dutch began to draw more benefit from our trade, they would lend more cheerfully.

The British Ministry have not yet authorized Mr. Hartley to consent to any thing as to commerce. They amuse him and us, and deceive themselves. I told him yesterday that they would find us like a globe—not to be overset. They wish to be the only carriers between their islands and other countries; and though they are apprised of our right to regulate our trade as we please, yet I suspect they flatter themselves that the different States possess too little of a national or continental spirit, ever to agree in any one national system. I think they will find themselves mistaken.

Believe me to be, dear sir,

Your affectionate friend,

JOHN JAY.

JAY TO KITTY LIVINGSTON.

PASSY, 20th July, 1783.

DEAR KITTY :

I have now your kind letter of the 24th May last before me, and sincerely thank you for it. It is a little singular that so few letters from us have reached you, especially as several of them have been written since the cessation of hostilities.

If God preserves my life and grants my prayers we shall see each other next June or July, and then, my dear Kate, we will exchange much interesting information. During the course of the late Revolution many have been put to a variety of trials, and I think I can better estimate the value both of men and things than I should otherwise have been able to do. It is to be lamented, however, that although experience generally adds to our prudence, it often diminishes our happiness, at least so far as respects this world. My future situation will excite but little envy, and as I shall stand in nobody's way, I shall cease to be exposed to those little machinations, which, though scarcely ever fatal to honest and prudent men, always cause a certain degree of trouble and indignation.

Mr. Morris it seems has postponed his resignation, and I rejoice at it. That resolution is fortunate for the public, and in my opinion conducive to his reputation. He has his enemies it is true, and so all men so circumstanced ever have had and ever will have.

Farewell, my good and faithful friend. Keep my boy for me, and believe me to be with the most sincere esteem and regard JOHN JAY.

JAY TO ROBERT R. LIVINGSTON.

DEAR SIR: PASSY, July 20, 1783.

The delays which have postponed the completion of
the definitive treaty have hitherto prevented my trying the effect of the waters of Bath for a pain in my
breast, which has continued in different degrees for a
year past. Were I much longer to neglect that only
probable chance of restoring my health, my little
family might have much reason to complain.

I fear that the fluctuating counsels of the British
Cabinet will protract that business until so late in the
season, as not to leave me sufficient time both to
give the waters a fair trial, and afterwards go to
Spain before the weather will become too inclement
for an invalid to travel such a distance in a country
so destitute of accommodations. Should that be the
case, I shall hope to be excused for not undertaking
it, especially as nothing of importance remains there
to be done, except preparing the draft of a treaty of
commerce, which I hoped to have been able to bring
with me to America in the spring, when it was my
fixed resolution to resign.

But as I should then pass the winter without being
useful to the public, Congress may not perhaps think
it reasonable that their allowance to me should be
continued. I think it my duty therefore to apprise
them of these circumstances, and to refer it to their
discretion to assign such earlier date to my resignation as they may think best. I must beg the favour
of you to request and to inform me of their decision

on this subject without delay, for as I shall not probably have an opportunity of sailing before June next, it is important to me to know by what rule I am to regulate the expenses of my family in the meantime.

As you know upon what principles I have devoted myself to the public for the last nine years, and as those motives would be questionable if after the war I did not return to a private station, I hope the propriety of my resolution to resign will appear manifest, especially when to these considerations are added the circumstances of certain individuals of my family, whose afflictions and whose relation to me give them the strongest claims to my care and attention.

Be pleased, sir, to present to Congress my warmest acknowledgments for the marks of confidence with which they have honoured me, and assure them that by becoming a private citizen I mean not to retreat from any duties which an American owes his country.

I have the honour to be, etc.

JOHN JAY.

ALEXANDER HAMILTON TO JAY.

PHILADELPHIA, 25th July, 1783.

DEAR SIR:

Though I have not performed my promise of writing to you, which I made when you left this country, yet I have not the less interested myself in your welfare and success. I have been witness with pleasure to every event which has had a tendency to advance you in the esteem of your country; and I may assure you with sincerity that it is as high as you could possibly wish. All have united in the warmest approbation of your conduct. I cannot forbear telling you this, because my situation has given me access to the truth, and I gratify my friendship for you in communicating what cannot fail to gratify your sensibility.

The peace, which exceeds in the goodness of its terms the expectations of the most sanguine, does the highest honour to those who made it. It is the more agreeable as the time was come when thinking men began to be seriously alarmed at the internal embarrassments and exhausted state of this country. The New England people talk of making you an annual fish-offering, as an acknowledgment of your exertion for the participation of the fisheries.

We have now happily concluded the great work of independence, but much remains to be done to reap the fruits of it. Our prospects are not flattering. Every day proves the inefficacy of the present confederation, yet the common danger being removed, we are receding instead of advancing in a disposition to amend its defects. The road to popularity in each State is to inspire jealousies of the power of Congress, though nothing can be more apparent than that they have no power; and that for the want of it the resources of the country during the war could not be drawn out, and we at this moment experience all the mischiefs of a bankrupt and ruined credit. It is to be hoped that when prejudice and folly have run themselves out of breath, we may return to reason and correct our errors.

After having served in the field during the war, I have been making a short apprenticeship in Congress ; but the evacuation of New-York approaching, I am preparing to take leave of public life to enter into the practice of the law. Your country will demand your services abroad. I beg you to present me most respectfully to Mrs. Jay, and to be assured of the affection and esteem of,

Dear sir,
Your obedient servant,
ALEXANDER HAMILTON.

BENJAMIN VAUGHAN TO JAY.

LONDON, Augt. 8th, 1783.

MY DEAR SIR:

I have not answered your letter, so kindly written to me, for reasons, which will bear me out to *you*, as they do to my conscience; for had I written confidentially and the whole of what I knew, I believe you are by this time convinced that I should have done mischief *prematurely*. I have not however been idle in that cause, which is the only one worth our notice, and which, as it was the foundatiou of our first happy acquaintance, will I flatter myself contribute to cement me to you while I live. I am not made for idleness, and I find new objects daily rising, though I am covert in my mode of forwarding them.

As I do not however look upon the post as a safe vehicle for matters of confidence between us, I shall go to the object of this letter, which is to introduce Mr. Dugald Stewart to you, after you have seen whom, you will have seen the most remarkable among the literary young men in Scotland. He is already their first rate mathematician and moral philosopher; and as his diligence and abilities and connections are equal to any thing, there is no knowing where he will stop; and I shall be glad you will have had an opportunity of seeing him, as he wants nothing but a little longer period of life to make him somewhat famous.

I do not *boast* of his politics. He is a very cautious man, and having turned his thoughts but little that way, he does not suffer himself to decide.—I found indeed so many other things to say, that I seldom talked politics with him. When I did, he was always candid, and inclined to what was right; at least when I was in habits with him.

I shall begin to make you many apologies for taking the liberty of introducing my friends to you, unless you take the same privilege on your side. As I respect you & yours in the utmost possible degree, I think, my dear sir, that you will meditate some employment for a person whom you have obliged and attached in the highest degree.

My father's family by the time you receive this, will probably be in America and under strong obligations for your introductions. When the larger mass has moved, Mr. Stewart could prove that the smaller cannot resist the attraction and remain at rest, where any other attraction subsists.

Mr. Stewart will introduce with himself his friend Lord Ancram, whom he represents as a pleasing, pretty young man, being the son of the Marquis of Lothian.

I have the honor to be, my dearest sir, with the highest respect and much gratitude,

Your affectionate humble serv^{t.}

BENJN. VAUGHAN.

P. S.—I hope Mrs. Jay has received a little box from me. I beg to present my very respectful regards to her through you, knowing that in that way they will be most acceptable.

COUNT DE VERGENNES TO JAY.

M. de Vergennes begs that Mr. Jay, Minister Plenipotentiary of the United States of America, will do him the honor of dining with him at Versailles on Wednesday next, 3d of September.[1]

VERSAILLES, August 28th, 1783.

BENJAMIN FRANKLIN TO JAY.

PASSY, September 10, 1783.

SIR:

I have received a letter from a very respectable person in America, containing the following words, viz.

"It is confidently reported, propagated and believed by some among us, that the Court of France was at bottom

---

[1] The day on which the definitive treaty was signed.

against our obtaining the fishery and territory in that great extent in which both are secured to us by the treaty ; that our Minister at that Court favoured, or did not oppose this design against us ; and that it was entirely owing to the firmness, sagacity and disinterestedness of Mr. Adams, with whom Mr. Jay united, that we have obtained those important advantages."

It is not my purpose to dispute any share of the honour of that treaty which the friends of my Colleagues may be disposed to give them ; but, having now spent fifty years of my life in public offices and trusts, and having still one ambition left, that of carrying the character of fidelity at least to the grave with me, I cannot allow that I was behind any of them in zealous faithfulness. I therefore think that I ought not to suffer an accusation, which falls little short of treason to my Country, to pass without notice, when the means of effectual vindication are at hand. You, Sir, was a witness of my conduct in that affair. To you and my other Colleagues I appeal by sending to each a similar letter with this, and I have no doubt of your readiness to do a brother Commissioner justice, by certificates that will entirely destroy the effect of that accusation.

I have the honour to be, with much esteem, Sir,
   Your most obedient
    and most humble Servant,
      B. Franklin.

JAY TO BENJAMIN FRANKLIN.

Sir :   Passy, 11 September, 1783.

I have been favoured with your letter of yesterday, and will answer it explicitly.

I have no reason whatever to believe that you were averse to our obtaining the full extent of boundary and fishery secured to us by the treaty. Your conduct respecting them throughout the negotiation indicated a strong and steady attachment to both those objects, and in my opinion promoted the attainment of them.

I remember that in a conversation which M. de Rayneval, the first Secretary of Count de Vergennes, had with you and me in the summer of 1782, you contended for our full right to the fishery, and argued it on various principles.

Your letters to me when in Spain, considered our territory as extending to the Mississippi, and expressed your opinion against ceding the navigation of that river, in very strong and pointed terms.

In short, sir, I do not recollect the least difference in sentiment between us respecting the boundaries or fisheries.   On the contrary, we were unanimous and united in adhering to, and insisting on them, nor did I ever perceive the least disposition in either of us to recede from our claims, or be satisfied with less than we obtained.

I have the honour to be with great respect and esteem, sir, your most obedient and very humble servant.

JOHN JAY.

JAY TO EGBERT BENSON.

MY GOOD FRIEND :   PASSY, 12 September, 1783.

Is it not almost time for me to expect a letter from you ?—the one enclosing letters of August was the last.

Mrs. Jay gave me another daughter last month, and you are her godfather; I hope next summer to introduce her to you. Do tell me something about my family; I have not heard of them since my last.

I am preparing despatches to Congress, and therefore cannot write long letters.

Your irregular and violent popular proceedings and resolutions against the tories hurt us in Europe. We are puzzled to answer the question, how it happens that, if there be settled governments in America, the people of town and district should take upon themselves to legislate. The people of America must either govern themselves according to their respective constitutions and the confederation, or relinquish all pretensions to the respect of other nations. The newspapers in Europe are filled with exaggerated accounts of the want of moderation, union, order, and government which they say prevails in our country.

I hope our affairs will soon assume a different aspect; the waves will run high for some time after a storm; these matters give me more regret than surprise, but I do not wonder at their appearing very extraordinary in those countries where the tone of government is high.

We have the fullest assurances that New York will be evacuated without delay. I am impatient for that event; our remonstrances to the British Minister on that subject have been strong and frequent.

I am, dear Benson, your affectionate friend,

JOHN JAY.

JAY TO CHARLES THOMSON.

PASSY 12th September, 1783.

DEAR SIR:

Mr. Thaxter, who returns unspoiled, is the bearer of the definitive treaty, and will deliver you this.

Mr. Hartley expects soon to confer with us about commerce, and says he is persuaded that Britain will be liberal. I should not doubt it if it was certain that the States would act like one nation.

I think all commercial treaties should observe exact reciprocity. Mr. Hartley wishes that the American carrying places (why only the carrying places?) on both sides of the boundary line may be in common *forever.* I doubt the policy of our agreeing to it, except for limited terms or during the duration of the treaty of commerce, which, in my opinion, should be temporary, unless very extensively free and reciprocal, because such treaties, if unequal and full of restrictions, may in time be very disadvantageous, though at present convenient. Dr. Franklin wishes to provide against privateering and depredations on unarmed people in future wars. I agree with him perfectly, except that I wish every army invading us may be a licentious, predatory one, for in that case the inhabitants would oppose them with more vigour and perseverance.

It is my determination to return next summer, and therefore I hope my friends will not think of employing me in Europe in any way that might interfere with it.

The prints herewith enclosed relate to a subject

which excites universal attention ; they will explain themselves.

Mrs. Jay, who is just getting out of the straw, presents her compliments to you and Mrs. Thomson.

With great regard and attachment, I am, dear sir, your friend and servant,

JOHN JAY.

JAY TO ROBERT MORRIS.

PASSY, 12th September, 1783.

DEAR SIR :

The definitive treaty is concluded, and we are now, thank God, in the full possession of peace and independence. If we are not a happy people it will be our own fault.

We daily expect the commission for a treaty of commerce. I wish that the sentiments of our country on that important subject may be fully stated in the instructions which will accompany it. I think all our treaties of commerce should be temporary. The circumstances of our country may be greatly changed in twenty or thirty years, and what may now be advantageous may possibly be then inconvenient. Besides, as we increase in wealth and power, we shall find it less difficult to mould treaties to our minds. In my opinion we should constantly look forward to a commercial intercourse with all the ports and places on the American continent and American islands to whomsoever belonging. Perpetual treaties of commerce now made would probably exclude us from that prospect.

In a late letter to G. Morris I conclosed him an account of the invention of globes, wherewith man may literally soar above the clouds. I herewith send you two prints containing representations of the rise and descent of one of them.

I hear your boys go on exceedingly well at Geneva, and have reason to believe that they are in very good hands.

Mrs. Jay has another daughter ; both of them are doing well, except that the child has a bad cold. I hope next summer to see you, and to brighten at the hills the chain which I flatter myself will always connect us. Let not, therefore, any idea of keeping me longer in Europe be encouraged. Be pleased to assure Mrs. Morris of our constant regard, and believe me to be, dear sir, your affectionate friend,

JOHN JAY.

JAY TO ROBERT R. LIVINGSTON.

PASSY, 12th September, 1783.

DEAR ROBERT :

At your farm, with your family, in peace and in plenty, how happy is your situation ! I wish you may not have retired too soon. It is certain you may do much good where you are, and perhaps in few things more than in impressing, by precept, influence, and example, the indispensable necessity of rendering the Continental and State government vigorous and orderly.

Europe hears much and wishes to hear more of divisions, seditions, violences, and confusions among us. The tories are generally and greatly pitied, more indeed than they deserve. The indiscriminate expulsion and ruin of that whole class and description of men would not do honour to our magnanimity or humanity, especially in the opinion of those nations who consider, with more astonishment than pleasure, the terms of peace which America has obtained. General Washington's letter does him credit as a soldier, patriot, and Christian. I wish his advice may meet with the attention it merits.

Mr. Hartley has gone to London, and expects soon to return and resume the discussion of commercial regulations, etc.; he has assured us officially that Britain is not resolved to adhere to the line marked out in their proclamation respecting the West India trade. I doubt their knowing themselves what they mean to do. In my opinion we should adhere to exact reciprocity with all nations, and were we well united they would yield to it. He assured us also that orders were gone for the evacuation of New York.

On the 13th of last month Mrs. Jay was delivered of a daughter; we have called her Ann, after my sister, about whom I am very anxious, having heard nothing of her or any other of my family these three months. You will oblige me exceedingly by accounts of them. I hope to see you and them next summer. We have had much cool weather lately, and I find myself the better for it.

All the people are running after air globes. The invention of them may have many consequences, and who knows but travellers may hereafter literally pass from country to country on the wings of the wind. One of enclosed prints is no less true than laughable. Assure your good family of our sincere regard, and believe me, to be, dear Robert, your affectionate friend,

JOHN JAY.

JAY TO BENJAMIN VAUGHAN.

PASSY, 13th September, 1783.

DEAR SIR:

I am greatly in your debt on the account of letters, but I hope next month to answer them in person, unless unforeseen obstacles to my leaving this place should again occur.

Mrs. Jay received the box you were so kind as to send her, and is exceedingly obliged by that polite and friendly mark of attention. She has another daughter, who, except a bad cold, is well, and she is regaining strength, though slowly.

Our independence treaty is concluded, but your court declined comprehending in it certain objects which, in my opinion, merit their regard as much as ours. We are soon to begin negotiations for a treaty of commerce, but I confess I am not so sanguine as to expect that they will be unembarrassed by the partial politics which seem to prevail in your Cabinet.

With sincere and great regard and esteem, I am, dear sir, your friend,

JOHN JAY.

JAY TO GEÑERAL SCHUYLER.

PASSY, 16th September, 1783.

DEAR SIR :

The day before yesterday I was favoured with your friendly letter of 1st July.

To whatever cause the suspension of our correspondence may have been owing, I am persuaded that it did not originate either with you or with me. How far my conjectures on that subject may be well founded, will be ascertained when we meet.

Had your reason for retiring been less urgent than that of ill-health, I should have thought it premature. While government remains relaxed, and the laws have yet to acquire a due degree of respect and obedience, men of talents, weight, and influence should exert themselves to establish and maintain constitutional authority and subordination.

No less wisdom and perseverance are necessary to preserve and secure what we have gained, than were requisite in the acquisition ; and experience informs us that internal commotions and confusion are as injurious to the peace and happiness of society as war and enemies from abroad. Well-ordered government is essential to the duration and enjoyment of the tranquillity and leisure you promise yourself at Saratoga, and therefore domestic as well as public considerations call upon you for such a degree of attention to these subjects as your health will admit of.

I hope and expect next summer to return. Not only my family and my private concerns require it, but also the principles which led me into public life. But if, on my return, I find it my duty to devote more of my time to the public, they shall have it, though retirement is what I ardently desire.

I am not surprised that men of certain characters should censure the terms of peace. There are men who view subjects only on the dark side; there are others who find fault to show their discernment; and we meet with some whose opinions are wholly decided by ideas of convenience and personal politics. I am happy, however, to hear that the great majority are content. In the opinion of Europe, they have great reason to be so.

Your affectionate and very humble servant,

JOHN JAY.

JAY TO GOUVERNEUR MORRIS.

PASSY, 24th September, 1783.

DEAR MORRIS :

The sight of your friendly letter of the 25th of July last, and of those it recommends, gave me much pleasure. Marks of remembrance from old acquaintances, and the society of fellow-citizens in a foreign country, excite agreeable sensations. I have, as yet, met with neither men nor things on this side of the water which abate my predilection, or, if you please, my prejudices, in favour of those on the other. I have but few attachments in Europe much stronger than those we sometimes feel for an accidental fellow-traveller, or for a good inn and a civil landlord. We

leave our approbation, and good wishes, and a certain
degree of regard with them, by way of paying that
part of the reckoning and travelling expenses which
money cannot always defray. My affections are
deeply rooted in America, and are of too long standing to admit of transplantation. In short, my friend,
I can never become so far a citizen of the world as to
view every part of it with equal regard ; and perhaps
nature is wiser in tying our hearts to our native soil,
than they are who think they divest themselves of
foibles in proportion as they wear away those bonds.
It is not difficult to regard men of every nation as
members of the same family ; but when placed in that
point of view, my fellow-citizens appear to me as my
brethren, and the others as related to me only in the
more distant and adventitious degrees.

I am glad my letter by Mr. Grigby gave you reason
to infer an alteration for the better in the state of my
health, because I flatter myself it afforded pleasure to
my friends. The fact is, that my disorder has been
gradually declining ever since I left the city ; but
although the pain in my breast has diminished, it still
continues, and daily tells me *memento mori.* As to
the fever which the influenza left me, it has at last,
thank God, taken its leave. During all my sickness
I have been happy in preserving a constant flow of
spirits ; and cheerfulness, that agreeable companion,
has never forsaken me. I hope a trip to Bath will so
patch up my "house of clay" as to render it tenanta-
ble a good while longer ; a thorough repair I do not
promise myself.

Your account of my son pleases me. I expect and wish to see him next summer; for it is time to lay the foundation of those habits and principles by which I am desirous that his conduct through life should be influenced. Nature has not given to children any instinctive affections for their parents; and youth, that fair season of virtue and ingenuousness, presents the only opportunity for our perfectly gaining their hearts. This conspires with a great variety of other considerations to call me home; and I should not be satisfied with myself if I prolonged my excursion from private life beyond the term which, for public reasons, I at first prescribed it. When a man's conduct ceases to be uniform and consistent, it ceases to be proper. My little girls are well, and their mother is not much otherwise. So much for domestic matters; now for a few lines on politics.

While there are knaves and fools in the world, there will be wars in it; and that nations should make war against nations is less surprising than their living in uninterrupted peace and harmony.

You have heard that the Ottoman and Russian empires are on the point of unsheathing the sword. The objects of the contest are more easy to discern than the issue; but if Russia should extend her navigation to Constantinople, we may be the better for it. That circumstance is an additional motive to our forming a treaty of commerce with her. Your commercial and geographical knowledge render it unnecessary for me to enlarge on this subject. But whatever we may have to do abroad, it is of little consequence when compared to what we have to do at home.

I am perfectly convinced that no time is to be lost in raising and maintaining a national spirit in America. *Power to govern the confederacy, as to all general purposes, should be granted and exercised.* The governments of the different States should be wound up, and become vigorous. America is beheld with jealousy, and jealousy is seldom idle. Settle your boundaries without delay. It is better that some improper limits should be fixed, than any left in dispute. In a word, every thing conducive to union and constitutional energy of government should be cultivated, cherished, and protected, and all counsels and measures of a contrary complexion should at least be suspected of impolitic views and objects.

The rapid progress of luxury at Philadelphia is a frequent topic of conversation here ; and what is a little remarkable, I have not heard a single person speak of it in terms of approbation.

Believe me to be your friend and servant,

JOHN JAY.

GOUVERNEUR MORRIS TO JAY.

PHILADELPHIA, 25 Sep^r·, 1783.

DEAR SIR:

I have received your letter of the twelfth of March by Mr. Penn, sixth of April by Mr. Redford and twenty-ninth of July by Mr. Hunt for all which I am to thank you. Let me also thank you for your letter of the seventeenth of July. Personally, I shall be very happy to see you in the spring, but I confess that I do not very clearly see how it can prove advantageous either to yourself or to your Country if, as you have written to others, the want of health is among the reasons for your return, I cannot but doubly lament it. Remember me affectionately to all my friends who may be in your circle of acquaintance and particularly present my love to Mrs. Jay.

The British employ themselves about the evacuation of New York, but that business goes on slowly. I am however informed from tolerable authority that they will be gone by the begining of November. If, as you suppose, the British Ministry imagine that we cannot retaliate their restrictions, they are deceived, for their conduct will itself give Congress a power which they might not otherwise be possessed of. Indeed my friend nothing can do us so much good as to convince the eastern and southern States how necessary it is to give proper force to the federal government; and nothing will so soon operate that conviction as foreign efforts to restrain the Navigation of the one, and the Commerce of the other. But for my own part, I have no desire to retaliate commercial restrictions. It is my fixed opinion that a Nation can by such restrictions do nothing more than injure herself; nor is an injury the less because it affects more the remote members than it does the head of the empire. The sovereign may collect, and ought to have revenue from all his dominions which are in condition to afford it, but he acts weakly as well as wickedly if he cramps one part of the community that he may draw more easily the blood and juices from another part. The late prohibition of trade with the British Islands, unless in British bottoms, can do us no harm and can do them no good. Our produce they must and will have and if they employ half a million in carrying on the navigation at a great expence, which we should have performed at a less expence, for two hundred thousand, our two hundred thousand will be left for other operations, even to speculate on their produce and our own, so as to make them pay the speculator a profit on every gallon of rum they sell and every barrell of flour they buy, in our ports. By making the subsistance of their people in the Islands more expensive, they aid the efforts of rival Nations to furnish the commodities of their Islands to others, and even to their own subjects. This kind of policy is so bad, that I am persuaded the British Minister cannot seriously intend the prohibition, altho' I am equally convinced that a regard to the national prejudices renders it unavoidable at present. I do not therefore think we should labor to undo what is done but leave things awhile to their own course; and as to a treaty of commerce, I think the best way is to make no treaty for some time to come, and if we tell them that we will make no treaty, they will be much more desirous of it than we ought to be.

Congress are, as you will have heard, already removed to an interior town, which by the bye has every disadvantage, without any advantage over this place; whether they will continue there, or remove to some other village, or come hither, are questions which I cannot resolve. It will, in my opinion, be necessary that they sit near to Philadelphia, but improper to reside within it. They ought not to be very distant from the Bank; nor ought they to be where the supreme authority is not in them. You and I can well remember, when every kind of insult was to be apprehended from being under the jurisdiction of an ungoverned (?) State. Happily, the rulers could see no advantage resulting to themselves from any injuries they might commit against Congress.

Mr. Adams seems to be in opinion with you, as to the necessity of sending a Minister to England, as indeed he does in some other points. He will I suppose be the man for sundry reasons which I might assign, but he will, I think, have serious cause to repent of the appointment ; under present circumstances, nothing could have more unfavorable effects, than to send a Minister who should feel himself attached or opposed to any of the parties by which that nation is rent asunder. He should hold them in equal indifference of sentiment, with equal appearance of confidence, paying to the *ins* a respect due to their places, but which neither *ins* or *outs* are, or can be, entitled to on the score of their merit and virtue, at least from us. As we may not easily find a man capable of this conduct, perhaps the best Minister is no Minister; for the want of one will shew that we are not precipitate in a desire of close connection, and that, however the old mercantile habits may have revived commercial intercourse, the government has a proper jealousy and caution. This circumstance also must work favorably on our politics with other powers, and give weight and dignity to the Ministers we do send.

As to Mr. Dana, he I know means well but I think it would be very wise for him to leave St. Petersburgh, as he went thither *incog ;* or if he should not, it would be very wise for Congress to recall him, as we have nothing to do with the Empress of all the Russias. We cannot conveniently carry on any traffic with her dominions, for various reasons which might be assigned, such (as for instance) that we produce commodities similar to her's, and very few to exchange with her—none indeed of consequence but rice —that the distance is too great, that the poverty both of her subjects and our own requires an advance of capital to each, &c. If her Ladyship should drive the Turk out of Europe, and demolish the Algerines and other piratical gentry she will have done us much good, for her own sake, and we may then find it convenient to meet the commodities of the Levant at some *entrepot*, such as Marseilles, Barcelona, Mahon, or Gibraltar. But it is hardly possible that the other powers will permit Russia to possess so wide a door into the Mediteranean. I may be deceived, but I think England herself would oppose it. As an American, it is my hearty wish that she and the Emperor may effect their schemes, for it will be a source of great wealth to us, both immediate and future. Adieu.

Believe me yours,
Gouvern^{r.} Morris.

JAY TO ALEXANDER HAMILTON.

Passy, 28th September, 1783.

Dear Sir :

Mr. Carter lately delivered to me your friendly letter of the 25th of July last. You were always of the number of those whom I esteemed, and your correspondence would have been both interesting and agreeable. I had heard of your marriage, and it gave me pleasure, as well because it added to your happiness, as because it tended to fix your residence in a State, of which I long wished you to be, and remain a citizen.

The character and talents of delegates to Congress daily become more and more important, and I regret your declining that appointment at this interesting period. Respect, however, is due to the considerations which influence you ; but as they do not oppose your accepting a place in the Legislature, I hope the public will still continue to derive advantage from your services. Much remains to be done, and labourers do not abound.

I am happy to hear that the terms of peace, and the conduct of your negotiators, give general satisfaction ;

but there are some of our countrymen, it seems, who are not content, and that too with an article which I thought to be very unexceptionable, viz., the one ascertaining our boundaries. Perhaps those gentlemen are latitudinarians.

The American newspapers, for some months past, contain advices that do us harm. Violences, and associations against the tories, pay an ill compliment to government, and impeach our good faith in the opinions of some, and our magnanimity in the opinions of many. Our reputation also suffers from the apparent reluctance to taxes, and the ease with which we incur debts without providing for their payment. The complaints of the army—the jealousies respecting Congress—the circumstances which induced their leaving Philadelphia—and the too little appearance of a national spirit, pervading, uniting, and invigorating the confederacy, are considered as omens which portend diminution of our respectability, power, and felicity. I hope that, as the wheel turns round, other and better indications will soon appear. I am persuaded that America possesses too much wisdom and virtue to permit her brilliant prospects to fade away for the want of either. But, whatever time may produce, certain it is that our reputation and our affairs suffer from present appearances.

The tories are as much pitied in these countries as they are execrated in ours. An undue degree of severity towards them would, therefore, be impolitic as well as unjustifiable. They who incline to involve that whole class of men in indiscriminate punishment and ruin, certainly carry the matter too far. It would be an instance of unnecessary rigour, and unmanly revenge, without a parallel, except in the annals of religious rage, in times of bigotry and blindness. What does it signify where nine tenths of these people are buried? I would rather see the sweat of their brows fertilizing our fields than those of our neighbours, in which it would certainly water those seeds of hatred which, if so cultivated, may produce a hedge of thorns against us. Shall all be pardoned then? By no means. Banish and confiscate the estates of such of them as have been either faithless or cruel, and forgive the rest.

Victory and peace should, in my opinion, be followed by clemency, moderation, and benevolence, and we should be careful not to sully the glory of the revolution by licentiousness and cruelty. These are my sentiments, and however unpopular they may be, I have not the least desire to conceal or disguise them.

Be pleased to present my best compliments to Mrs. Hamilton, and believe me to be, with great esteem and regard, dear sir, your most obedient, humble servant,

JOHN JAY.

REVEREND JOHN PRICE TO JAY.

GREAT BOURTON, NEAR BANBURY, OXFORDSHIRE,
October the 29th, 1783.

HONOURED SIR:

Permit a Welchman to congratulate you and Congress, on your freedom, liberty, and independency. May Heaven incline the hearts of Britons and Americans to be truly thankful, for the blessings of Peace, and may both parties beg God's pardon, for the blood spilt and treasures spent in the late war. This application may, perhaps, appear strange to you, especially as it comes from a graduate of the University of Oxford, and a Clergyman of the Church of England; but sir, when you are informed that I, and many more, are so much oppressed, that we cannot bear much longer, as we have no hopes of relief or redress left, the wonder ceases.

I should be infinitely obliged to your Excellency to favour me with a letter, informing me therein, whether or no I can have the honour and pleasure of waiting upon you, and paying my respectful Compliments personally, to the greatest of Embassadors, on the 18th or 19th of November next in London, or elsewhere, as I, with many more of the principality of Wales, intend, if God willing, to cross the Atlantic to a Land of freedom and Liberty where the meanest person is made more happy, if not greater, than Generals, Kings, Emperors, or Popes, by the conduct and Bravery of the Great and Immortal Washington, who has outshined, and Eclipsed, all Asiatic, African, and European Generals, and Commanders from the Creation of the World, to this Day. We humbly hope Congress will give us all reasonable and proper encouragements to emigrate, and become their subjects. Our Submission to the Crown of England for almost five centuries past may be sufficient to recommend us to any Nation or Court on Earth. Our Ancestors were brave and have withstood the force and strength of Rome, Saxony, Normans, Danes, Scots, &c, and we still retain our language in some measure, with some notion of inheritance. Shall conclude subscribing myself

Your Excellency's most devoted h'ble servant,

JOHN PRICE.

P. S.   Direct for the Revd. Jn. Price
         at Borton near Banbury, Oxfordshire.

ROBERT MORRIS TO JAY.

PHILADELPHIA, Nov. 4th, 1783.

DEAR SIR:

I hear your health is mended since the date of your last letter of the 20th of July, and rejoice at it. Your distant friends suffer irreparable injury if you are indisposed to write; those who write so well should write often, and even your short letters say so much in so few words, that it is impossible not to wish for them, if longer ones cannot be had. I acknowledge the force of all your observations on my intended resignation, and know the necessity of perseverance so long as there is a prospect of being useful; but you must also acknowledge that it is folly in the extreme to continue in the drudgery of office after you see clearly that the public cannot be benefited; your own affairs suffering, your feelings daily wounded, and your reputation endangered by the malice and misrepresentation of envious and designing men. During the war, I was determined to go through with the work I had undertaken, and although my resignation was made before the signing of the provisional treaty was known, yet I made no hesitation to declare to a committee of Congress, that if the war lasted I would continue. The war, however, ceased—Congress feared to dismiss their army without some pay; they had not money, and could only make payment by paper anticipation, and even this could not be effected without my assistance. I was urged to continue, and forced into that anticipation. The army was dispersed, and since their departure, the men who urged these measures most, and who are eternally at war with honour and integrity, have been continually employed in devising measures to prevent my being able to fulfil my engagements, in hopes of effecting my ruin in case of failure. I must, however, in justice to the majority of Congress, which has ever been composed of honest men, declare that the faction I allude to is but inconsiderable in numbers, although

they make themselves of some consequence by this assiduity.
You know the . . ., &c. : I should disregard these men
totally, if I found a disposition in the several Legislatures
to support national faith, credit, and character ; but, unhappily, there is at present a total inattention on their parts.
I am, however, persuaded, that sooner or later, the good
sense of America will prevail, and that our governments
will be intrusted in the hands of men whose principles will
lead them to do justice, and whose understandings will teach
the value of national credit. This may be too long in coming to pass, at least for me, and therefore you may rest
assured, that I quit all public employ the moment my engagements are fulfilled.

The court of France having refused the last sum asked, I
do not wish to trouble them further. I am not sensible of
having at any time made an improper application, either as
to *substance* or *manner*. Those who are solicited in such
cases, are in the situation to make whatever objections they
find convenient. I wish, however, that the ministers in
France were sensible of one truth, which is, that my administration either saved them a good deal of money, or
a great deal of disgrace; for if I had not undertaken it when
I did, they must either have advanced ten times the amount
I received, or have deserted America, after having undertaken her cause, and perhaps have been obliged to subscribe
to very indifferent terms of peace for themselves.

It is happy for me that the loan in Holland stepped in to
our relief, after the refusal of the court to grant the moderate sum of 3,000,000 livres as the concluding point. This
refusal was ill-timed and impolitic. I could show resentment with some effect, if I were so disposed ; but so far
from it, I retain a grateful remembrance of past favours,
and make a point to promote the commercial intercourse
between France and this country. I must also show my
sense of the obligations conferred on us by the Hollanders.

We hear that the definitive treaty is signed. I long to see it; for you may depend that unless some new articles are added respecting our intercourse with the British West Indies, it will be both a work of difficulty and time to carry measures that will justify your opinion of us. I thank you for the kind sentiments which you express of me in several parts of your letters. I will endeavour to deserve them. I do not know whether Gouverneur writes to you by this opportunity; you must cherish his friendship, it is worth possessing. He has more virtue than he shows, and more consistency than anybody believes. He values you exceedingly, and hereafter you will be very useful to each other. Mrs. Morris will write to Mrs. Jay, and say for herself what she has to say; though I don't believe she will tell her, as she does to everybody else, the high estimation in which she holds Mrs. Jay and yourself. Permit me also, my worthy friend, to assure you both of the sincerity of that affection with which I profess myself

Your most obedient and humble servant,

ROBERT MORRIS.

JAY TO CHARLES THOMSON.

LONDON, 14th November, 1783.

DEAR SIR:

I have been here a month, and well only two days. I came in quest of *health*, but "*seek and you shall find*" does not, it seems, always extend to that of the body.

The Parliament is sitting. The king's speech and its echoes you will see in the papers. I have not had any conversation on politics with either of the ministers. In my opinion, no plan or system of conduct respecting America is yet decided upon by the Cabinet, in which the jarring principles of whig and tory still strive and ferment. The latter persuade themselves that we shall not be able to act as a nation, that our governments are too feeble to command respect, and our credit too much abased to recover its reputation, or merit confidence. I hope better things. We are not without friends in this country, but they have more inclination than power to be friendly. We have also enemies, and bitter ones. If we act wisely and unitedly, we have nothing to fear. It is in our power finally to make a navigation act, and prevent British vessels carrying our productions ; provided we should execute it, we would find it of as much value as many treaties of commerce. Let us act, however, with temper ; it is more easy to make sores than to heal them. But if Britain should adopt and persist in a monopolizing system, let us retaliate fully and firmly. This nation, like many others, is influenced more by its feelings than reasonings. I am, dear sir, your affectionate friend and servant,

JOHN JAY.

ROBERT MORRIS TO JAY.

PHILADELPHIA, November 27th, 1783.

MY DEAR SIR :

I congratulate you on the signing of the definitive treaty, and on the evacuation of New-York, which took place on Tuesday. Our friend Gouverneur Morris is there. He has been gone about eighteen days, and I expect him back very soon ; he will then give you the detail, and inform you of such things as you may wish to know respecting any of your particular friends.

If Great Britain persists in refusing admittance to our ships in their islands, they will probably have great cause to repent, for I shall not be surprised to see a general prohibition to the admittance of theirs into our ports ; and if such a measure is once adopted, they may find it very difficult to obtain any alteration, and in that case the advantages of carrying will be much against them. Should the court of France pursue the same policy, we shall fall in with the Dutch, and probably have more connexions in commerce with them than with any other people. I have received the prints of the rise and fall of the *balloon*. Pray cannot they contrive to send passengers with a man to steer the course, so as to make them the means of conveyance for despatches from one country to another, or must they only be sent for intelligence to the moon and clouds ?

We are dismissing the remains of our army, and getting rid of expense, so that I hope to see the end of my engagements before next May, but I doubt whether it will be in my power to observe that punctuality in performing them, which I wish and have constantly aimed at.

I am sending some ships to China, in order to encourage others in the adventurous pursuits of commerce, and I wish to see a foundation laid for an American navy.

I am, dear sir,

Your affectionate friend and humble servant,

ROBERT MORRIS.

ROBERT R. LIVINGSTON TO JAY.

NEW-YORK, 29th Nov., 1783.

DEAR JOHN:

I am two letters in your debt, and am conscious that I shall make an ill return for them in offering you this product of a midnight hour, after a day spent in the fatigue of business and ceremony that our present situation exacts. But having just been informed by Mr. Platt that he sails to-morrow morning, I cannot permit him to go, without offering you my congratulations on an event which you have so greatly contributed to bring about, the evacuation of this city by the British on Tuesday last.

Our enemies are hardly more astonished than we are ourselves, and than you will be when you hear that we have been five days in town without the smallest disturbance; that the most obnoxious royalists that had sufficient confidence in our clemency to stay had not met with the least insult. Their shops were opened the day after we came in, and Rivington himself goes on as usual. The State of New York Gazette is as well received as if he had never been printer to the king's most excellent majesty. So that your friends in Europe will find their apprehensions ill-founded, and that the race of tories will not, after all, be totally extinct in America. Perhaps, by good training and by crossing the breed frequently (as they are very tame), they may be rendered useful animals in a few generations.

I thank you for your prints of the air-balls; but wish to have some fuller account of their composition, and the use proposed to be made of them. As an architect, I cannot but be curious about the first castles in the air that promise to have some stable use.

Receive my congratulations on the birth of your daughter, and make my compliments to Mrs. Jay on the occasion.

I had hardly finished the last line, when I was alarmed by a very loud rumbling noise, accompanied by a quick tremulous motion of the earth. The family are too much alarmed to permit me to add more. Adieu.

R. R. LIVINGSTON.

THE COUNTESS OF HUNTINGDON TO JAY.

The Countess of Huntingdon's best Compliments wait on his Excellency, Mr. Jay. She takes this early opportunity of making her most acceptable thanks to him for his politeness and most obliging attentions in the pleasure of seeing him. She hopes, from the advantages of the waters and change of scene being made useful and agreeable, Bath may have the credit of retaining him longer the subject of such advantages.

BATH, Saturday, Dec$^{br.}$ 6 [1783].

JAY TO THE COUNTESS OF HUNTINGDON.

BATH, December 7th, 1783.

Mr. Jay presents his respectful compliments to the Countess of Huntingdon and is exceedingly obliged by the very polite note which her Ladyship did him the honour to write yesterday. When persons of rank become dignified by virtue and distinguished for active benevolence, they naturally command esteem and excite attention. These considerations give particular value to the kind wishes which her Ladyship is pleased to express for Mr. Jay's health. He begs her Ladyship to be assured of his perfect respect and esteem, and of the pleasure it would give him to have frequent opportunities of evincing both.

JAY TO KITTY LIVINGSTON.

BATH, 24th December, 1783.

DEAR KITTY :

Why so long silent, my good friend ? Many months have elapsed since we have been favoured with a line from you. I hope want of health has not obliged you to deny us that satisfaction. Want of inclination, I am sure, has not. Of that we have received too many unequivocal proofs to entertain the most distant doubt. You have long been my faithful, steady friend. I know the value of your esteem and regard, and be assured that you possess mine in a very high degree. Much do I wish for the happy moment when we shall all meet, and when we shall communicate to each other many things, which, however interesting, must be very sparingly trusted to paper. The necessity of this caution has imposed upon us a long and painful reserve, for between friends few things are more agreeable, as well as useful, than free and undisguised communications. This is a pleasure to which I have been greatly a stranger since I left America, and it is in that country alone that I expect again to enjoy it. Experience has taught me reserve, but it has also taught me that with you it will be unnecessary. This is a pleasant idea, and my mind dwells upon it with great satisfaction. How few there are in this world, my dear Kate, capable of a firm, uniform attachment—much fewer, I assure you, than I once thought,—but youth is credulous, and consequently must be often disappointed. I hope my disappointments are nearly at an end ; for I expect very little, except from you and a few others.

I have letters from Sally almost every week. Thank God, she continues well. She tells me our little girls grow charmingly. My absence from her has been much longer than I expected. On coming to London I was taken ill of a dysentery, and afterwards with a sore throat. Some remains of the latter still trouble me. Upon the whole, however, I am better, and the waters of this place have done me good. I propose next week to return to London, and from thence make the best of my way to France. I am impatient to be with my little family, and to have my sweet little girls upon my knee, while their mother tells me the domestic occurrences which have happened in my absence. Believe me to be, with great and sincere regard,

Your friend and servant,

JOHN JAY.

KITTY LIVINGSTON TO JAY.

ELIZABETH TOWN, Dec. 30th, 1783.

Permit me, my dear Sir, to wish you and sister the Compliments of the season, and to assure you that no one more sincerely wishes the ensuing year may be propitious to your every wish than your friend who has now the pleasure of writing to you.

The Church disputes, far from subsiding, rage with more violence than ever. The Whigs finding the Moore-ans, or in plain English the tories, the strongest party are determined to petition the Legislature for their interposition. They will never stop short of depriving Mr. Moore of the rectorship, in which, though I am no Churchwoman, I think they are perfectly right. They ought indeed to go farther. They should silence Mr. Moore altogether. I am no friend to persecution, but I think in the present critical situation of their City, the Tories will have no reason to complain if we do nothing more than prevent their holding any office which may give them influence, until they can consent, to lay aside their hankering after the flesh pots of Britain.

Yesterday opened the election for their City Members; a very contested one was expected. I am sorry to hear that some men bid fair to succeed who are very unequal to the task of Legislation.

The dancing assembly met with great opposition, some from religious and some from political motives opposed it, but the loyal Managers, (Augustus Van Courtland and Daniel Ludlow), resigning and expunging some of their rules, appeased the populace, and they have carried them into execution. A private ball at the Chancellor's, another at uncle P. V. B. Livingston's in compliment to his Excellency, Gen'l Washington, (as he quartered there), are all I have heard of.

Your friend, Dr. Bancroft, spent some time with us going and returning from New York. Mr. Holker introduced him and has assured us that the Dr. has not had for several years so agreeable a relaxation from politicks. When I last heard from Philadelphia that gentleman was preparing to sail for Charleston, but the weather setting in very severe shortly after probably has detained him. The Dr. did not leave us without a promise to repeat his visit in the Spring. I shall consider his doing it a mark of approbation of the reception we gave him. A more agreeable visitor we could not have entertained, as he gave us a more particular account respecting your health and family than any we have received since your residence in France. I believe I mentioned in a former letter that we had not the pleasure of seeing Mrs. Izard. Col. Ogden, if I may judge from his remissness, must make another Voyage to Europe to be instructed in good breeding.

Mr. Robt. Morris I hear seems determined to quit the first of next May ; then G. M. will I suppose return to his Mammy. We never have been so at a loss to tell where you are as at present, not having received any letters of a later date than August. Are Mr. and Mrs. Ridley in Paris or London ? The Dr. and Mr. Holker differed on that subject. If it be not premature will you wish them joy for me. I wrote to Mr. Ridley the same time I wrote to sister and intended it to go from Philadelphia that you should hear from us before the arrival of Sir Guy [Carleton]. Sister's letter I detained to go with Major Upham at his particular request. Mr. Holker thought proper to bring back the letter and send it in the L'Orient Packet, which must have occasioned its very late arrival.

The Legislature of this State having risen, we are hourly expecting my Father home. By the enclosed letter you will see it's determined that Master Peter stays with us this Winter. He is very ambitious to write equal to his Aunt Susan, his instructress. This morning as I was looking over him I read his copy for the day, " Commend virtuous deeds." " I must do more than that," says he, " I must imitate them." He has read *Robinson Crusoe* and *Don Quixote*. He is now reading *Nature Delineated*, and is exceedingly pleased with the natural history they contain. He begins the exercises of the day and closes the same with reading a few Chapters in the Bible. He has learnt many of the hymns in the book you sent him, and frequently expresses a great desire to see you and his Mamma. He enjoys good health and is often complimented with having his Mammas complextion. It is indeed sun and frost proof. . . .

Kiss Sally and your sweet babes for me and I'll pay you with interest when we have the pleasure of meeting. Mamma, Susan, and Peter unite with me in love to sister and you.

Your affectionate friend and sister, KITTY.

GOUVERNEUR MORRIS TO JAY.

PHILADELPHIA, 10th January, 1784.

DEAR JAY :

I write to acknowledge your letter of the 24th September. Being uncertain where you are, and consequently what course this letter may take, and through what hands it will pass, I shall not say so much as I otherwise might. I will direct to the care of Dr. Franklin.

Your attachment to America, when removed from it, is the old story of travellers ; but when it comes from one in whose feelings we feel an interest, *decies repetita placebit.* Of your health you speak despondingly, yet you say your spirits are good. Believe me, my friend, good spirits will both make and preserve good health. I mean to extend the observation generally, but not universally. Whatever lot betides us, I wish you at least one happy year, and I hope that Heaven will do you the justice to grant a long succession of them. Make my good wishes acceptable to Mrs. Jay, and present me tenderly to your children.

I was lately in New-York, and have the pleasure to tell you that all your friends were well. Things there are now in that kind of ferment which was rationally to have been expected ; and I think the superior advantages of our constitution will now appear in the repressing of those turbulent spirits who wish for confusion, because that in the regular order of things they can only fill a subordinate sphere.

This country has never yet been known to Europe, and God knows whether it ever will be so. To England it is less known than to any other part of Europe ; because they constantly view it through a medium either of prejudice or of faction. True it is, that the general government wants energy ; and equally true it is that this want will eventually be supplied. A national spirit is the natural result of national existence ; and although some of the present generation may feel colonial oppositions of opinion, that generation will die away, and give place to a race of Americans. On this occasion, as on others, Great Britain is our best friend; and by seizing the critical moment when we were about to divide, she has shown clearly the dreadful consequences of division. You will find that the States are coming into resolutions on the subject of commerce; which, if they had been proposed by Congress on the plain reason of the thing, would have been rejected with resentment, and perhaps contempt.

With respect to our taste for luxury, do not grieve about t. Luxury is not so bad a thing as it is often supposed to be; and if it were, still we must follow the course of things, and turn to advantage what exists, since we have not the power to annihilate or create. The very definition of luxury is as difficult as the suppression of it.

Do not condemn us till you see us. Do not ask the British to take off their foolish restrictions. Let them alone and they will be obliged to do it themselves. While the present regulation exists, it does us more of political good than it can possibly do of commercial evil. Adieu.

Believe me always yours,

GOUVERNEUR MORRIS.

CHARLES THOMSON TO JAY.

ANNAPOLIS, Jan. 14, 1784.

DEAR SIR:

.   .   .   .

I sincerely congratulate you on the return of peace, and it is my most ardent prayer that the United States may improve the opportunity now afforded of becoming a happy people. The treaty was this day ratified, being the first day we have had nine States since the last of October. The ratification is forwarded by Col. J. Harmar, the bearer.

whom I beg leave to recommend to your particular attention and civility. Mrs. Thomson desires to be remembered to Mrs. Jay, to whom you will please to make my most respectful compliments.

I am with sincere esteem and regard,

Your most obedient and most humble servant,

CHAS. THOMSON.

CHARLES THOMSON TO JAY.

ANNAPOLIS, Jany. 15, 1784.

DEAR SIR :

Though I am sensible that Lieut-Col. D. S. Frank, who is the bearer of this, needs no introduction or recommendation to you, yet I cannot suffer him to go without a line from me. He is intrusted with a triplicate ratification of the definitive treaty, which passed yesterday, the first time we have had nine States represented since Octr. last, and which was done with the unanimous consent not only of every State but of every member in Congress. The proclamation and recommendation of which he carries copies passed also with a like unanimous consent; So that I have strong hopes the treaty will be carried into full effect, and that when the passions of the people are cooled, a spirit of conciliation will prevail. But considering what many have suffered, whose feelings are still alive and whose wounds are not yet closed, and considering that our new established governments have not attained their full tone and vigour, it can hardly be expected that people will in a moment forget what is past and suddenly return to an interchange of friendly offices with those whom for years past they have considered as their most bitter enemies. My apprehensions are greatest from your own State where the people have suffered most, and yet there is such a spirit and vigour in that government, that I trust matters will be conducted with prudence and moderation.

We have had no delegates from that State since the first Monday in November, occasioned, I am informed by a law of the State which prevented the meeting of the Assembly till the City was evacuated. However, as the Assembly is now met we expect delegates will soon be present. There has been a scene for six months past over which I would draw the veil. I may perhaps have an opportunity of explaining myself further. However, the prospect begins to brighten and as I love to indulge a hope which corresponds with my fond wishes, I flatter myself that prudence and good sense will prevail.

I am, with sincere esteem and affection, Dear Sir,
Your Obedient and humble Servant,
CHAS. THOMSON.

SILAS DEANE TO JAY.

LONDON, Jan. 21st, 1784.

SIR:

I called at your lodgings in November last, but your servant told me you were not within, and that you intended to set out for Bath in a day or two; on which, being exceedingly desirous of an interview with you, I sent you a letter requesting that favour; but going out of town myself a few days after, and having received no answer, I am at a loss what to conclude on, whether my letter might have failed, or that you do not incline to favour me with an interview; and hence I am induced to trouble you with this, and to request that you will simply inform me by a line, if you received my letter of November, and if an interview will be agreeable or not. I wish to obviate and remove any late prejudices which you may have entertained against me, from the most gross misrepresentations of my conduct since my arrival in England; and I submit to you the propriety of giving me an opportunity for doing this; and am, with great respect, Sir,

Your most obedient and very humble Servant,

SILAS DEANE.

ROBERT R. LIVINGSTON TO JAY.

NEW-YORK, 25th January, 1784.

DEAR JOHN:

The quiet, which in my last I mentioned to have prevailed here, still continues with very few interruptions; though the imprudence of the tories has, in some instances, given disgust to the warm whigs, particularly in a contest for the government of the church corporation, to the exclusion of those out of the lines, and in appointing Mr. Moore rector, in order to fill the church, a few days before we came in. The Legislature have interposed, and the government of the church is transferred to the whigs.

Our parties are, first, the tories, who still hope for power, under the idea that the remembrance of the past should be lost, though they daily keep it up by their avowed attachment to Great Britain. Secondly, the violent whigs, who are for expelling all tories from the State, in hopes, by that means, to preserve the power in their own hands. The third are those who wish to suppress all violences, to soften the rigour of the laws against the loyalists, and not to banish them from that social intercourse which may, by degrees, obliterate the remembrance of past misdeeds; but who, at the same time, are not willing to shock the feelings of the virtuous citizens, that have at every expense and hazard fulfilled their duty, by at once destroying all distinction between them and the royalists, and giving the reins into the hands of the latter; but who, at the same time, wish that this distinction should rather be found in the sentiments of the people, than marked out by the laws. You will judge to which of these parties the disqualifications contained in our election bill has given the representation, when I tell you that the members for this city and county are Lamb, Harper, Sears, Van Zandt, Mallone, Rutgers, Hughes, Stag, and Willet. I must, however, do all parties the justice to say, that they profess the highest respect for the laws, and that, if we except one or two persons, they have, as yet, by no act contradicted that profession.

You will receive with this a ratification of the treaty. Congress are now convened at Annapolis in consequence of their curious resolution to have two places of residence, of which they are by this time ashamed and tired.

We are very angry here with Great Britain, on account of her West India restrictions (from which, by-the-bye, they suffer greatly), and are fulminating resolutions to prohibit all intercourse with her, which I think will probably be the case ere long.

Thus have I given you a sketch of our politics, which will only be interesting to you if, as I sincerely hope, you mean to return soon to us.

Politics has extended this letter to such an unreasonable length, that I dare not hazard a subject nearer my heart than either, but must, at this time, confine all its dictates to simple assurances of the firm and tender affection with which I am, and ever shall be,

Dear John, your friend,
ROBT. R. LIVINGSTON.

JAY TO GOUVERNEUR MORRIS.

PARIS, 10th February, 1784.

DEAR MORRIS:

Your letter of the 25th September came to my hands in England on the 8th December last; and since my return, I have received that of the 7th

November, which, though containing only three lines, I prefer to most of the others. Perhaps you have forgot it :

It is now within three minutes of the time when the mail is made up and sent off. I cannot, therefore, do more than just to assure you of the continuance of my love. Adieu. Yours,

G. M.

That this letter was so short I ascribe to procrastination ; that it was written at all I ascribe to your heart ; your head evidently had no concern in it, for, if consulted, it would have intimated that they who live near a post-office find no good excuse for singular brevity in the mails being to be sent off in a few minutes after they sit down to write, unless, indeed, some circumstance just occurred should make the subject of the letter. But, be that as it may, I would rather receive one little effusion from your heart than twenty from your head, though I hope to derive much pleasure from both. We shall have much to say to each other, and I think both of us will be gainers by it. Why I think so must not be discussed in letters, whose seals will not be respected.

You suppose that ill-health induces me to resign. You are mistaken. It seldom happens that any measure is prompted by one single motive, though one among others may sometimes have decisive weight and influence. Many motives induce me to resign, but of those many there is one which predominates, and that is this : When I embarked in the public service, I said very sincerely that I quitted private life with regret, and should be happy to return to it when the objects which called me from it should be attained. You know what those objects were, and that, on the peace, they ceased to operate. To be consistent, therefore, I must retire. The motive is irresistible. Superadded to this are the education of my son, the attention I owe to the unfortunate part of my family, and the happiness I expect from rejoining my friends. Pecuniary considerations ever held a secondary place in my estimation. I know how to live within the bounds of any income, however narrow, and my pride is not of a nature to be hurt by returning to the business which I formerly followed : but professions of this sort are common, and facts only can give unequivocal evidence of their sincerity.

I have passed between three and four sad months in England. Bad weather and bad health almost the whole time. On my arrival a dysentery and fever brought me low, and a sore-throat, which still plagues me, succeeded. Bath has done me good, for it removed the pain in my breast, which has been almost constant for eighteen months.

I had many excellent opportunities of writing to my friends from London and Bristol, but I was enjoined to abstain as much as possible from pen and ink.

It is natural that you should expect to find some news in this letter. I will tell you a little, though it is probable that your sagacity has prevented its being unexpected. The institution of the Order of Cincinnatus does not, in the opinion of the wisest men whom I have heard speak on the subject, either do credit to those who formed and patronized or to those who suffered it.

I am indebted to our excellent friend, Robert Morris, for a very obliging letter. He shall soon hear from me. In the meantime let him share with you in this adieu.

Yours sincerely,

JOHN JAY.

GENERAL SCHUYLER TO JAY.

NEW-YORK, Feb. 18th, 1784.

DEAR SIR:

By Colonel Hamilton, who made me a visit at Albany on the 26th instant, I had the pleasure of your favour of the 16th September last. Persuaded you never convey sentiments to your friends, which flow merely from the head, and in which the heart does not participate, I have not words to express how pleasingly mine was affected in the perusal.

I think I hear you wish to be advised of what is passing in your native country, at a juncture when the decisions of government must determine the philosophers and politicians of Europe to form their opinion of our wisdom or our folly. Having been exceedingly indisposed, I have not attended until a few days ago, and am consequently, as yet, not in a situation to speak decidedly ; but I have reason to apprehend, however, from the complexion of the members, that our conduct will be such as to afford occasion to the friends of mankind to drop a tear on the intemperance of mankind ; and to reflect, with pain, that a people who have hardly been emancipated from a threatened tyranny, forgetting how odious oppression appeared to them, begin to play the tyrant, and give a melancholy evidence, that however capable we were of bearing adversity with magnanimity, we are too weak to support, with propriety, the prosperity we have so happily experienced.

I am led to this conclusion from observing that too many, not contented with a peace, glorious and advantageous beyond the expectations of the most sanguine real patriot, and that, too, obtained at a period when the complexion of our national affairs was alarming in the extreme, wish to evade the positive stipulations, few and inconsiderable as they are, in favour of those who adhered to Britain ; and carry their views even so far beyond that, as totally to deprive all those who remained within the power of the British troops from the rights of citizens, upon the false conclusion that all who remained in were zealous adherents to the then enemy, and all who were not, disinterested and real patriots. I think you and I could point out some who looked at both sides of the question whilst the contest was doubtful, and who probably did not wish it to terminate as it has done ; and yet these are the very characters who are now most vociferous against that set of people, to whom, but a few months before the annunciation of the provisional articles, they still paid court. I hope, however, when the present scramblers for the honours and the emoluments of the States are satisfied, that our affairs will take another turn, and that we shall not irretrievably lose our national character. Among those claimants and scramblers you will not include some whose zeal for the common cause, from the first stage of the contest to the close, are justly entitled to the attention of government—such as Mr. Duane, who has the mayoralty of this city, and some others.

When I assure you that I am anxious for your speedy return to your native country, and that it is more than a selfish wish, I am very sincere ; for I believe your influence would tend much to promote its true interest.

Permit me to entreat your lady to participate with you in wishes which come from the heart, for your health and happiness, and for your speedy and safe arrival on these shores, where you will find friends who love and esteem you, and where all ought to revere you who are capable of being penetrated with gratitude for the most eminent services. For my part, I never think of you without emotions too delicate for communication. God bless you.

I am, affectionately and sincerely

Your obedient servant,

PHILIP SCHUYLER.

JAY TO SILAS DEANE.

CHAILLOT, NEAR PARIS, 23d February, 1784.

SIR :

Your letter of the 21st of January was delivered to me this morning. It is painful to say disagreeable things to any person, and especially to those with whom one has lived in habits of friendship ; but candour on this subject forbids reserve. You were of the number of those who possessed my esteem, and to whom I was attached. To me, personally, you have never given offence ; but, on the contrary, I am persuaded you sincerely wished me well, and was disposed to do me good offices.

The card you left for me at Mr. Bingham's, and also the letter you mention, were both delivered to me, and I cannot express the regret I experienced from the cruel necessity I thought myself under, of passing them over in silence ; but I love my country and my honour better than my friends, and even my family, and am ready to part with them all whenever it would be improper to retain them. You are either exceedingly injured, or you are no friend to America; and while doubts remain on that point, all connection between us must be suspended. I wished to hear what you might have to say on that head, and should have named a time and place for an interview, had not an insurmountable obstacle intervened to prevent it. I was told by more than one, on whose information I thought I could rely, that you received visits from, and was on terms of familiarity with General Arnold. Every American who gives his hand to that man, in my opinion, pollutes it.

I think it my duty to deal thus candidly with you, and I assure you, with equal sincerity, that it would give me cordial satisfaction to find you able to acquit yourself in the judgment of the dispassionate and impartial. If it is in your power to do it, I think you do yourself injustice by not undertaking that necessary task. That you may perform it successfully whenever you undertake it, is the sincere wish and desire of, sir, your most obedient humble servant,

JOHN JAY.

JAY TO ROBERT MORRIS.

PARIS, 25th February, 1784.

MY GOOD FRIEND:

Your favour of the 4th November last found me in England, where, though I suffered much sickness, I left the pain in my breast; but a sore-throat I caught there still remains obstinate and troublesome.

The resolution of Congress of 1st October last did

not reach me until in December. On my return here last month, I wrote in pursuance of it to Mr. Carmichael to come here without delay with the books and vouchers. I daily expect to hear from him, and shall be happy to see that business settled before I embark, which I hope will be in April, but from or to what port, and in what vessel, is as yet uncertain.

There is no doubt but that you have had much to struggle with, and will have more. Difficulties must continue inseparable from your office for some time yet, and they will be the means either of increasing or diminishing your reputation. In my opinion you must go on. Success generally attends talents and perseverance, and these thorns will in due season probably bear flowers, if not fruit.

There are parts of your letter on which, though I concur with you in sentiment, I forbear to make remarks, because this may not pass to you uninspected. I hope we shall meet in the course of a few months more, and then reserve will cease to be necessary.

What you say of Gouverneur accords with my opinion of him. I have never broken the bands of friendship in my life, nor when once broken have I ever been anxious to mend them. Mine with him will, I hope, last as long as we do, for though my sentiments of mankind in general are less favourable than formerly, my affection for certain individuals is as warm and cordial as ever.

Mrs. Jay presents her affectionate compliments to you and Mrs. Morris, to whom we join in sincerely wishing all the happiness with which amiable merit should be ever blesed. Tell Gouverneur I long to take him by the hand, and believe me to be, my dear sir, with constant attachment, your affectionate friend and servant, JOHN JAY.

JAY TO BENJAMIN VAUGHAN.

CHAILLOT, NEAR PARIS, 21st March, 1784.

DEAR SIR,

The violence of your political storm seems to have abated, but I should not be surprised if you should frequently have March weather.

Accounts from America lead me to suspect that your commercial negotiations with us will not be facilitated by delay; and I should not be surprised if a system should then be adopted which would render European proclamations of very little importance to that country. It appears more probable that England will outwit herself. There is a tide in human affairs which, like other tides, turns only to run in an opposite direction.

I am preparing to go to New York by the first good vessel that may sail for that port. I more than wish to see you there. They who know the nature of man expect perfection nowhere. There are certain degrees in refinement and arts, which are more favourable than others to those principles and manners which wise men prefer. In this, as well as in some other circumstances, we have the advantage of other countries. Various causes conspire to give every man his weight, and I believe the old maxim of *"quisque suæ faber est fortunæ"* has fewer exceptions in

America than elsewhere. They who bring with them ideas borrowed from the regions of fancy and romance will be disappointed. The golden age will not cease to be a fable until the millennium; until that period for separating life from death, pleasure from pain, virtue from vice, and wisdom from folly, every society and country will continue to partake more or less of the heterogeneous and discordant principles, which seem to be the seeds both of moral and natural evil.

Were I in your situation, I would see for myself, and then determine. To avoid mistakes, it is necessary to see things as being what they really are. Minutiæ are often omitted, or imperfectly drawn in representations. Great part of the good within our reach depends on minutiæ; they merit more attention than many apprehend.

Be pleased to present my respectful compliments to Lord and Lady Shelburne. I hope his gout has left him. Remember me also to our patriot friend, Doctor Price.

   Adieu, my dear sir,

       Yours, sincerely,

         John Jay.

JOHN WITHERSPOON TO JAY.

London, March 27, 1784.

Dear Sir:

 I had some expectations of seeing you before this in Paris, which was the cause of my not writing since my arrival in London. Suffer me to inform you that the trustees of our College [Princeton] very much contrary to my judgment were induced by some things they had heard to suppose that this would not be an improper time to solicit benefactions for the College which is known to have suffered so much by being seated in the centre of the theatre of the late War. They therefore insisted upon my accompanying Gen. Reed to Europe, giving us a joint commission to make application for this purpose both in England and France.

There is little or no prospect of success here, and though I should be well pleased to visit Paris for my own satisfaction I am somewhat unwilling to add to the charge unless there be some reason to hope it may be useful. I have letters of introduction to the Comte de Vergennes and the Comte de Sanfield from the Minister of France with us and also other letters from Mr. Marbois and Gen[l.] Washington. Those letters, however, I suppose are general and not relating to the purpose above mentioned. What I would particularly request of you is to give your opinion freely and candidly whether in case of my going to Paris it would be at all proper to make application to any persons for the College either as to subscriptions, books, or apparatus. I will be governed in this matter by your opinion and that of Dr. Franklin to whom I have also written, and will either not go to Paris at all, or when there, be entirely silent on this business and only gratify my curiosity and pay my compliments where they are due.

Though I did not trouble you with a letter of thanks, I have ever retained a grateful sense of your friendship and attention to my son John who sailed with you from America. He has made frequent mention of it, and also spoke much of the propriety and fortitude of Mrs. Jay's conduct on your disastrous voyage.

Please to make my respectful compliments to Mrs. Jay. Her father was one of the last persons I saw in America, and left him very well. I have the honor to be,

Dear Sir, Your most obedient humble Servant,
JNO: WITHERSPOON.

JOHN ADAMS TO JAY.

THE HAGUE, April 2d, 1784.

MY DEAR FRIEND:

I blush to acknowledge that I received your favour of the 6th February, in its season, and in good condition, and that I have not answered it.

By leading a quiet life, and by great care and regular exercise, I have happily recovered a little health, and if you think it necessary, I might now venture on a journey to Paris But I should be glad to wait here six weeks longer, that I may increase my stock of strength a little more, if possible, provided you will give me leave. I should be glad to know what you have upon the carpet, and how advanced, in brief, if you please.

The money for the payment of Mr. Morris's bills is happily secured, but we were a long time in bringing the loan to bear.

I have received several letters from Boston and Philadelphia, from very good hands, which make very honourable and affectionate mention of you. You have erected a monument to your memory in every New England heart. My regards to your good family, and believe me,

Your sincere friend,

JOHN ADAMS.

JAY TO JOHN WITHERSPOON.

CHAILLOT, NEAR PARIS, 6th April, 1784.

DEAR SIR:

I had last evening the pleasure of receiving your favour of the 27th ult. I congratulate you on your safe arrival, and sincerely wish that the same good fortune may attend your return.

While our country remained part of the British empire, there was no impropriety in soliciting the aid of our distant brethren and fellow-subjects for any liberal and public purposes. It was natural that the younger branches of the political family should request and accept the assistance of the elder. But as the United States neither have, nor can have, such relations with any nations in the world ; as the rank they hold, and ought to assert, implies ability to provide for all the ordinary objects of their government ; and as the diffusion of knowledge among a republican people is and ought to be one of the constant and most important of those objects, I cannot think it consistent with the dignity of a free and independent people, to solicit donations for that or any other purpose, from the subjects of any prince or state whatever.

The public, with us, are, in my opinion, so deeply interested in the education of our citizens, that universities, etc., ought no longer to be regarded in the light of mere private corporations. The government should extend to them their constant care ; and the State treasuries afford them necessary supplies.

The success which might attend such applications in this country can only be matter of conjecture. The raising money by subscription has not been so customary in France as in Britain, and my opinion is that you would collect very little. If indeed the court should set the example, and really wish to promote it, the thing would then become fashionable ; and I am inclined to think that even the fashion of giving would have a great run for a few weeks. As to books, the consideration that every American student who in a long lapse of years might open those books would read the name of the donor, added to the vanity of authors, and others who may be zealous to extend the reputation of French literature, would probably procure you some. As to apparatus, the best instruments and machines are made in England; and the greater as well as better part of those used here are, I am told, brought from thence. I am much mistaken if Europe, in general, does not wish that we were less knowing than we are already. But if it was probable that such applications would be attended with ever so great success, yet, as I think they can be properly made only in the United States, I could not prevail upon myself to advise the experiment.

If, however, you should visit Paris, I assure you it will give me great pleasure to see you, and to be instrumental in rendering it agreeable to you. We have been fellow-labourers in the same field, and if you come, we will rejoice together in celebrating "harvest home."

With respect to the disagreeable voyage in which your son shared with us, I won't say *jubes renovare dolorem*, because I am habituated to reflect on events of that sort with tranquillity. It was one of those, however, which tried all who were concerned in it; and I must do your son the justice to say that none of us preserved more equanimity and good-humour throughout the whole than he did, and he had a full share of unpleasant circumstances, as well as some others of us. I am, dear sir,

Your most obedient and very humble servant,

JOHN JAY.

JAY TO KITTY LIVINGSTON.

CHAILLOT, NEAR PARIS, 7th April, 1784.

My Good Friend :

It gave me pleasure to receive your obliging letter of the 30th December, and the more so as the one to Sally which accompanies it contains agreeable accounts of your health. Accept my thanks for the kind wishes which the season gave you occasion to offer. In your sincerity I have full confidence, and in your happiness I feel that interest which long-confirmed esteem and attachment never fails to create.

If the ensuing summer should bring us all together in health and spirits, I shall think the day of my arrival one of the most fortunate of my life. After having passed so many years in scenes of trouble and difficulty of various kinds, I look forward with emotion not to be described to that peaceful circle of my friends and family, where I again expect to meet the enjoyments which have so long deserted me. God only knows what futurity may have in store for us, or what adverse events may still continue to teach us lessons of resignation. It is happy for us, however, that hope is our constant companion, and that new expectations constantly succeed the disappointment of preceding ones.

Having expected that Mr. Carmichael would have arrived with the public accounts in time to have them settled before the April packet engaged her passengers, I had taken steps for going in her ; but he did not reach Paris till the 27th ult., and Mr. Barclay, who is to settle them, being then and still absent, I must necessarily be detained here till in May. I hope, but am not sure, that I shall then embark. In matters which do not depend upon myself, or people like you, I dare not be sanguine. Such of our baggage as is not in immediate use is already packed up.

Your accounts of my dear boy please me. Tell him his endeavours to gain knowledge and practise virtue will increase and secure my affection for him.

Remember me to all the family, and believe me to be, dear Kate,

Your affectionate friend and brother,

JOHN JAY.

JAY TO CHARLES THOMSON.

CHAILLOT, NEAR PARIS, 7th April, 1784.

DEAR SIR:

On the 5th inst. Mr. Norris gave me your obliging letter of the 26th September last. I regret that he did not come here sooner, for it will always give me pleasure to have opportunities of evincing my esteem and regard for you by attention to those who possess yours. Mr. Carmichael, whom I had long expected with the public accounts, did not arrive until the 27th ult., when Mr. Ridley had just gone to England, and Mr. Barclay, who had been long there, was and still is absent. Nothing but the settlement of those accounts now detains me here, and a mortifying detention it is, considering that the best season for being at sea is passing away. While I stay, Mr. Norris shall perceive that he could have brought few recommendations to me so acceptable as yours, and those amiable qualities for which you commend him. I wish he may return as uncorrupted as he came. Paris is a place better calculated for the improvement of riper years; and, in my opinion, very young men should not visit it. Our country has already sent some here, who will return the worse for their travels. I hope your young friend may escape. If he should, you may congratulate him on having made the choice of Hercules, for he will be tempted. On the 1st instant I received your favour of January last by Colonel Harmer. I flatter myself that the delays attending the ratification of the treaty will not occasion difficulties, especially as one of the ministers who made the peace is now at the head of the British administration. If European commercial restrictions produce unanimity and tend to raise a *national* spirit in our country, which probably will be the case, I shall think them blessings. It is time for us to think and act like a sovereign as well as a free people, and by temperate and steady self-respect to command that of other nations. It is but too much the fashion to depreciate Congress, and I fear that, as well as many other of our new fashions, will cost us dear.

Be pleased to present our compliments to Mrs. Thompson. With great and sincere regard and esteem, I am, dear sir, your most obedient servant,

JOHN JAY.

CHARLES THOMSON TO JAY.

DEAR SIR: PHILADELPHIA, June 18, 1784.

I have the pleasure to inform you that on the 7th of May Congress elected you Secretary for Foreign Affairs. I do not know how you will be pleased with the appointment, but this I am sure of—that your country stands in need of your abilities in that office. I feel sensibly that it is not only time, but highly necessary for us to think and act like a sovereign, as well as a free, people; and I wish this sentiment were more deeply impressed on the members of every State in the Union. The opportunities you will have of corresponding not only with the executives but with the several legislatures, in discharging the duties of your office, will I trust greatly contribute to raise and promote this spirit; and this is a reason why I wish you were here to enter on the business.

On the same day that you were elected to the Office for Foreign Affairs, Congress appointed Mr. Jefferson, in addition to Mr. J. Adams and Mr. Franklin, for the purpose of negotiating commercial treaties with the powers of Europe.

I am, Dear Sir, Yours Affectionately,

CHAS. THOMSON.

OFFICIAL CONGRATULATIONS FROM NEW YORK CITY TO JAY.[1]

To the honourable JOHN JAY, *Esquire, late one of the ministers plenipotentiary of the United States of America for negotiating a peace.*

SIR:

Be pleased to accept the congratulations of the Mayor, Aldermen, and Commonalty of the city of New-York, on your safe return to the place of your nativity.

---

[1] Closing up his affairs connected with the Treaty of Peace, and settling his public accounts with Mr. Barclay, special agent appointed by Congress, Mr.

The revolution, which hath secured our liberties and independence, will not be more celebrated for the illustrious events which have marked its progress, than for the roll of statesmen and heroes by whose wisdom and valour, under the Divine favour, it hath been established on the most solid basis.

Among these worthy patriots you, sir, are highly distinguished. In our own convention, in our first seat of justice, as a member and as president of the United States in Congress assembled, and as a minister plenipotentiary both in Spain and France,—you have executed the important trusts committed to you with wisdom, firmness, and integrity, and have acquired universal applause.

While you thus possess the national confidence and esteem for a series of eminent services, we, your fellow-citizens, feel a singular pleasure in embracing this opportunity to present you with the freedom of your native city, as a public testimony of the respectful sentiments we entertain towards you, and as a pledge of our affection, and of our sincere wishes for your happiness.

[July 24, 1784.]

JAY TO THE PRESIDENT OF CONGRESS.

NEW YORK, July 25, 1784.

SIR :

Having waited until the settlement of the public accounts was completed, I left Paris the 16th of May last, and on the 1st of June embarked with my family at Dover, on board the ship *Edward*, Captain

---

Jay left Paris in the latter part of May, 1784, and sailed for America, from Dover, on the first day of June. Upon his arrival at New York, July 24th, he was feelingly greeted by his fellow-citizens, and the Corporation presented him the above address of welcome, accompanied by the " freedom of the City " enclosed in a gold box. In one of his first letters after landing, he wrote : " At length, my good friend, I am arrived at the land of my nativity ; and I bless God that it is also the land of light, liberty, and plenty. My emotions cannot be described."

Couper, in which we arrived here yesterday. Mr. Barclay has transmitted, or will soon transmit, to Mr. Morris a state of the above-mentioned accounts ; and as it will thence appear that some of the bills drawn upon me have been twice paid, it becomes necessary for me to inform your Excellency of the particular and cautious manner in which that business was transacted on my part. Soon after the arrival of the first bills, I directed Mr. Carmichael to prepare and keep a book, with the pages divided into a number of columns, and to enter therein the dates, numbers, and other descriptive particulars of every bill that might be presented to me for acceptance, and to which on examination he should find no objection. I made it an invariable rule to send every bill to him to be examined and entered previous to accepting it ; and from that time to the day I left Spain, I never accepted a single bill until after it had been inspected and sent to me by him to be accepted. Further, to avoid mistakes and frauds, I also made it a constant rule that every bill presented for payment should undergo a second examination by Mr. Carmichael, that if he found it right he should sign his name to it, and that the bankers should not pay any bill unless so signed.

The bills twice paid, or rather the different numbers of the same set, stand entered in different places in the book above mentioned ; and I can only regret that the entries of the numbers first presented and accepted were not observed by him, either at the time when the subsequent ones were offered for acceptance, or at the time when they were afterwards brought for payment.

It gives me pleasure to inform your Excellency that the British and American ratifications of the treaty of peace were exchanged a few days before I left Paris. The day of my departure I received, under cover from Dr. Franklin, a copy of the British ratifications, which I have the honour to transmit herewith enclosed.

With great respect and esteem, I have the honour to be, etc.

JOHN JAY.

P. S.—I shall send with this letter to the post office, several others which were committed to my care for your Excellency.

ROBERT R. LIVINGSTON TO JAY.

CLAREMONT, 30th July, 1784.

Permit me, my dear friend, to congratulate you on your return to your native shore, and to the friendly embraces of those who love you in every situation in which you have been or can be placed. My impatience to see you led me to New-York about three weeks since, where, from the time you had set for sailing, I thought it probable that you must have arrived before this. An unfortunate accident which has happened to my eldest daughter, who a few days ago broke her arm, obliges me to send you these cold expressions of my friendship, rather than comply with my wishes in offering them and receiving yours, in person. Having, as I hope, *concluded my political career*, I have no other wish left but that of spending the remainder of my life with those who have contributed so much to the happiness of its gayest period. Whether you entertain the same moderate wishes, whether you content yourself with the politics of this State, or whether you will engage in the great field that Congress have again opened to you, I shall still have the consolation to reflect that seas do not roll between us, that I may sometimes see you, and frequently hear from you. If you are not cured of your ambition, you have every thing to hope for both in the State and Continental line. I need not tell you, that I only wish to know your objects *that I may concur in them.*

Believe me, dear John,
Most sincerely and warmly your friend,
R. R. LIVINGSTON.

JAY TO ROBERT R. LIVINGSTON.

NEW YORK, August 18, 1784.

Your kind letter of the 30th ult. was delivered to me yesterday by Mr. Lewis. I thank you very sincerely for your friendly congratulations on my return, and assure you that among the pleasures I have long promised myself from it, that of renewing our former intercourse and correspondence is not the least. I lament the unfortunate accident which has happened to your oldest daughter, and which has deprived me of the satisfaction of meeting you here.

I have had, and have, so many applications about papers and business, respecting causes in which I was formerly concerned, that I shall be obliged to pass a fortnight or three weeks here. When it will be in my power to pay you a visit is uncertain. I consider it as a pleasure to come, and shall endeavour to realize it as soon as possible.

When I resigned my appointments in Europe, I purposed to return to the practice of the law; what effect the unexpected offer of Congress (of which I was ignorant until after my arrival here) may have on that design as yet remains undecided. How far either of us have been, or may be, under the influence of ambition are questions which, however clear to ourselves, must necessarily be less so to others.

Present my affectionate compliments to your mother and Mrs. Livingston. Remember me to all the family.

Yours sincerely,
JOHN JAY.

JAY TO BENJAMIN VAUGHAN.

NEW YORK, 2d September, 1784.

DEAR SIR:

The far greater part of my time since my arrival has been passed in the country, so that several vessels have lately gone to Europe without letters from me to our friends there.

The health of my family and myself is better than usual, and I begin to flatter myself that if you and Mrs. Vaughan could enjoy this country in only half the degree that I do you would not greatly regret leaving Old England. I am more contented than I expected. Some things, it is true, are wrong, but more are right. Justice is well administered, offences are rare, and I have never known more public tranquillity or private security. Resentments subside very sensibly, though gradually. I have met with whigs and tories at the same table. The spirit of industry throughout the country was never greater. The productions of the earth abound. Prices have fallen since my arrival, though still much higher than formerly, especially the wages of mechanics and labourers, which are very extravagant. House-rent is more than double what it was before the war.

Yours sincerely,

JOHN JAY.

MARQUIS DE LAFAYETTE TO JAY.

ALBANY, October 7, 1784.

MY DEAR SIR :

I am very unfortunate in my attempts to meet you, but I hope at last to have better success, and sincerely wish it to happen about the middle of next month, when I hope to wait upon Congress at their next meeting.

Until a few days ago, I had no doubt but to hear you had accepted the appointment conferred upon you. My fears, however, have been raised, and with my usual frankness I assure you that your refusal could not but be attended with very bad circumstances. Setting compliments apart, I am sensible of the great injury such a denial would cause to the public, not only on account of the loss made by the United States in your person, but also for other motives. I hope you will accept ; I know you must ; but in case you are not determined I had rather change my plans than not to see you before I write to Congress. I wish much to hear from you at New-York, where I expect to be about the 22nd. My most affectionate respects wait upon Mrs. Jay. With every sentiment of regard & attachment, I have the honour to be your sincere friend,

LAFAYETTE.

WILLIAM BINGHAM TO JAY.

PARIS, Oct. 16th, 1784.

DEAR SIR :

I have just heard that a French packet is on the point of departure for New York.

I cannot permit it to sail without forwarding you a few lines expressive of the pleasure I received on hearing of your safe arrival.

The services you have rendered your country will naturally secure you a very welcome reception. The only circumstance that can be productive of disagreeable sensations is the situation of your State, exposed to such political convulsions. However, I hope it will soon be restored to harmony and good-temper.

I hope your public appointment will prove an agreeable surprise to you on your arrival, and that you will be able to reconcile the acceptance of it to every consideration of private interest and convenience, as well as public duty.

The British seem to recede every day more and more from the paths of conciliation. A certain nation, to whom we are indebted for political favours will endeavour to cherish this disposition, as she is sure to benefit by such growing feuds and divisions.

From the observations I have made since my arrival here, I can discover the necessity of very complying conduct on the part of those Americans who have public business to transact with this Court. Such conformity to the opinions of others is not easily reconcilable to the feelings and manly deportment of republicans.

No one is better acquainted than you are with the system of *this Court,* and no one is more jealous of their country's honour, in essential points. You may well imagine, then, that your appointment was *not regarded with satisfaction,* nor will the congratulations that you will receive on it from certain persons be *sincere*.

With great esteem and regard, believe me to be, dear sir, your sincere friend and obedient humble servant,

WILLIAM BINGHAM.

JAY TO BENJAMIN VAUGHAN.

PHILADELPHIA, 30th November, 1784.

DEAR SIR:

A sufficient number of members to form a Congress not having arrived at Trenton, I passed on to this place ten days ago, to visit my friends. I found your family well, and am happy in this opportunity of cultivating their acquaintance.

Your obliging letter of the 5th August lately came to hand. Accept my thanks for it, and for the pamphlets enclosed with it.

The policy of Britain respecting this country is so repugnant to common sense that I am sometimes tempted to think *it must be so ;* and the old adage of *quos Deus*, etc., always occurs to me when I reflect on the subject.

The India business never appeared to me a difficult one. Do justice, and all is easy. Cease to treat those unhappy natives as slaves, and be content to trade with them as with other independent kingdoms. On such an event, advantageous though fair treaties might be made with them, and you might leave, with their consent, force sufficient in circumscribed limits to secure the benefit and observance of them. Your tribute, indeed, would be at an end, but it ought not to have had a beginning ; and I wish it may ever prove a curse to those who impose and exact it in any country.

Our affairs are in such a state as, all circumstances considered, might naturally have been expected ; far better than many represent them, though not so well as they ought to be.

Congress is convened at Trenton, and I join them to-morrow. In the course of six or eight weeks a judgment may be formed of their prevailing sentiments and views.

It is certain that we are trading at a wild rate ; and it is no less true that your people are giving most absurd credits to many, who neither have or ought to have any at home. This delirium cannot last. Adieu, my dear sir.

Yours sincerely,
JOHN JAY.

JAY TO BENJAMIN FRANKLIN.

TRENTON, 13th December, 1784.

DEAR SIR :

The Marquis de Lafayette is so obliging as to take charge of this letter. He has seen much of our country since his arrival, and having had many opportunities of knowing our true situation, will be able to give you full information on the subject. I think he is (and has reason to be) convinced that the attachment of America to him has not been abated by the peace, and that we are now as little disposed to break friendship with France as we were during the war. This is a most favourable season for her to relax the severe commercial restrictions which oppose our trade to her islands. Her liberality would be contrasted to British ill-humour, and unavoidably produce correspondent impressions.

The present Congress promises well. There are many respectable members here. Federal ideas seem to prevail greatly among them, and, I may add, a strong disposition to conciliation and unanimity. Your letter on the subject of leave to return is, with a variety of foreign papers, referred to a committee. They have as yet made no report, and, therefore, I can give you no satisfactory intelligence on that head. I lately saw Mrs. Bache in good health and spirits at Philadelphia, and I am persuaded no less anxious for your return than you can be. Mrs. Jay and our little family are at Elizabethtown, and her last letters inform me they were all well. Be pleased to make my compliments to your grandsons.

I am, dear sir,

Your obliged and obedient servant,

JOHN JAY.

FRANCIS HOPKINSON TO JAY.

PHILAD^A., Janu^y. 12, 1785.

DEAR SIR:

Confiding in the place I flatter myself I hold in your good opinion I take the liberty of suggesting an idea which many of my friends have urged to me, viz. that I might be proposed as one of the Commissioners for building the Federal City of Congress. I have indeed no great technical knowledge in Architecture, but as I have a good deal of leisure, some little taste and a talent for contrivance I think

I could be of some use. I am the more induced to this application, as I am determined to purchase a lot to build and fix my Residence under this new jurisdiction; and have already taken some preparative steps for enabling me to do so. I look forward to this City as an Asylum from the rage and rancour of party, and as the seat of polite arts in America.

Excuse this liberty, and whether my present inclination shall be gratified nor not, be assured that I shall think myself honour'd by your esteem and future correspondence, and that I am,

Dear Sir,

Your sincere friend and very humble servant,

F. HOPKINSON.

JAY TO THE MARQUIS DE LAFAYETTE.

NEW YORK, 19th January, 1785.

DEAR SIR :

It was not before this morning that I was informed that the bearer of this letter was going to France, and to sail to-morrow ; and business and company have not till now (late in the evening) permitted me to sit down to write to you. I cannot, however omit this opportunity of sending you a few lines, which, though not very interesting, will nevertheless evince my attention to a correspondence, from which I promise myself much pleasure as well as much information. The removal of Congress to this place necessarily occasioned a suspension of business, and delayed their maturing several matters which they had under consideration. They have, within a few days past, made a house, and as they possess both talents and temper, there is reason to presume that the Union will derive advantage from their measures.

Advices from Kentucky inform us that they are threatened with an Indian war; and there is some room to conjecture that such an event would not be disagreeable to our western neighbours, who, if they do interfere, will certainly be more cunning than wise. That settlement increases with a degree of rapidity heretofore unknown in this country, and increase it will, notwithstanding any attempt of anybody to prevent it.

Federal ideas begin to thrive in this city, and I suspect in a few days to communicate to you a circumstance which will strongly manifest it.

Although we cannot be immediately interested in the war, which it is thought will take place between the emperor and the Dutch, yet we may be affected by its consequences, and, therefore, must wish to know who will, and who will not, probably take sides with this or that party, in case of a rupture.

Have we any reason to flatter ourselves that you will encourage us to drink your wines, by permitting your islands to eat our bread? or will Bordeaux (as is said) constrain Versailles to patronize a provincial monopoly at the expense of a more liberal policy? Commercial privileges, granted to us by France, at this season of British ill-humour, would be particularly grateful; and afford conclusive evidence against its being the plan of the two kingdoms to restrain our trade to the islands. We know how uneasy we are under these restraints, and we confide fully in your exertions to remove them. I write very freely, but you are my fellow-citizen, and therefore it does not appear to me necessary to attempt to dress my ideas *à la mode de Paris.*

Believe me to be, dear sir, with great regard and esteem, your most obedient and very humble servant,

JOHN JAY.

JAY TO DR. BENJAMIN RUSH.

SIR : NEW YORK, 24 March, 1785.

Such has been the state of my official business and of that which arose from my long neglected private affairs, that ever since the removal of Congress to this place I have been obliged to trespass on my usual punctuality in private correspondences. Hence it happened that I have so long denied myself the pleasure of replying to your friendly letter of the 16th January. Accept my warmest acknowledgments for the kind and very obliging manner in which you mention my services abroad ; and permit me to congratulate you on the success of the application to Congress on behalf of Dickenson College, which you appear zealously to patronize. I consider knowledge to be the soul of a republic, and as the weak and the wicked are generally in alliance, as much care should be taken to diminish the number of the former as of the latter. Education is the way to do this, and nothing should be left undone to afford all ranks of people the means of obtaining a proper degree of it at a cheap and easy rate.

I thank you for the pamphlet you sent me; there is good sense and just reasoning in it. I wish to see all unjust and all unnecessary discriminations everywhere abolished, and that the time may soon come when all our inhabitants of every colour and denomination shall be free and equal partakers of our political liberty. I am, sir, with great respect and esteem, your most obedient servant,

JOHN JAY.

JAY TO JOHN ADAMS.[1]

OFFICE FOR FOREIGN AFFAIRS,
31st March, 1785.

DEAR SIR:

I have the honour of transmitting to you herewith enclosed a certified copy of an act of Congress of the 21st instant, instructing you to communicate to Mr. St. Saphorin the high sense the United States, in Congress assembled, entertain of the liberal decision made by his Danish Majesty, on the question proposed to his minister by you, respecting the ordination of American candidates for holy orders in the Episcopal Church, commonly called the Church of England.[2]

Congress has been pleased to order me to transmit copies of your letter, and the other papers on this subject, to the executives of the different States; and I am persuaded they will receive with pleasure this

---

[1] Now American Minister to Great Britain.

[2] In a circular letter of the same date, March 31st, to the Governors of the States, Jay informs them that "the Bishops of Denmark will confer holy orders on American Candidates without any tests which (like those insisted on in England) would be improper for Americans to comply with."

mark of your attention, and of his Danish Majesty's friendly disposition.

I have the honour to be, with great respect and esteem, dear sir, your most obedient and very humble servant,

JOHN JAY.

JAY TO MR. GRAND.

NEW YORK, 28th April, 1785.

DEAR SIR :

I received last evening the two letters you did me the honour to write on the 8th February last, and congratulate you sincerely on the birth of your grandson.

I have accepted the office which Congress was pleased to offer me, and shall be much obliged to you for such intelligence from time to time as you may think useful for me to receive, and prudent for you to communicate. As a public man, I shall always remember your attachment and services to the United States ; and as a private one, it will always give me pleasure to acknowledge the friendly attention which has so long marked your conduct towards me and my family. In both capacities, therefore, I shall be happy to give you better evidence of my esteem and regard, than compliments or professions can possibly afford.

Mr. Morris' resignation is a great loss to this country, and yet I am not without hopes that the department of finance will become properly arranged. The *nature* of our governments, as well as the circumstance of their being *new*, exposes our operations to delay, and renders the best systems slow in forming, as well as slow in executing. In my opinion, one superintendent or commissioner of the treasury is preferable to any greater number of them ; indeed, I would rather have each department under the direction of one able man than of twenty able ones. All things, however, in this world have their bright as well as their dark sides ; and there are few systems so imperfect as not to have some conveniences. Many reasons induce me to disapprove of committing the treasury to the management of *three* persons ; and yet one very great convenience results from it, viz., that our jealous republicans will have more confidence in *three* gentlemen coming from different parts of the continent than they would place in any one single man. Confidence, you know, is always followed by credit, and credit is the forerunner of money.

I am, dear sir, your most obedient and very humble servant,

JOHN JAY.

JAY TO JAMES LOWELL.

DEAR SIR:

OFFICE FOR FOREIGN AFFAIRS,
10th May, 1785.

I have been favoured with your obliging letter of the 18th of March, and should sooner have thanked you for it had n't a variety of matters concurred in constraining me to postpone that pleasure till now. My endeavours I assure you shall not be wanting to

put the affair of Mr. Saderstrom in such a train as
that it may be terminated to the satisfaction both of
that gentleman and of his creditors. The report on
his case was entirely dictated by public considerations ; for considering the feeble state of our federal
government it appeared to me highly expedient that
its tone should not only be prevented from becoming
more relaxed, but that it should be invigorated in
every manner and degree which our union and general interest might require, and a due regard to our
constitutions and equal rights permit. It is my first
wish to see the United States assume and merit the
character of one great nation, whose territory is
divided into countries and townships for the like purposes. Until this be done the chain which holds us
together will be too feeble to bear much opposition
or exertion, and we shall be daily mortified by seeing
the links of it giving way and calling for repair one
after another. Accept my sincere acknowledgments
for the very obliging terms in which you mention my
appointment to the office I now hold, and be assured
of the esteem and regard with which I am, dear sir,
your most obedient and humble servant,

JOHN JAY.

ROBERT MORRIS TO JAY.

DEAR SIR : PHILADELPHIA, May 19, 1785.
On my return here I found your obliging letter of the
13th, which arrived during my absence. Our ship from
China [1] does tolerably well for the concerned ; she has

---

[1] The vessel mentioned by Mr. Morris was the ship *Empress*, the first ever
sent from the United States to China. So important was this enterprise

opened new objects to all America. A mandarin signs a passport for all European ships, directed to the commanders of two of the emperor's forts on the river of Canton, nearly in the following words :—" Permit this barbarian boat to pass ; she has   guns and   men, consequently can do the emperor no harm." If the government of America could concentrate the force of the country in any one point when occasion required, I think our mandarins might grant similar passports to the rest of the world.

I beg my compliments to the ladies, and am, with warm attachment,

Dear Sir,
Your obedient and humble servant,
ROBERT MORRIS.

SAMUEL SHAW TO JAY.

NEW YORK, 19th May, 1785.

SIR :

The first vessel that has been fitted out by the inhabitants of the United States of America for essaying a commerce with those of the empire of China, being, by the favour of Heaven, safe returned to this port, it becomes my duty to communicate to you, for the information of the fathers of the country, an account of the reception their Citizens have met with, and the respect with which their flag has been treated in that distant region ; especially as some circumstances have occurred which had a tendency to attract the attention of the Chinese towards a people of whom they have hitherto had but very confused Ideas, and which serve in a peculiar manner, to place the Americans in a more conspicuous point of view, than has commonly attended the

---

deemed, that an official account of the voyage was addressed by the supercargo to the Secretary, who laid it before Congress, and that body passed a resolution expressing their satisfaction at this successful attempt to establish a direct trade with China.—" Life of Jay," vol. i., p. 192.

introduction of other Nations into that ancient and extensive Empire.

The Ship employed on this occasion is about three hundred and sixty tons burthen, built in America and equipped
with forty-three persons, under the command of John
Green, Esq. The subscriber had the honor of being appointed agent for their Commerce by the Gentlemen, at
whose risk this first experiment has been undertaken.

On the 22 of Feby., 1784, the Ship sailed from New York,
and arrived the 21 March at St. Iago, the principal of the
Cape de Verd islands. Having paid our respects to the
Portuguese viceroy, and with his permission taken such re-
freshments as were necessary, we left those islands on the
27th, and pursued our voyage. After a pleasant passage,
in which nothing extraordinary occurred, we came to
anchor in the straits of Sunda on the 18th July. It was
no small addition to our happiness on this occasion to meet
there two ships belonging to our good allies the French.
The commodore, Monsieur D'Ordelin, and his officers, welcomed us in the most affectionate manner ; and as his own
ship was immediately bound to Canton, gave us an invitation to go in company with him. This friendly offer we
most cheerfully accepted, and the commodore furnished
us with his signals by day and night, and added such
instructions for our passage through the Chinese seas as
would have been exceedingly beneficial had any unfortunate accident occasioned our separation. Happily, we
pursued our route together. On our arrival at the island of
Macao, the French consul for China, Monsieur Vieillard,
with some other gentlemen of his nation, came on board to
congratulate and welcome us to that part of the world ; and
kindly undertook the introduction of the Americans to the
Portuguese governor. The little time that we were there
was entirely taken up by the good offices of the consul, the
gentlemen of his nation, and those of the Swedes and Im-

perialists who still remained at Macao. The other Europeans had repaired to Canton. Three days afterward we finished our outward-bound voyage. Previous to coming to anchor, we saluted the shipping in the river with thirteen guns, which were answered by the several commodores of the European nations, each of whom sent an officer to compliment us on our arrival. These visits were returned by the captain and supercargoes in the afternoon ; who were again saluted by the respective ships as they finished their visit. When the French sent their officers to congratulate us, they added to the obligations we were already under to them, by furnishing men, boats, and anchors to assist us in coming to safe and convenient moorings. Nor did their good offices stop here; they insisted further that until we were settled, we should take up our quarters with them at Canton.

The day of our arrival at Canton, August 30, and the two following days, we were visited by the Chinese merchants, and the chiefs and gentlemen of the several European establishments. The Chinese were very indulgent towards us. They styled us the *new people ;* and when by the map we conveyed to them an idea of the extent of our country, with its present and increasing population, they were highly pleased at the prospect of so considerable a market for the productions of theirs.

The situation of the Europeans at Canton is so well known as to render a detail unnecessary. The good understanding commonly subsisting between them and the Chinese was in some degree interrupted by two extraordinary occurrences ; of which I will, with your permission, give a particular account.

The police at Canton is at all times extremely strict, and the Europeans residing there are circumscribed within very narrow limits. The latter had observed with concern some circumstances which they deemed an encroachment upon their rights. On this consideration they determined to apply for redress to the *hoppo*, who is the head officer of the customs, the next time he should visit the shipping. Deputies accordingly attended from every nation, and I was desired to represent ours. We met the hoppo on board an English ship, and the causes of complaint were soon after removed.

The other occurrence, of which I beg leave to take notice, gave rise to what was commonly called the *Canton war*, which threatened to be productive of very serious consequences. On the 25th November an English ship in saluting some company that had dined on board, killed a Chinese, and wounded two others in the mandarin's boat alongside.

It is a maxim of the Chinese law that blood must answer for blood; in pursuance of which they demanded the unfortunate gunner. To give up this poor man was to consign him to certain death. Humanity pleaded powerfully against the measure. After repeated conferences between the English and the Chinese, the latter declared themselves satisfied, and the affair was supposed to be entirely settled. Notwithstanding this, on the morning after the last conference (the 27th), the supercargo of the ship was seized while attending his business, thrown into a sedan-chair, hurried into the city, and committed to prison.

Such an outrage on personal liberty spread a general alarm; and the Europeans unanimously agreed to send for their boats, with armed men from the shipping, for the security of themselves and property until the matter should be brought to a conclusion. The boats accordingly came, and ours among the number; one of which was fired on, and a man wounded. All trade was stopped, and the Chinese men-of-war drawn up opposite the factories. The Europeans demanded the restoration of Mr. Smith, which the Chinese refused, until the gunner should be given up.

In the mean while the troops of the province were collecting in the neighborhood of Canton—the Chinese servants were ordered by the magistrates to leave the factories—the gates of the suburbs were shut—all intercourse was at an end—the naval force was increased—many troops were embarked in boats, ready for landing—and every thing wore the appearance of war. To what extremities matters might have been carried, had not a negotiation taken place, no one can say. The Chinese asked a conference with all the nations except the English. A deputation (in which I was included for America) met the *Fuen*, who is the head magistrate of Canton, with the principal officers of the province. After setting forth, by an interpreter, the power of the emperor and his own determination to support the laws, he demanded that the gunner should be given up within three days, declaring that he should have an impartial examination before their tribunal, and if it appeared that the affair was accidental, he should be released unhurt.

In the mean time he gave permission for the trade, excepting that of the English, to go on as usual; and dismissed us with a present of two pieces of silk to each, as a mark of his friendly disposition. The other nations, one after another, sent away their boats under protection of *a Chinese flag*, and pursued their business as before. The English were obliged to submit, the gunner was given up, Mr. Smith was released, and the English, after being forced to ask pardon of the magistracy of Canton in presence of the other nations, had their commerce restored.

On this occasion I am happy that we were the last who sent off our boat, and that *without a Chinese flag;* nor did she go till the English themselves thanked us for our concurrence with them, and advised the sending her away. After peace was restored, the chief and four English gentlemen visited the several nations (among whom we were included), and thanked them for their assistance during the troubles. The gunner remained with the Chinese, his fate undetermined.

Notwithstanding the treatment we received from all parties was perfectly civil and respectful, yet it was with peculiar satisfaction that we experienced on every occasion from our good allies the French the most flattering and substantial proofs of their friendship. "If," said they, "we have in any instance been serviceable to you, we are happy; and we desire nothing more ardently than further opportunities to convince you of our affection."

We left Canton the 27th December, and on our return refreshed at the Cape of Good Hope, where we found a most friendly reception. After remaining there five days, we sailed for America, and arrived in this port on the 11th instant.

To every lover of his country, as well as to those more immediately concerned in commerce, it must be a pleasing reflection that a communication is thus happily opened between us and the eastern extremity of the globe; and it adds very sensibly to the pleasure of this reflection, that the voyage has been performed in so short a space of time, and attended with the loss only of one man. To Captain Green and his officers every commendation is due, for their unwearied and successful endeavours in bringing it to this most fortunate issue, which fully justifies the confidence reposed in them by the gentlemen concerned in the enterprise.

Permit me, sir, to accompany this letter with the two pieces of silk presented to me by the *Fuen* of Canton, as a mark of his good disposition towards the American nation. In that view I consider myself as peculiarly honoured, in being charged with this testimony of the friendship of the Chinese, for a people who may in a few years prosecute a commerce with the subjects of that empire under advantages equal, if not superior, to those enjoyed by any other nation whatever.

I have the honour to be,
With the most perfect respect, sir,
Your most obedient and very humble servant,
SAMUEL SHAW.

JAY TO THE PRESIDENT OF CONGRESS.

OFFICE FOR FOREIGN AFFAIRS,
19 May, 1785.

SIR :

It is well known that these countries prior to the late war carried on a valuable trade with Honduras and Campeachy, and employed above one hundred vessels in exchanging, at the English settlements, beef, pork, and other kinds of provision for logwood, mahogany, sarsaparilla, etc.

It being the policy of Spain to keep other nations at a distance from their American dominions, she beholds these settlements with pain and jealousy. The uneasiness which subsists at present between those two nations on that subject seems to offer us an opportunity of negotiating with the English for a participation in their right to cut logwood, or at least to trade with them there as formerly. It is not improbable that they may consent to strengthen their footing in those parts by interesting us in the advantages resulting from their continuing to maintain it. To sound their ministry in the first instance informally and inexplicly on the subject can cost us little.

If Congress should think proper to take this matter into consideration, and instruct their ministers or permit me to write to them about it, secrecy will, I think, be particularly necessary ; for there is reason to apprehend that Spain and France would not consider our obtaining that object to be so consistent with their views as it appears to me to be with our interest.

I have the honour to be with great respect, your Excellency's most obedient and very humble servant,

JOHN JAY.

GENERAL SCHUYLER TO JAY.

DEAR SIR: ALBANY, May 30, 1785.

The person, at present in the chair of Government, so
evidently strives to maintain his popularity at the expense
of good Government, that it has given real concern to many,
as well as to myself, both here and in the Southern part
of the state.   Not only the lowest but the most unworthy
characters are countenanced by him and thro' his influence
placed in offices of trust.   Great part of the magistracy of
this and the adjacent Western and Northern Counties are
wretches that would disgrace the most despicable of all
governments,—these serve his turn ; and he abets a faction
(privately as he thinks, but sufficiently notorious to those
who have taken some pains to be informed) which wishes
to destroy both public and private Credit, and whose sole
aim is to rise into importance on the ruin of others.   Happily the spirit of this and the County of Montgomery has
been called forth and crushed some of the leaders of the
faction at the late election.   Indeed they were not able to
carry a single Candidate.   But notwithstanding this check
it is conceived how that the business of a reform in a government cannot be accomplished unless Mr. Clinton is
ousted, and it is therefore determined to attempt a change
and almost every character of respectability and indeed a
great majority of all ranks will support the attempt.   But
who is to be the person?   It is agreed that none have a
chance of succeeding but you, the Chancellor or myself.
The second on account of the prejudices against his family
name, it is believed would fail.   With respect to me, altho'
I should carry a majority of at least fifteen hundred voices
in this and Montgomery County and some in Washington,
yet I am so little known in the Southern part of this state
that I should fail there.   Besides this reason, which suffices
with my friends here as well as myself, there is another
arising from my great and many bodily infirmities which
render me incapable of that attention which the office

requires. I therefore could not accept of it even if unanimously offered. Hence the wishes of me and my friends are directed to you, and we have not only sanguine but well founded hopes, that you will obtain a great majority. Those in this quarter will all decide for you who would otherwise vote for me. In Ulster, Dutchess and Orange there will probably be such a diversity of opinion as nearly to balance between you and Mr. Clinton. In Westchester we believe you will generally carry it and so with Richmond. How Long Island will stand we cannot form any opinion of. From New York we have been privately sounded and it was justly observed that if both you and I were held up both would fail, and I afforded satisfaction in declining for reasons above stated. As the party in the Metropolis who wish you is respectable we have reason to believe that you would have a very considerable majority there and from the high estimation you stand in with all ranks it is not improbable but that you would obtain almost all the suffrages there. But, My Dear Sir, to succeed in a mission of this kind, time must be improved ; every day is of importance and we therefore wish you to communicate to me, in the confidence of sacred friendship whether you will accede to our wishes or whether you would, rather than risk any thing, permit the chair to be filled as it is at present ; for unless you can be opposed to him, it will be needless to attempt a change. Even if it would be carried in my favor, I am wholly incapable of the burthen. That we most earnestly wish and intreat you to be the man I hope you will entertain no doubt of. Let me then conjure you not to hesitate in opening yourself to me ; not a word shall transpire, that those impressed with the highest sense of propriety, can condemn, not a step taken but what prudence, and the most sacred attention to your reputation shall justify.

Adieu. I am Dear Sir affectionately and sincerely your obedient servant,   PH. SCHUYLER.

JAY TO WILLIAM BINGHAM.

JAY TO WILLIAM BINGHAM.

New York, 31 May, 1785.

Dear Sir :

I have been favoured with yours of the 12th February, containing a copy of 16th October last, for which accept my cordial thanks.

Your observations in France respecting a certain event coincide exactly with what I expected on that subject. Indeed, the many interesting remarks spread through your letter appear to me to have weight.

Our last accounts give us reason to suppose there will be no war between the Emperor and the Dutch, so that the continuance of a general peace begins again to appear probable.

Our frontier posts still have British garrisons, and we are impatient to hear *why* they are not evacuated. Mr. Adams, I suppose, is by this time in London ; his letters will remove our suspense on that head.

The African States have alarmed us, but we hope peace with them may be obtained. Your attention to that subject is commendable, and you may do good by communicating the result of your inquiries to Mr. Adams.

Our affairs are settling by degrees into order. If power be given to Congress to regulate trade and provide for the payment of their debts, all will be well. Difficulties on those points still exist, but several ideas daily gain ground. The people of Boston resent British restrictions, and if the same spirit should become general it will probably influence the States to enable Congress to retaliate and extend their powers accordingly. The *Empress of China* has made a fortunate voyage and it is said many are preparing to embark in that commerce. The spirit of enterprise and adventure runs high in our young country, and if properly directed by a vigorous and wise government would produce great effects.

A rage for emigrating to the western country prevails, and thousands have already fixed their habitations in that wilderness. The Continental Land Office is opened, and the seeds of a great people are daily planting beyond the mountains.

Mrs. Jay desires me to assure you of her regard. Make our best compliments to Mrs. Bingham, and believe me to be, dear sir, with great esteem and regard,

Your most obedient servant,

JOHN JAY.

JAY TO GENERAL SCHUYLER.

DEAR SIR :   NEW YORK, 10th June, 1785.

What you say on a certain subject argues a degree of confidence and friendship which excites my warmest acknowledgments, and which shall always be returned on my part.

I sincerely and frankly declare to you that my being and having long been employed by Congress, whose attachment and attention to me has been uniform, and who, in my absence and without my knowledge or desire, gave me the place I now fill, will not permit me to quit their service, unless their conduct towards me should change, or other circumstances occur which might render such a step consistent with my ideas of propriety. This is my deliberate and mature opinion: a servant should not leave a good old master for the sake of a little more pay or a prettier livery. Were I at present to accept the government if offered, the world would naturally be led to say, and to believe, that I did it from some such paltry motives.

Although I apprehend that this my answer will not correspond with the wishes which your friendly partiality for me suggests, yet when you put yourself in my stead, and consider what you would do on such an occasion, I think the same reasons which operate upon me would have a similar influence upon you. The conduct of men is so generally (and so often with reason) imputed to interest or ambition that they who are actuated by neither must expect such imputations, whenever circumstances expose their principles of action to doubt and question ; the present case strikes me in that point of light. The place I hold is more laborious, requires more confinement and unceasing application, and is not only less lucrative but also less splendid than that of the government. To exchange worse for better does not seem very disinterested ; and when professions and facts give opposite evidence, it is easy to foresee which will obtain the most credit.

If the circumstances of the State were pressing, if real disgust and discontent had spread through the country, if a change had in the general opinion become not only advisable but *necessary*, and the good expected from that change depended on me, then my present objections would immediately yield to the consideration that a good citizen ought cheerfully to take any station which, on such occasions, his country may think proper to assign him, without in the least regarding the personal consequences which may result from its being more or less elevated ; nor would there then be reason to fear that Congress might consider my leaving their service as being inconsistent with that degree of delicacy and gratitude which they have a right to expect, and which respect for myself as well as for them demands from me.

With sentiments of great and sincere regard, I am, dear sir,

Your obliged and affectionate friend,

JOHN JAY.

JAY TO THE GOVERNORS OF THE STATES.

[Circular-letter.]

OFFICE FOR FOREIGN AFFAIRS,
14 June, 1785.

SIR :

I have the honour of informing your Excellency that Congress have received a letter from His Most Christian Majesty, dated the 27th of March last, announcing the birth, on that day, of a prince, whom he had named Duke of Normandy.

As this event adds to the happiness of a king and a people who have given many important proofs of friendship for our nation, it must naturally excite that pleasure which generous minds always derive from the prosperity of their friends and benefactors.

I have the honour to be, with great respect,
Your Excellency's most obedient servant,

JOHN JAY.

JAY TO DON DIEGO GARDOQUI.[1]

OFFICE FOR FOREIGN AFFAIRS,
21st June, 1785.

SIR :

I have received the letter you did me the honour to write on the 2d June instant.

The etiquette which will be observed on your reception by Congress is as follows, viz. : At such time as may be appointed by Congress for a public reception the Secretary for Foreign Affairs will conduct you to the Congress Chamber, to a seat to be placed for you, and announce you to Congress, the President and members keeping their seats and remaining covered. Your commission and letters of credence are then to be delivered to the Secretary of Congress, who will read a translation of them, to be prepared by the Secretary for Foreign Affairs from the copies to be left with the President. You will then be at liberty to speak (and if you please deliver to the Secretary of Congress in writing) what you may think proper to Congress, who will take what you may say into consideration, and through the Secretary for Foreign Affairs will communicate whatever

---

[1] The newly appointed Minister from Spain to the United States. Jay had met him in the course of his negotiations at Madrid.

answer they may resolve upon. When you retire you will be reconducted by the Secretary for Foreign Affairs. A visit will be expected by every member of Congress, as well those who may be in town, as others who may afterwards arrive during your residence here.[1]

I hope the state of your health will soon be such as to admit of your coming on to this city before the heats of summer render travelling disagreeable. It will give me great pleasure to take you by the hand and to assure you in person of the esteem and regard with which I am, dear sir,

Your most obedient and very humble servant,

JOHN JAY.

To Señor DON DIEGO GARDOQUI,
    The Plenipotentiary of His Catholic Majesty,
        charged with his affairs at the United
        States of America in Congress assembled.

DR. RICHARD PRICE TO JAY.

NEWINGTON GREEN, NEAR LONDON,
July 9th, 1785.

DEAR SIR:

I hope you will excuse the liberty I take in introducing to you the bearer of this letter, M r. Curtauld. He and his Mother and Sisters have for several years made a part of my congregation at Haukney, and his character is unexceptionable. He has converted his little property into money which he intends to employ in purchasing land in some

---

[1] The Spanish Minister was received by Congress at noon of July 2d. On the previous day Jay wrote to him :

" I shall have the honour of accompanying and introducing you to Congress, and for that purpose we will proceed together from my house in my carriage so near twelve o'clock as to be at the Congress Chamber exactly at the time appointed."

of the interior parts of America with no other view than to occupy it himself and to become an industrious farmer. Any information or assistance which you may be so good as to give him will confer an obligation upon me as well as upon him. The United States must be in some danger from needy and worthless adventurers who will be often going over to them from Europe. There is, in the present instance, no danger of this kind, for Mr. Curtauld's views are laudable, and he will, I am fully persuaded, make an honest and useful member of the United States.

I directed to you in autumn last some copies of my pamphlet on the American Revolution.

This was an effort of my zeal to promote, according to the best of my judgment, the improvement and happiness of mankind in general and of the United States in particular. The recommendations in it of measures to abolish gradually the Negro-trade and Slavery and to prevent too great an inequality of property have I find offended some of the leading men in South Carolina; and I have been assured from thence that such measures will never be encouraged there. Should a like disposition prevail in many of the other States, it will appear that the people who have struggled so bravely against being enslaved themselves are ready enough to enslave others; the event which had raised my hopes of seeing a better state of human affairs will prove only an introduction to a new scene of aristocratical tyranny and human debasement; and the friends of liberty and virtue in Europe will be sadly disappointed and mortified.

I rely, Dear Sir, on your candour and goodness to excuse the liberty I now take with you. I am afraid that the acquaintance which I had the happiness to commence with you when in London is not sufficient to warrant it. With every good wish and great respect for your character, I am,

Your most obedient and humble servant,

RICHARD PRICE.

JAY TO THE MARQUIS DE LAFAYETTE.

OFFICE FOR FOREIGN AFFAIRS,
15th July, 1785.

DEAR SIR :

Accept my thanks for your interesting letter of the 19th March, which was immediately communicated to Congress. I consider it as a new proof of that constant and useful attention to our affairs, from which the United States have so often derived both pleasure and advantage. Let me request the continuance of your correspondence, and be assured that it will always give me pleasure to communicate to you such intelligence respecting American occurrences as may appear interesting.

Don Diego Gardoqui is arrived, and has been received so much in the spirit of friendship, that I hope his master and himself will be well pleased. Our negotiations with him will soon commence, and I sincerely wish that the issue of them may be satisfactory to both countries. To prepare for war, and yet be tenacious of peace with all the world, is, I think, our true interest. I wish Mr. Gardoqui's instructions may be sufficiently extensive to admit of a settlement of our boundaries, etc., on principles which alone can create and perpetuate cordiality.

The British show no disposition to evacuate our frontier posts. What their real designs are can at present be only inferred and conjectured from appearances ; and present appearances induce a suspicion that they mean to hold them. The letters we expect from Mr. Adams will probably remove all doubts on that head. It is certain that they pay great attention to the Indians, and give great encouragement to emigrants from us. Their expectations from the latter circumstance will fail them. I wish that every acre of ground they hold in America was settled by natives of the United States. They would transplant their love of liberty, their spirit of enterprise, and their attachment to republicanism into countries in which it is our interest that such plants should be propagated and flourish ; in time they will bear fruit.

The commercial class of our people sensibly feel the restraints on our trade, and look up to Congress for a remedy. Good will come out of evil ; these discontents nourish federal ideas. As trade diminishes, agriculture must suffer ; and hence it will happen that our yeomen will be as desirous of increasing the powers of Congress as our merchants now are. All foreign restrictions, exclusions, and unneighbourly ordinances will tend to press us together, and strengthen our bands of union.

I send you herewith a number of gazettes, from which you will discern something of the spirit which prevails.

Congress go on doing business with great concord, temper, and harmony. I enclose a copy of the ordinance for regulating the Land Office. They are now on the subject of requisitions ; and I flatter myself, that as the highest respect for good faith prevails in the House, exertions will be made by the States to preserve the public credit.

Governor Livingston was appointed for the Hague, but declining that place, Governor Rutledge has been elected for it. His answer has not yet reached.

When, my dear sir, will your court send us a minister? Our having one at Versailles affords reason to expect one from thence. The report of Mons. De Montiers' coming over in that capacity dies away. From the little I saw of him in Paris, I am inclined to think he would be an agreeable as well as an able minister.

I am, dear sir, your most obedient servant,

JOHN JAY.

JAY TO THE MARCHIONESS DE LAFAYETTE.

NEW YORK, 13th August, 1785.

MADAM :

I have received the letter which you did me the honour to write on the 15th April last. Few circumstances could have given me more pleasure than such evidence of my having a place in the remembrance and good opinion of a lady, whose esteem derives no less value from her discernment than from the delicacy of her sentiments.

Accept, therefore, madam, of my sincere and cordial acknowledgments for honouring me with a place among your correspondents, which was the more obliging as you were to afford more pleasure *by* than you could expect to receive *from* it. You know it is an old observation, that ladies write better letters than gentlemen, and therefore, independent of other considerations, a correspondence between them is always so far on unequal terms.

I can easily conceive that you, whose predilection for your husband was always conspicuous, should experience so much satisfaction on seeing him return from this, his field of glory, with additional honours; and I can, with equal ease, form an idea of his emotions when, on that as on former occasions, those honours promoted him to higher rank in your estimation.

Your remarks on the Marquis' affection for his children, and the value you set on domestic enjoyments, must be pleasing to those who are capable of feeling their force.

I assure you I rejoice in the prospect you have of extending, through your branch, the reputation of both your families; and you have my best wishes that the latest historian may say of your descendants that all the men were as valiant and worthy as their ancestor, who will probably be distinguished by the appellation of *Americanus*, and all the women as virtuous and amiable as *his* lady.

If you were not what you are I would not encourage the desire you express of accompanying the Marquis on his next visit to this country, for I am sure you would be disappointed.

We have few amusements to relieve travellers of that weight of time and leisure which oppresses many of them. Our men, for the most part, mind their business, and our women their families; and if our wives succeed (as most of them do) in "making home man's best delight," gallantry seldom draws their husbands from them.

Our customs, in many respects, differ from yours, and you know that, whether with or without reason, we usually prefer those which education and habit recommend. The pleasures of Paris and the pomp of Versailles are unknown in this country, and their votaries must unavoidably experience a certain vacuity or blank here, which nothing but good sense, moderate desires, and a relish for less splendid, less various, but not less innocent or satisfactory enjoyments can supply. Though not a Frenchman, I should, nevertheless, be too polite to tell these things to those whom they might restrain from visiting us. On you they will have a contrary effect. It would gratify the friends of the Marquis, viz., the citizens of the United States, to have the honour of a visit from you. I flatter myself that consideration will afford a strong additional inducement.

My little family is well. Mrs. Jay desires me to assure you of her remembrance and regard; and permit me to add that I am, with sincere esteem and respectful attachment,

Madam, your most obedient and

Very humble servant,

John Jay.

JAY TO JOHN ADAMS.

Office for Foreign Affairs,
6th September, 1785.

Dear Sir :

The frequent solecisms, observable for some years past in the politics of the Court of London, render it exceedingly difficult to divine how they will think and act under almost any given circumstances.

It is manifestly as much their interest to be well with us as it is ours to be well with them ; and yet the gratification of resentments, occasioned by disappointment, seems to take the lead of more elevated and useful principles of action.

They expect much from the trade of America, and yet they take pains to cut off every source within their reach by which we may make remittances. It is strange that they should wish us to buy, and yet be so industrious to put it out of our power to pay. Such a system must cause loss of money to their merchants and loss of reputation to ours. I wish most sincerely that credit was at an end, and that we could purchase nothing abroad but for ready money. Our exportations would then be equally profitable, and as our importations would be diminished, we should have less to pay. Domestic manufactures would then be more encouraged, and frugality and economy become more prevalent.

What impression the conduct of Captain Stanhope may make on the minister to me appears uncertain. Certain however it is, that mutual civility and respect must, in the nature of things, precede mutual benevolence and kindness. The manner of your reception and treatment indicates their attention to this consideration, and yet the detention of the posts, the strengthening their garrisons in our neighbourhood, the encouragement said to be given to settlers in those parts, and various other circumstances speak a language very different from that of kindness and good-will.

They may hold the posts, but they will hold them as pledges of enmity ; and the time must and will come when the seeds of discontent, resentment, and hatred, which such measures always sow, will produce very bitter fruit.

I am well informed that some of the loyalists advise and warmly press the detention of the posts. It is strange that men, who for ten years have done nothing but deceive, should still retain any credit. I speak of them collectively ; among them there are men of merit : but to my knowledge some of the most violent, the most bitter and implacable, and yet most in credit, are men who endeavoured to play between both parties, and vibrated from side to side as the appearance of success attracted them. Nay, the very accounts of losses which many of them have presented afford conclusive evidence of their inattention to truth and common decency. Such, however, has been the infatuation of British counsels, that what was manifest to others was problematical, if not entirely dark, to them.

As to their present minister, he has neither been long enough in administration, nor perhaps in the world, for a decided judgment to be formed either of his private or public character. He seems to possess firmness as well as abilities, and if to these be added information, and comprehensive as well as patriotic views, he may be worthy of his father. England will probably be either much the better or much the worse for him.

We are anxious to receive letters from you on the subject of the posts, that in either event we may be

prepared. In the one case, I should think it very justifiable in Congress to take a certain step, that would
be longer and more sensibly felt by Britain than the
independence of these States.

Mr. Arthur Lee has been elected to the vacant
place at the Board of Treasury.

Governor Rutledge declines going to Holland.
The affair of Longchamps is adjusted ; he stays where
he is.

> With great respect and esteem, I am
> Your very obedient and very humble servant,
> JOHN JAY.

GENERAL WASHINGTON TO JAY.

MOUNT VERNON, 27th Sept. 1785.

DEAR SIR :

Mr. Taylor presented me the honour of your favour of
the 25th ult., and gave me the pleasure of hearing that Mrs.
Jay and yourself were well when he left New-York.

Upon your safe return to your native country, after a
long absence, and the important services you have rendered
it in many interesting negotiations, I very sincerely congratulate you and your lady.

It gave me great pleasure to hear of your appointment as
secretary of the United States for the department of foreign
affairs ; a happier choice in my opinion could not have been
made, and I shall always rejoice at any circumstance that will
cor ribute either to your honour, interest or convenience.

c will always give me pleasure to hear from you. Mrs.
Washington joins me in respectful compliments to, and best
wishes for Mrs. Jay and yourself.

I am, dear sir,
> Your most obedient and most humble servant,
> GEORGE WASHINGTON.

JAY TO DR. RICHARD PRICE.

New York, 27th September, 1785.

Dear Sir :

I have had the pleasure of receiving the letter of the 9th of July last which you wrote me by Mr. Curtauld. Your recommendation will be of great use to him and you may rely on my readiness to do him any friendly offices in my power. . . .

I hope my letter, in answer to the one which enclosed a number of your political pamphlets, has reached you by this time. I do not recollect the date, but it went in one of the last vessels.

The cause of liberty, like most other good causes, will have its difficulties, and sometimes its persecutions, to struggle with. It has advanced more rapidly in this than in other countries, but all its objects are not yet attained ; and I much doubt whether they ever will be, in this or any other terrestrial state. That men should pray and fight for their own freedom, and yet keep others in slavery,is certainly acting a very inconsistent as well as unjust and, perhaps, impious part ; but the history of mankind is filled with instances of human improprieties. The wise and the good never form the majority of any large society, and it seldom happens that their measures are uniformly adopted, or that they can always prevent being overborne themselves by the strong and almost never-ceasing union of the wicked and the weak.

These circumstances tell us to be patient, and to moderate those sanguine expectations which warm and good hearts often mislead even wise heads to entertain on those subjects.   All that the best men can do is, to persevere in doing their duty to their country, and leave the consequences to Him who made it their duty; being neither elated by success, however great, nor discouraged by disappointments however frequent and mortifying.

With sincere esteem and regard, I am, dear sir,

Your most obedient servant,

JOHN JAY.

JAY TO BENJAMIN FRANKLIN.

NEW YORK, 4 October, 1785.

DEAR SIR :

Your grandson, whom it gave me great pleasure to see, delivered to me a few days ago your kind letter of the 21st of last month.

Your being again with your family, the manner in which the French Court parted with you, the attention you experienced from your English friends, and the reception you met with from your fellow-citizens, are circumstances that must give you great satisfaction.

It strikes me that you will find it somewhat difficult to manage the two parties in Pennsylvania.   It is much to be wished that union and harmony may be established there; and if you accomplish it much honour and many blessings will result from it.   Unless you do it, I do not know who can, for independent of experience and talents you possess their confidence; and your advice and measures must derive very great weight from the reputation and consideration you enjoy.

Why your letters respecting your grandson have not been more efficacious I cannot explain. The appointment of persons in the foreign department has, *in no instance*, been referred to me for my advice or opinion. Jealousy of power and *influence* in individuals as well as bodies seems to characterize the spirit of the times and has much operation both on men and measures.

We are happy to find that you think of visiting New York. By the road from Burlington and Amboy, which is smooth and but short, you might doubtless come with very little inconvenience, especially as you may travel at your leisure and take as many days for it as your ease and the weather may require. Mrs. Jay is exceedingly pleased with this idea, and sincerely joins me in wishing to see it realized. Her attachments are strong, and that to you, being founded in esteem and the recollection of kind offices, is particularly so. I suspect your little friend has forgotten your person—your name is familiar to her, as indeed it will be to every generation.

With the best wishes I am, dear sir, your obliged and affectionate servant,

JOHN JAY.

JAY TO THE PRESIDENT OF CONGRESS.

OFFICE FOR FOREIGN AFFAIRS,
13th October, 1785.

SIR :

Your Excellency will find herewith enclosed a letter from Chevalier Jones of 6th August, and a copy of a letter (which is the same that is published in the Philadelphia paper of 11th instant) from Mons. Sontangés, dated 14th July last, to the judges and consuls of Nantes, informing that the Algerines had declared war against the United States.

As their late peace with Spain has rendered their armaments unnecessary against that power, they probably choose to turn them against us to prevent their being useless, and in hopes of acquiring considerable booty. This peace, if the public accounts of it are true, gives those pirates just matter of triumph ; and in this moment of their exultation I am inclined to think that an advantageous treaty with them is not to be expected. This war does not strike me as a great evil. The more we are ill-treated abroad the more we shall unite and consolidate at home. Besides, as it may become a nursery for seamen, and lay the foundation for a respectable navy, it may eventually prove more beneficial than otherwise. Portugal will doubtless unite with us in it, and that circumstance may dispose that kingdom to extend commercial favours to us further than they might consent to do if uninfluenced by such inducements. For my own part, I think it may be demonstrated, that while we bend our attention to the sea, every naval war, however long, which does not. do us essential injury, will do us essential good.

I have the honour to be, with great respect and esteem, your Excellency's most obedient and very humble servant,

JOHN JAY.

JAY TO JOHN ADAMS.

NEW YORK, 14th October, 1785.

DEAR SIR:

. . . I perfectly concur with you in sentiment respecting what ought to be the conduct and policy of the United States, and I am not without hopes that they will gradually perceive and pursue their own interests. There certainly is much temper as well as talent in Congress, and although it is not in their power to do all that should be done, yet they are willing and industrious to do whatever depends upon them. Your letters I am sure are useful ; they disseminate those federal ideas which cannot be too forcibly inculcated or too strongly impressed. Our federal government is incompetent to such objects, and as it is in the interest of our country, so it is the duty of her leading characters to co-operate in measures for enlarging and invigorating it. The rage for separation and new States is mischievous ; it will, unless checked, scatter our resources, and in every view enfeeble the Union. Your testimony against such licentious, anarchical proceedings would, I am persuaded, have great weight.

Your letters as yet are silent respecting the evacuation of our frontier posts. I do not mean to press you either to do or say any thing *unseasonably* about it, for there are times and tides in human affairs to be watched and observed. I know your attention, and therefore rest satisfied that we shall hear from you on this interesting subject as soon as you ought to write about it. During the ensuing sessions of the Legislature, I shall watch them each, and endeavour to send you such as may respect the interests of the Union. I find it extremely difficult to collect them. When I first came into this office, I wrote a circular-letter to the Governors requesting them among other things to send me from time to time printed copies of their acts; but whatever may have been the cause, it has so happened that, except in two or three instances, that request has been entirely neglected.

With the newspapers herewith sent, you will find the requisition of Congress; what its success will be cannot yet be determined. The Algerines, it seems, have declared war against us. If we act properly, I shall not be very sorry for it. In my opinion it may lay the foundation for a navy, and tend to draw us more closely into a federal system. On that ground only we want strength, and could our people be brought to see it in that light, and act accordingly, we should have little reason to apprehend danger from any quarter.

Mr. De Marbois has left us and is gone to St. Domingo, where he has an intendancy. Mr. Olto succeeds him, and appears well disposed. As yet your place at the Hague is vacant; several gentlemen are in nomination, among whom I hear are Mr. Izard and Mr. Madison.

Dr. Franklin is happy at Philadelphia. Both parties are assiduous in their attentions to him, and it is thought more than probable that he will succeed Mr. Dickinson. I fear, in the language of our farmers that a day so remarkably fine for the season may prove a *weather breeder*, that is, that he will find it difficult to manage both parties; for if he gives himself up to one, he must expect hostility from the other. I wish he may be able to reconcile them, and thereby restore that State to the degree of strength and respectability which from its population, fertility, and commerce it ought to possess.

I congratulate you on the issue of your discussions with their High Mightinesses. Mr. Dumas gave us an account of it, and we are all pleased to find that it terminated as it did.

With great and sincere esteem and regard, I am, dear sir, your most obedient and humble servant,

JOHN JAY.

WILLIAM T. FRANKLIN TO JAY.

PHILADA. 16th Oct., 1785.

DEAR SIR:

Mr. Hudon, of whom you have heard me speak, will have the honor of delivering you this. He is lately returned from Virginia where he has been fulfilling the object of his coming to America in modelling the bust of Genl. Washington in which he has been singularly successful.

He is now about returning to France by the way of N. York. I have persuaded him to take with him the Gen'ls bust, that he has given us, in order to shew Congress what he is capable of doing, and thereby obtaining the Preference in being employ'd to make the Equestrian Statue voted long since.

I beg leave to recommend M. Hudon to your Civilities and I am persuaded his merit will procure him your good Offices.

I cannot close this, without returning you my sincerest thanks for the many Marks of favor and friendship you gave me lately at York. I have added them to those you formerly conferr'd on me, and shall ever retain a grateful remembrance of both.

Permit me to assure Mrs. Jay of my respect, and to make her my most thankful Acknowledgements for the Civilities and attention she so kindly shew'd me.

With great respect, Esteem and Affection,

I am, Dear Sir,

Your most obedient and obliged humble Servant

W. T. FRANKLIN.

JAY TO JOHN ADAMS.

DEAR SIR :   NEW YORK, 1st November, 1785.

My last to you was of the 14th ult. by the ship *Betsey*, Captain Thomas Watson. Since that time I have had the pleasure of receiving and laying before Congress your dispatches of the 6th, 8th, and 10th of August last.

We concur so perfectly in sentiment, respecting public affairs and what ought to be done, that I find no occasion to enlarge on those heads.

In a late report I have called the attention of Congress to this serious question, viz., whether the United States should withdraw their attention from the ocean and leave foreigners to fetch and carry for them, or whether it is more their interest to look forward to naval strength and maritime importance, and to take and persevere in the measures proper to attain it.

The diversity of opinions on this point renders it necessary that it should be well considered and finally decided. The Eastern and Middle States are generally for the latter system, and though the others do not openly aver their preferring the former, yet they are evidently inclined to it. Hence it is that the most of the leading men in Congress from that quarter do not only not promote measures for vesting Congress with power to regulate trade, but, as the common phrase is, throw cold water on all such ideas.

Having few or no ships of their own, they are averse to such duties on foreign ones as will greatly advance the price of freight ; nor do they seem much disposed to sacrifice any present proffer for the sake of their neighbours who have these and wish to have more.

We hear much of the Algerines having declared war against the United States. None of our advices were official, but as the intelligence comes directly from Nantes, Bordeaux, and Orient, there seems to be much reason to fear it is true. The public papers herewith sent will inform you of our common occurrences, and I wish it was in my power to tell you what Congress mean to do respecting many matters on which they are to decide. The representation is at present slender, and will, I suspect, continue so till the new members come on.

I have the honour to be, etc., JOHN JAY.

JAY TO THE PRESIDENT OF CONGRESS.

OFFICE FOR FOREIGN AFFAIRS,
24th November, 1785.

SIR :

Mr. Temple presented me this morning the commission which I have now the honour of transmitting to your Excellency herewith enclosed. It appoints

him Consul-General of His Britannic Majesty throughout the United States of America.

Two questions arise on this occasion :

1. Whether he is to be received *de jure*.

2. Whether it will be expedient to receive him
de gratia.

The first question is settled by Vattel in the following paragraph, viz. :

" Among the modern institutions," etc., page 131.

The second question appears to me to be an important one, for, however determined, interesting
consequences will result from its decision. In considering it a secondary question presents itself, viz.,
whether the rejection or reception of this consul will
most dispose his nation to the terms of commercial
intercourse which we wish. To this point the fable
of the north wind and the sun seems applicable.

It appears to me that the admission of a consul
here is not a matter of so much importance to Britain
as to induce that nation to purchase or obtain by any
compliances which they would not *otherwise* make.
Severity, or *summum jus* on small points, may irritate,
but they very seldom coerce. Retaliatory restrictions
on trade and navigation are great objects, and very
consistent with the pride and dignity, as well as
interest, of a nation ; but under such ideas to refuse
to receive a consul would, whatever might be the
true motives, be generally ascribed to a degree of
pique and irritation which, though nations may feel,
they ought not expressly or impliedly to declare.

In my opinion, therefore, this consul ought to be
received, but in such a manner as to be and to

appear as a matter of favour, and not as a matter of course.

I have the honour to be your Excellency's most obedient and very humble servant,

JOHN JAY.

JAY TO THOMAS JEFFERSON.

OFFICE FOR FOREIGN AFFAIRS, NEW YORK,
9th January, 1786.

DEAR SIR:

Since my last of 7th December last, and indeed for some time before that, Congress has been composed of so few States actually represented as not to have it in their power to pay that attention to their foreign affairs which they would doubtless otherwise have done. Hence it has happened that no resolutions have been entered into on any of the important subjects submitted to their consideration. This obliges me to observe a degree of reserve in my letters respecting those subjects which I wish to be free from, but which is nevertheless necessary, lest my sentiments and opinions should be opposed to those which they may adopt and wish to impress.

There is reason to hope that the requisition will be generally complied with; I say generally, because it is not quite clear that every State, without exception, will make punctual payments.

Although a disposition prevails to enable Congress to regulate trade, yet I am apprehensive that, however the propriety of the measure may be admitted, the manner of doing it will not be with equal ease agreed to.

It is much to be regretted that the confederation had not been so formed as to exclude the necessity of all such kind of questions. It certainly is very imperfect, and I fear it will be difficult to remedy its defects, until experience shall render the necessity of doing it more obvious and pressing.

Does France consider herself bound by her guarantee to insist on the surrender of our posts? Will she second our remonstrances to Britain on that head? I have no orders to ask these questions, but I think them important.

Spain insists on the navigation of the great River, and that renders a treaty with her uncertain as yet.

Among the public papers herewith sent you will find the speech of the Governor of New York to the Legislature, and the answer of the Senate. A spirit more federal seems to prevail than that which marked their proceedings last year.

You will also perceive from the papers that Massachusetts begins to have troubles similar to those which this State experienced from Vermont. North Carolina suffers the like evils, and from the same causes. Congress should recollect the old maxim, " Obsta principiis."

I wish the negotiations with the Barbary Powers may prove successful, because our country in general desires peace with them. For my part I prefer war to tribute, and that sentiment was strongly expressed in my report on that subject.

Our Indian affairs do not prosper. I fear Britain bids higher than we do. Our surveys have been checked, and peace with the savages seems somewhat precarious. That department might, in my opinion, have been better managed.

With great respect, I have the honour to be, dear sir, your most obedient and very humble servant,

JOHN JAY.

JAY TO THE PRESIDENT OF CONGRESS.

SIR : NEW YORK, Jan. 20th, 1786.

As the attention of the American merchants begins to turn to the China and India trade, and several of their vessels will probably be employed in it in the course of this year, I take the liberty of submitting to the consideration of Congress the propriety of appointing a consul and vice-consul general for Canton and other ports in Asia. Such officers would have a degree of weight and respect which private adventurers cannot readily acquire, and which would enable them to render essential services to their countrymen on various occasions. More credit would be given by strangers to men who bring such evidence of their merit, than to others whose characters cannot be so soon and so certainly known ; and their commission would give them more ready access to a greater influence with princes, governors, and magistrates than private merchants can in general expect.

I have the honour to be, with great respect, Your Excellency's most obedient and humble servant,

JOHN JAY.

THOMAS JEFFERSON TO JAY.

DEAR SIR: PARIS, Jan. 25th, 1786.

I received on the 18th instant your private favour of
December 9th, and thank you for the confidence you are so
good as to repose in me, of which that communication is a
proof; as such it is a gratification to me, because it meets
the esteem I have ever borne you. But nothing was
needed to keep my mind right on that subject, and, I
believe I may say, the public mind here. The sentiments
entertained of you in this place are too respectful to be
easily shaken. The person of whom you speak in your
letter arrived here on the 19th, and departed for Warsaw on
the 22d. It is really to be lamented that after a public
servant has passed a life in important and faithful services
—after having given the most plenary satisfaction in every
station,—it should yet be in the power of every individual
to disturb his quiet, by arraigning him in a gazette, and by
obliging him to act as if he needed a defence—an obligation
imposed on him by unthinking minds which never give
themselves the trouble of seeking a reflection unless it
be presented to them.[1] Your quiet may have suffered for
a moment on this occasion, but you have the strongest of
all supports, that of the public esteem; it is unnecessary to
add assurances of that with which I have the honour to be,
dear sir,

Your most obedient and most humble servant,

TH. JEFFERSON.

JAY TO FREDERICK JAY.

DEAR FADY : ——,1786.

My official situation with respect to foreign ministers, renders it improper for me to place myself under
personal obligations to any of them, and consequently

---

[1] Jefferson refers in this note to an abusive attack made upon Mr. Jay's
integrity by a young man named Littlepage, who had lived with him in Spain.
The correspondence in the case appears in "Life of Jay," vol. i., pp. 204-229.

to request their personal favours.   I flatter myself you will perceive as clearly as I do, the propriety of observing this delicacy, and therefore that you will impute my declining to apply to Mr. Gardoqui, on the subject mentioned in your note of last evening, to that consideration, and not to any reluctance to serve you ; for as I shall always rejoice in your welfare, so I shall always regret every obstacle which may restrain me from measures tending to promote it.[1]

Your affectionate brother,

JOHN JAY.

JAY TO GOVERNOR CLINTON.

NEW YORK, 26th January, 1786.

SIR :

Experience convinces me that to do justice to my official business, it is necessary to devote all my time and attention to it ; as it hence becomes improper for me to engage in any affairs that must necessarily call me off from the duties of my office, I find myself constrained to resign the appointment with which I have been honoured by this State as one of their agents for managing their controversy with Massachusetts.[2] The number and acknowledged abilities of the other agents render this resignation of no further importance than that it deprives me of the satisfaction I always derive from serving my native State, to which

---

[1] This note appears in reply to one from Jay's brother Frederick, who desired a recommendation from the Spanish minister to secure the sale of the cargo of a Spanish vessel lately arrived at New York in distress.

[2] Respecting boundaries and the proprietorship of the western part of New York State.

I have been long and repeatedly indebted for strong and flattering marks of confidence.

I have the honour to be, with great respect,
Your Excellency's most obedient and humble servant,

JOHN JAY.

JAY TO JOHN ADAMS.

NEW YORK, Febuary 22, 1786.

DEAR SIR :

Nine States are not yet represented in Congress, and therefore the affairs of this department continue in the same state that they were in at the date of my last.

The public papers will enable you to see the complexion of the times. Federal opinions grow, but it will be some time before they bear fruit ; and, what is not the case with most other fruits, they will, to judge from present appearances, ripen slower in the *South* than in the *North.*

The packet will sail next week. I shall then write to you again. With great and sincere esteem and regard,

I have the honor to be, dear Sir,
Your most obedient and humble servant

JOHN JAY.

FRANCIS HOPKINSON TO JAY.

PHILADELPHIA, March 11, 1786.

MY DEAR SIR :

Our friend, Mr. Jefferson having requested me to furnish him with the newspapers and other prints of this city, I have hitherto sent those packages by the French packet, but he has found, as I foresaw he would, that mode of conveyance too expensive, and has now desired me to send them to you, to be forwarded as merchandize, and not as papers or letters. I presume he has written to you on the subject. Agreeably to this plan, I send a package herewith, which you will please to transmit according to his desire.

May I ask how you come on in your political family. Our *Law office* is at present open, and the debates and proceedings there afford ample room for amusement, speculation and observation. The two parties of our State are so nearly ballanced in the House of Assembly, that neither are sure of carrying a point.[1] This situation excites the Orators and leading men of the House to the most vigorous exertions, and those who have leisure to attend the debates are sure to be highly gratified. When both parties unite in a measure, it is a thousand to one that it is a salutary and proper measure. Pennsylvania hops along upon her *one leg* better than I expected. I never liked our Constitution ; yet the above metaphor suggests one advantage which I did not think of before: viz : That having but one branch of Legislature—or if you please, but one leg to support her, the old lady is obliged to be very attentive and circumspect in her positions and motions, lest she should fall and break her nose. Those who have two to depend upon, are apt to trip thro' carelessness. Your Constitution, I think, hobbles on one leg and a stick. But enough of this nonsense.

I shall be glad of a line from you when you have nothing else to do. I shall always think myself honored by your esteem and happy in your friendship.

Adieu,

Yours Sincerely,

Fr. Hopkinson.

---

[1] The two parties in the Pennsylvania Assembly referred to were known as the " Republicans " and " Constitutionalists "—the latter conservative, and opposed to changes in the existing governmental machinery of the State, whose Legislature was composed of but one House.

JAY TO R. LUSHINGTON.

NEW YORK, 15th March, 1786.

SIR :

I have been favoured with your letter of the 22d ult., and immediately communicated it to the Committee of our Society for promoting the liberation of slaves and protecting such as may be manumitted.[1] They are taking proper measures on the occasion, and I flatter myself that our Legislature will interpose to prevent such enormities in future.

It is much to be wished that slavery may be abolished. The honour of the States, as well as justice and humanity, in my opinion, loudly call upon them to emancipate these unhappy people. To contend for our own liberty, and to deny that blessing to others, involves an inconsistency not to be excused.[2] Whatever may be the issue of the endeavours of

---

[1] This Society was organized early in 1785, and held its first quarterly meeting on May 12th of that year at the "Coffee House" in New York. Its officers were *President*, John Jay ; *Vice-President*, Samuel Franklin ; *Treasurer*, John Murray, Jr. ; *Secretary*, John Keese. In 1808 it was incorporated under special act of the Legislature, and supported a free school for the education of negro children, which in 1807 had an attendance of about one hundred.

Mr. R. Lushington, to whom Jay wrote the above, was a benevolent Quaker, of Charleston, S. C., who had reported the case of a negro kidnapped in New York and sold at Charleston. He had expressed the hope to Jay that "some mode might be adopted to prevent and deter people from pursuing so vilainous a practice."

[2] Jay favored, and with others petitioned for, the total prohibition of the exportation of slaves from New York to the Southern States in order to prevent, as far as possible, the separation of families and increase of their miseries. As to slavery at home he believed in gradual or considerate emancipation, and followed out his theory in practice, as in the case of the negro boy he purchased in the West Indies in 1779 and released in 1787. " Life of Jay," vol. i., p. 230. On Oct. 1, 1798, he wrote : " I purchase slaves and manumit them at proper ages, and when their faithful services shall have afforded a reasonable return.'

you and others to promote this desirable end, the reflection that they are prompted by the best motives affords good reasons for persevering in them.

I am, sir, your most obedient and humble servant,

JOHN JAY.

JAY TO GENERAL WASHINGTON.

NEW YORK, March 16, 1786.

DEAR SIR:

Although you have wisely retired from public employment, and calmly view from the temple of fame the various exertions of that sovereignty and independence which Providence has enabled you to be so greatly and gloriously instrumental in securing to your country, yet I am persuaded that you cannot view them with the eye of an unconcerned spectator.

Experience has pointed out errors in our national government which call for correction, and which threaten to blast the fruit we expected from our tree of liberty. The convention proposed by Virginia may do some good, and would perhaps do more if it comprehended more objects. An opinion begins to prevail that a general Convention for revising the Articles of Confederation would be expedient. Whether the people are yet ripe for such a measure, or whether the system proposed to be attained by it is only to be expected from calamity and commotion, is difficult to ascertain. I think we are in a delicate situation, and a variety of considerations and circumstances give me uneasiness.

It is in contemplation to take measures for forming a general convention ; the plan is not matured. If it should be well concerted and take effect, I am fervent in my wishes that it may comport with the line of life you have marked out for yourself to favour your country with your counsels on such an important and signal occasion. I suggest this merely as a hint for consideration, and am with the highest respect and esteem, dear sir,

Your most obedient and very humble servant,

JOHN JAY.

JAY TO FRANCIS HOPKINSON.

NEW YORK, 29th March, 1786.

DEAR SIR :

I have had the pleasure of receiving your letter of the 11th inst., with the packet for Mr. Jefferson. He has omitted to write to me on the subject, but I shall take care to forward it to him in the manner you point out. It is probable he will find some difficulty in getting such parcels sent to him from *L'Orient* under the denomination of merchandizes, uninspected. In such governments the transmission of republican letters and papers is neither encouraged nor facilitated.

You and other manufacturers of laws more generally consult the prevailing fashions and predilections of the day than the utility of their goods to those who are to wear them. What will fetch most popularity, or may be exchanged for most personal advantages, are common questions, and the answers to them often determine the colour and the kind of stuff to be fabricated. So it is here, and so I believe it is, and always has been, everywhere, in greater or lesser degrees.

It appears to me that the people are exactly represented in most of their assemblies, and that the various classes of wise, weak, etc., out of the House, have their due proportion of representatives in it. It is hard to tell whether your government gets on with one leg, or runs on those of the Executive Council. I like our Constitution better than yours because in my opinion it is more capable of being well administered, and less capable of being ill administered. I suspect your sage pilot will find use for all his experience to navigate safely between your parties; I wish *they* would unite in wise and temperate measures.

With great esteem and regard I am, dear sir,
Your affectionate and humble servant,
JOHN JAY.

JAY TO LORD LANSDOWNE.

My Lord :
NEW YORK, 16th April, 1786.

Accept my thanks for the letter you did me the honour to write on the 4th September last, and for your obliging interposition in behalf of the person alluded to in it.

Your Lordship's conjectures respecting the new principles of trade and finance will probably be realized. We hear of several circumstances which look and promise well. The extent of those principles, and the system of commerce to be reared on them, are subjects, however, on which no decided judgment can here be formed, for want of information more minute and unquestionable than we at present have.[1]

Various, my Lord, are the conjectures of this country respecting the real disposition and intentions of yours on these and some other interesting points. While such doubts and apprehensions exist, a degree of jealousy will naturally continue to operate against mutual confidence. For my part, I sincerely wish to see good-humour prepare the way for friendly intercourse, and by degrees incline both countries rather to promote than retard each other's welfare. It gives me pleasure to reflect that our wishes on this head correspond, and that the time may yet come when your abilities and liberality will produce all the public benefits which may justly be expected from them. Mr. Pitt's views as to America, are yet to be ascertained : I wish they may be such as to increase the reputation and affection which his father's memory

---

[1] England's restrictive policy in trade matters, especially the closing of her West India ports to the Americans immediately after the Revolution, was deprecated by several of her leading statesmen, of whom Lansdowne was one. In his letter to Jay of Sep. 4, 1785, he writes :

" I have great pleasure in telling you that the new principles regarding both trade and finance, are making an evident progress among the publick. It must be expected that they will meet with some interruption from the influence of old prejudices and the activity of present parties. But I have no doubt of their overcoming both, if they are not precipitated or too vigorously pushed in every instance.

" I am anxious to hear that the government of United States has taken a solid consistence upon those wise and comprehensive foundations which you stated to me. I shall always look upon this Country as deeply interested in whatever regards your prosperity and reputation and above all your interior tranquillity."

enjoys among us. It strikes me that a minister of any nation, much connected with this, will always find advantage in possessing the esteem and confidence of America.

To what events this country may in future be instrumental, is indeed uncertain ; but I cannot persuade myself that Providence has created such a nation, in such a country, to remain like dust in the balance of others. We are happy, my Lord, in the enjoyment of much more interior tranquillity than the English newspapers allow, or their writers seem to wish us. In free states, there must and ought to be a little ferment. When the public mind grows languid, and a dead calm, unmarked by the least breeze of party, takes place, the vigour of a republic soon becomes lost in general relaxation. We perhaps are yet too distant from that point ; for although our laws and manners now give us as much personal security as can elsewhere be found, and although the same may in a great, though less, degree be said of our property, yet our federal government has imperfections, which time and more experience will, I hope, effectually remedy.

I have the honour to be, my Lord, with great respect and esteem, your Lordship's

Most obedient and very humble servant,

JOHN JAY.

JAMES MUNROE TO JAY.

SIR, NEW YORK, April 20, 1786.

The Committee to whom it is referred to report the plan of a temporary government for such States as shall be erected under the acts of cession from individual States, previous to their admission into the Confederacy, as also to organize the Indian department, request the favor of your attendance and advice upon those subjects upon Saturday next in Congress chamber at half after ten in the morning. The first question which arises with respect to the government is, Shall it be upon Colonial principles, under a governor, council and judges of the U. S., removeable at a certain period of time and they admitted to a vote in Congress with the common rights of the other States, or shall they be left to themselves until that event? In the former instance how the correspondence or superintendence of such colony or colonies, shall be systematically preserved and presented to the view of Congress? The same question occurs with respect to the Indian department. These subjects altho' not immediately within your province we consider as intimately connected with it, and shall be happy in your assistance in forming those arrangements which will become necessary respecting them.

I have the honor to be with great respect and esteem, your most obedient servant,

JAS. MONROE.

JAY TO LORD LANSDOWNE.

NEW YORK, 20th April, 1786.

MY LORD:

Mr. Ansley this morning delivered the letter you did me the honour to write on the 26th of February last. Every opportunity of manifesting my attention to your Lordship's recommendations will give me pleasure, and that inducement will conspire, with others of public nature, to ensure to Mr. Ansley my friendly endeavours to facilitate the execution of his commission, and render his residence here agreeable to him.

I perfectly agree in sentiment with your Lordship, that it much concerns the honour and future intercourse of both countries to have the treaty of peace duly and faithfully executed. It is to be lamented that wars like the last usually leave behind them a degree of heat which requires some time and prudence to allay. Minds like yours will not be susceptible of it, but the mass of the people commonly act and reason as they feel, and have seldom sufficient temper and liberality to perceive that peace should draw a veil over the injuries of war, and that when hostilities cease, no other contest should remain, but that of who shall take the lead in magnanimity and manly policy. Although these remarks apply to both countries, yet, whatever may be said or written to the contrary, there is certainly, my Lord, more temper in this country than it has credit for; and I am persuaded it would become more manifest, if less discouraged by irritating proceedings here and abroad. In the Legislature of this State there are this day members sitting, who, it is well known, are disqualified by law for their conduct during the late contest; and an act has lately passed for restoring all such of the gentlemen of the law as, for the same reason, had been suspended from the exercise of their profession. The execution of all laws of this sort becomes more and more relaxed, and of the many persons returned to this State from exile, and living in their former neighbourhoods, I have not heard of one that has met with any molestation. There are, indeed, certain characters who can never return with safety; but the

greater part of them are such as merit no other attention from any country than what national policy may
exact. With respect to the generality of these people, the public mind daily becomes more and more
composed. It is true that our affairs are not yet
perfectly arranged ; some former acts are to be done
away, and more proper regulations to be introduced.
There is reason, however, to hope that things will
gradually come right, and I am persuaded that a little
more good-nature on the part of Britain, would produce solid and mutual advantages to both countries.

My Lord, I write thus freely from a persuasion that
your ideas of policy are drawn from those large and
liberal views and principles, which apply to the future
as well as the present, and which embrace the interests
of the nation and of mankind, rather than the local
and transitory advantages of partial systems and individual ambition ; for your Lordship's plans on the peace
were certainly calculated to make the revolution produce only an exchange of dependence for friendship,
and of sound and feathers for substance and permanent benefits. How greatly would it redound to the
happiness as well as honour of all civilized people,
were they to consider and treat each other like fellow-
citizens ; each nation governing itself as it pleases,
but each admitting others to a perfect freedom of
commerce. The blessings resulting from the climate
and local advantages of one country would then become common to all, and the bounties of nature and
conveniences of art pass from nation to nation without being impeded by the selfish monopolies and

restrictions with which narrow policy opposes the extension of Divine benevolence. It is pleasant, my Lord, to dream of these things, and I often enjoy that pleasure ; but though, like some of our other dreams, we may wish to see them realized, yet the passions and prejudices of mankind forbid us to expect it.

I have the honour to be, with great respect and sincere regard, my Lord,

Your Lordship's most obedient
And very humble servant,
JOHN JAY.

JAY TO JOHN ADAMS.

NEW YORK, 4th May, 1786.

DEAR SIR :

I have been favoured with your letter, in which you mention Mr. Warren. Your opinion of that gentleman, added to the merits of his family, cannot fail to operate powerfully in his favour. I have communicated that letter to Mr. King, an able and valuable delegate from Massachusetts, who, I have reason to think, wishes well to you, and to all who, like you, deserve well of their country.

Our friend Gerry has retired from Congress with a charming, amiable lady, whom he married here. I regret his absence, for he discharged the trust reposed in him with great fidelity, and with more industry and persevering attention than many are distinguished by. Mr. King has also married a lady of merit, and the only child of Mr. Alsop, who was in Congress with us in 1774. I am pleased with these intermarriages; they tend to assimilate the States, and to promote one of the first wishes of my heart, viz., to see the people of America become one nation in every respect; for, as to the separate legislatures, I would have them considered, with relation to the Confederacy, in the same light in which counties stand to the State of which they are parts, viz., merely as districts to facilitate the purposes of domestic order and good government.

With great and sincere regard, I am, dear sir,
Your friend and servant,
JOHN JAY.

GENERAL WASHINGTON TO JAY.

MOUNT VERNON, 18th May, 1786.

DEAR SIR:

In due course of post I have been honoured with your favours of the 2d and 16th of March, since which I have been a good deal engaged, and pretty much from home.

I coincide perfectly in sentiment with you, my dear sir, that there are errors in our national government which call for correction,—loudly I will add: but I shall find myself happily mistaken if the remedies are at hand. We are certainly in a delicate situation; but my fear is, that the people are not yet sufficiently misled to retract from error! To be plainer, I think there is more wickedness than ignorance mixed with our councils. Under this impression, I scarcely know what opinion to entertain of a general Convention. That it is necessary to revise and amend the articles of confederation, I entertain *no* doubt; but what may be the consequences of such an attempt is doubtful. Yet something must be done, or the fabric must fall; it certainly is tottering! Ignorance and design are difficult to combat. Out of these proceed illiberality, improper jeal-ousies, and a train of evils which oftentimes in republican governments must be sorely felt before they can be removed. The former, that is ignorance, being a fit soil for the latter to work in, tools are employed which a generous mind would disdain to use, and which nothing but time and their own puerile or wicked productions can show the inefficacy and dangerous tendency of. I think often of our situation, and view it with concern. From the high ground on which we stood, from the plain path which invited our footsteps, to be so fallen! so lost! is really mortifying. But virtue, I fear, has in a great degree taken its departure from our land, and the want of disposition to do justice is the source of the national embarrassments; for under whatever guise or colourings are given to them, this I apprehend is the origin of the evils we now feel, and probably shall labour under for some time yet.

With respectful compliments to Mrs. Jay, and sentiments of sincere friendship, I am, dear sir,

Your most obedient and humble servant,

GEO. WASHINGTON.

JAY'S REPORT TO CONGRESS ON A JOINT LETTER FROM ADAMS AND JEFFERSON.

OFFICE FOR FOREIGN AFFAIRS,
May 29, 1786.

The Secretary of the United States for the Department of Foreign Affairs, to whom was referred a joint letter from Mr. Adams and Mr. Jefferson, of 28th March last,[1] together with a motion of the Honorable Mr. Pinckney on the subject of it, reports:

---

[1] " Diplomatic Correspondence of the United States from 1783 to 1789," vol. ii.

That those gentlemen in this letter mention that in a conference with the Ambassador of Tripoli he informed them that 12,500 guineas to his constituents, with ten per cent. on that sum for himself, must be paid, if the treaty was made for only a period of one year.

That 30,000 guineas for his employers and 3,000 for himself were the lowest terms on which a perpetual peace could be made.

That Tunis would treat on the same terms, but that he could not answer for Algiers or Morocco.

They further observe that if Congress should order them to make the best terms they can with Tunis, Tripoli, Algiers, and Morocco, and to procure the money wherever they can find it, upon terms like those of the last loan in Holland, their best endeavours should be used, etc.

The motion in question proposes an instruction conformable to the above suggestion.

Two questions seem to arise on this letter :

1st. Whether these Ministers shall be authorized and instructed to make the best terms with those powers.

2d. Whether they shall be authorized and instructed to endeavour to borrow money in Europe for the purpose.

Your Secretary thinks full confidence may be reposed in the integrity and discretion of those Ministers, and therefore is of opinion that it would be expedient to leave the terms of the proposed treaties to their prudence.

As to authorizing and instructing them to endeavour to borrow money for the purpose in Europe, your Secretary much doubts the policy of it.

The probability of their borrowing so much money appears questionable.

Because those nations to whom our war with the Barbary States is not disagreeable will be little inclined to lend us money to put an end to it.

Because no funds are yet provided for paying even the interest of our former loans, either foreign or domestic.

Because the payments due France, though pressed, have not been completed.

Because the reluctance of the States to pay taxes, or to comply with the economical requisitions of Congress, or to give efficacy to their Federal Government, are topics of common conversation in Europe.

If a loan should be attempted and not succeed, the credit and respectability of the United States would be diminished by the attempt.

Your Secretary thinks that neither individuals nor States should borrow money without the highest probability at least of being able punctually to repay it ; and that States should never attempt a loan without having previously formed and arranged adequate funds for its discharge.

It appears to your Secretary improper to open such a loan, even if the success of it were certain.

Because, as the Federal Government, in its present state, is rather paternal and persuasive than coercive and efficient, Congress can make no certain dependence on the States for any specific sums to be required and paid at any given periods, and consequently are not in a capacity safely to pledge their honour and their faith for the repayment of any specific sums they may borrow at any given period, which must be the case if they should make this or any other loan.

Because, as the people or generality will never provide for the public expenses, unless when moved thereto by constitutional coercion, or by the dictates of reason, or by their feelings; and as the first of these motives is here out of the question, your Secretary thinks it probable that the States, on being applied to, will be more disposed to supply money to purchase these treaties of peace while they feel the evils resulting from the war, than they will to supply money to repay borrowed sums when all their fears and dangers from Sallee rovers, Algerine corsairs, and the pirates of Tunis and Tripoli are vanished and gone.

For these reasons your Secretary is much inclined to think that a fair and accurate state of the matter should be transmitted to the States, that they should be informed that the sum of ——— will be necessary to purchase treaties from the Barbary States, and that until such time as they furnish Congress with their respective portions of that sum, the depredations of those barbarians will, in all probability, continue and increase.

All which is submitted to the wisdom of Congress.

JOHN JAY.

JAY TO THE MARQUIS DE LAFAYETTE.

NEW YORK, 16th June, 1786.

DEAR SIR :

During your absence from France I omitted being
so regular in my correspondence as I should otherwise have been. I have been honoured with your
letters of the 18th April, and 6th September in the
last year, and with one of 11th February last. They
were all communicated to Congress.

The account of your German excursion is concise
and interesting. The sentiments and opinions respecting the United States and American affairs, which
you found there prevailing, appear to me very natural.
Successful revolutions and victorious arms have
always a degree of splendour about them which
shines at a great distance, and excites admiration,
whether well or ill founded. Few have been at the
pains of examining and understanding the merits of
the case between Great Britain and us, and nine
tenths of that few have taken their sides less from
conviction and opinion of right than from some of
the many other more common and more stimulating
motives, which usually govern the declarations and
conduct of the mass of mankind. It is equally natural that reports to our disadvantage, composed of
such proportions of truth and falsehood as might
render them probable and palatable, should be generally diffused and believed. There are very few
States, and very few ministers in them, who think
it convenient to magnify America either by word or
deed. Politicians, like critics, are often more disposed

to censure than to commend the works of others, and patriotic manœuvres *pro bono publico*, like pious frauds *pro salute animarum*, were never uncommon. As there is, and always was, and will be, an actual though involuntary coalition between the men of too much art and the men of too little, so they who either officially or from choice fabricate opinions for other people's use, will always find many to receive and be influenced by them. Thus errors proceeding from the invention of designing men are very frequently adopted and cherished by others, who mistake them for truths. It must be easy for the maritime nations to make the rest of Europe believe almost what they please of this country for some years yet to come, and I shall be much mistaken if fame should soon do us justice, especially as her trumpet is, in many places, employed and hired for other purposes.

Whence it happens, I know not, but so the fact is, that I have scarcely met with six foreigners in the course of my life who really understood American affairs. The cause of truth will probably be little indebted to their memoirs and representations, and when I consider what mistakes are committed by writers on American subjects, I suspect the histories of other countries contain but very imperfect accounts of them.

I can easily conceive that, at the German courts you visited, you have done us service, because I know how able, as well as how willing, you are to do it. I wish all who speak and write of us were equally well-informed and well-disposed. It is a common remark in this country that wherever you go you do us good. For my part, I give you credit, not merely for doing us good, but also for doing it uniformly, constantly, and upon system.

Do you recollect your letter of the 2d March, 1783, containing what passed between you and Count de Florida Blanca, respecting our western limits? I communicated that part of it some months ago to Mr. Gardoqui, in opposition to his pretensions and claims. He lately told me you had mistaken the Count, for that he never meant to convey to you anything like a dereliction of those claims, which, by-the-bye, are too extensive to be admitted.[1] In a word, they do not mean to be restricted to the limits established between Britain and us. Why should people, who have so much more territory than they know what to do with, be so solicitous to acquire more?

The moneys due by the United States to subjects of France have given occasion to applications by Mr. Marbois, and to reports on them by the board of treasury, which are now under the consideration of Congress. You, my dear sir, are not acquainted with the state of our finances, nor with the difficulties resulting from the inefficiency of our federal government. Time and more experience must and will cure these evils; when or how is less certain, and can only be conjectured.

---

[1] In reply, Lafayette wrote to Jay, October 25, 1786, enclosing a copy of the letter referred to, quoting Florida Blanca against Gardoqui, and added: "As to the navigation of the Mississippi, you know better than I what are the strong prejudices of that Court against it. But we know equally well that in a little time we must have the navigation one way or other, which I hope Spain may at last understand."

I had the honour last summer of writing a letter to the Marchioness, in answer to one she was so obliging as to favour me with ; did it ever come to hand ? Mrs. Jay writes to her by this conveyance. We and many others are pleased with the expectation of seeing you both here, and with the opportunity we shall then have of personally assuring you of our esteem and attachment,

I am, dear sir, your affectionate and obedient servant, JOHN JAY.

JAY TO GENERAL WASHINGTON.

PHILADELPHIA, June 27, 1786.

DEAR SIR :

Being deputed by the Church Convention of New York to attend a general one convened here, I brought with me your obliging letter of the 18th ult., that I might devote the first leisure hour to the pleasure of answering it. Congress having freed the papers, of which the enclosed are copies, from injunctions of secrecy, and permitted the delegates to make and send extracts from them to their different States, I think myself at liberty to transmit copies to you. These papers have been referred to me ; some of the facts are inaccurately stated and improperly coloured, but it is too true that the treaty has been violated. On such occasions I think it better fairly to confess and correct errors than attempt to deceive ourselves and others by fallacious, though plausible, palliations and excuses. To oppose popular prejudices, to censure the proceedings, and expose the improprieties of

States, is an unpleasant task, but it must be done. Our affairs seem to lead to some crisis, some revolution—something that I cannot foresee or conjecture. I am uneasy and apprehensive; more so than during the war. Then we had a fixed object, and though the means and time of obtaining it were often problematical yet I did firmly believe we should ultimately succeed, because I was convinced that justice was with us. The case is now altered; we are going and doing wrong, and therefore I look forward to evils and calamities, but without being able to guess at the instrument, nature, or measure of them.

That we shall again recover, and things again go well, I have no doubt. Such a variety of circumstances would not, almost miraculously, have combined to liberate and make us a nation for transient and unimportant purposes. I therefore believe that we are yet to become a great and respectable people; but when or how, the spirit of prophecy can only discern.

There doubtless is much reason to think and to say that we are wofully and, in many instances, wickedly misled. Private rage for property suppresses public considerations, and personal rather than national interests have become the great objects of attention. Representative bodies will ever be faithful copies of their originals, and generally exhibit a checkered assemblage of virtue and vice, of abilities and weakness.

The mass of men are neither wise nor good, and the virtue like the other resources of a country, can only be drawn to a point and exerted by strong circumstances ably managed, or a strong government ably administered.   New governments have not the aid of habit and hereditary respect, and being generally the result of preceding tumult and confusion, do not immediately acquire stability or strength. Besides, in times of commotion, some men will gain confidence and importance, who merit neither, and who, like political mountebanks, are less solicitous about the health of the credulous crowd than about making the most of their nostrums and prescriptions.

New York was rendered less federal by the opinions of the late President of Congress.   This is a singular, though not unaccountable fact—indeed, human actions are seldom inexplicable.

What I most fear is, that the better kind of people, by which I mean the people who are orderly and industrious, who are content with their situations and not uneasy in their circumstances, will be led by the insecurity of property, the loss of confidence in their rulers, and the want of public faith and rectitude, to consider the charms of liberty as imaginary and delusive.   A state of fluctuation and uncertainty must disgust and alarm such men, and prepare their minds for almost any change that may promise them quiet and security.

Be pleased to make my compliments to Mrs. Washington, and be assured that I am, with the greatest respect and esteem, dear sir,

Your obedient and humble servant,

JOHN JAY.

JAY TO THOMAS JEFFERSON.

NEW YORK, 14th July, 1786.

DEAR SIR :

Since my last to you of the 16th ult. I have been honoured with your letter of 23d and a joint one from you and Mr. Adams of 25th April.

Considering the importance of our commerce with Portugal, it gives me pleasure to learn that a treaty with that kingdom was so nearly concluded. Until our affairs shall be more perfectly arranged, we shall treat under disadvantages ; and therefore I am not surprised that our negotiations with Britain and Barbary are unpromising. To be respectable abroad, it is necessary to be so at home ; and that will not be the case until our public faith acquires more confidence, and our government more strength.

When or how these great objects will be attained, can scarcely be conjectured. An uneasiness prevails through the country, and may produce eventually the desired reformations, and it may also produce untoward events. Time alone can decide this and many other doubts ; for nations, like individuals, are more frequently guided by circumstances, than circumstances by them.

There are some little circumstances that look as if the Dutch regret our having found the way to China ; and that will doubtless be more or less the case with every nation with whose commercial views we may interfere. I am happy in reflecting, that there can be but little clashing of interests between us and France, and therefore that she will probably continue disposed to wish us well and do us good ; especially, if we honestly fulfil our pecuniary engagement with her. These engagements, however, give me much concern. Every principle and consideration of honour, justice, and interest calls upon us for good faith and punctuality ; and yet we are unhappily so circumstanced, that the moneys necessary for the purpose are not provided, nor in such a way of being provided as they ought to be. This is owing, not to anything wrong in Congress, but to their not possessing the power of coercion without which no government can possibly attain the most salutary and constitutional objects. Excuses and palliations, and applications for more time, make bad remittances, and will afford no inducements to our allies or others to afford us similar aids on future occasions.

With great respect I have the honour to be, dear sir,

Your most obedient and humble servant,

JOHN JAY.

GENERAL WASHINGTON TO JAY.

MOUNT VERNON, 15th Aug., 1786.

DEAR SIR :

I have to thank you very sincerely for your interesting letter of the 27th of June, as well as for the other communications you had the goodness to make at the same time.

I am sorry to be assured, of what indeed I had little doubt before, that we have been guilty of violating the treaty in some instances. What a misfortune it is, that Britain should have so well founded a pretext for its palpable infractions !

and what a disgraceful part, out of the choice of difficulties before us, are we to act!

Your sentiments, that our affairs are drawing rapidly to a crisis, accord with my own. What the event will be is also beyond the reach of my foresight. We have errors to correct. *We have, probably, had too good an opinion of human nature in forming our confederation.* Experience has taught us, that men will not adopt, and carry into execution, measures the best calculated for their own good, without the intervention of a coercive power. I do not conceive we can exist long as a nation, without having lodged somewhere a power which will pervade the whole Union, in as energetic a manner as the authority of the different State governments extends over the several States.

To be fearful of vesting Congress, constituted as that body is, with ample authorities for national purposes, appears to me the very climax of popular absurdity and madness. Could Congress exert them for the detriment of the public without injuring themselves in an equal or greater proportion? Are not their interests inseparably connected with those of their constituents? By the rotation of appointment, must they not mingle frequently with the mass of citizens? Is it not rather to be apprehended, if they were possessed of the powers before described, that the individual members would be induced to use them, on many occasions, very timidly and inefficaciously for fear of losing their popularity and future election? We must take human nature as we find it. Perfection falls not to the share of mortals. Many are of opinion, that Congress have too frequently made use of the suppliant, humble tone of requisition in applications to the States, when they had a right to assume their imperial dignity, and command obedience. Be that as it may, requisitions are a perfect nihility, where thirteen sovereign, independent, disunited States are in the habit of discussing and refusing compliance with them at their option. Requisitions are actually little better than a jest and a by-word throughout the land. If you tell the Legislature they have violated the treaty of peace, and invaded the prerogatives of the confederacy, they will laugh in your face. What, then, is to be done? Things cannot go on in the present train forever.

It is much to be feared, as you observe, that the better kind of people, being disgusted with the circumstances, will have their minds prepared for any revolution whatever. We are apt to run from one extreme into another. To anticipate and prevent disastrous contingencies would be the part of wisdom and patriotism.

What astonishing changes a few years are capable of producing! I am told that even respectable characters speak of a monarchical form of government without horror. From thinking proceeds speaking; thence to action is often but a single step. But how irrevocable and tremendous! What a triumph for the advocates of despotism to find that we are incapable of governing ourselves, and that systems founded on the basis of equal liberty are merely ideal and fallacious! Would to God that wise measures may be taken in time to avert the consequences we have but too much reason to apprehend.

Retired as I am from the world, I frankly acknowledge I cannot feel myself an unconcerned spectator. Yet, having happily assisted in bringing the ship into port, and having been fairly discharged, it is not my business to embark again on a sea of troubles. Nor could it be expected that my sentiments and opinions would have much weight on the minds of my countrymen. They have been neglected, though given as a last legacy in the most solemn manner. I had then perhaps some claims to public attention. I consider myself as having none at present.

With sentiments of sincere esteem and friendship,

I am, Dear Sir, Your most obedient
and affectionate humble servant,

GEO: WASHINGTON.

JAY TO THOMAS JEFFERSON.

NEW YORK, 18th August, 1786.

DEAR SIR :

It has happened, from various circumstances, that several reports on foreign affairs still lay before Congress undecided upon. The want of an adequate representation for long intervals, and the multiplicity of business which pressed upon them when that was not the case, have occasioned delays and omissions which, however unavoidable, are much to be regretted. It is painful for me to reflect that, although my attention to business is unremitted, yet I so often experience unseasonable delays and successive obstacles in obtaining the decision and sentiments of Congress, even on points which require despatch. But so it is, and I must be content with leaving nothing undone that may depend on me.

I have long thought, and become daily more convinced, that the constitution of our federal government is fundamentally wrong. To vest legislative, judicial, and executive powers in one and the same body of men, and that, too, in a body daily changing its members, can never be wise. In my opinion, these three great departments of sovereignty should be forever separated, and so distributed as to serve as checks on each other. But these are subjects that have long been familiar to you, and on which you are too well informed not to anticipate everything that I might say on them.

I have advised Congress to renew your commission as to certain powers. Our treasury is ill supplied—

some States paying nothing, others very little ; the impost not yet established ; the people generally uneasy in a certain degree, but without seeming to discern the true cause, viz., *want of energy both in State and Federal governments.* It takes time to make sovereigns of subjects.

I am, dear sir,

Your most obedient and very humble servant,

JOHN JAY.

BENJAMIN FRANKLIN TO JAY.

PHILAD. Aug. 24, 1786.

DEAR SIR :

I hear a treaty is compleated with Portugal. As soon as it may be made public you will oblige me much by favouring me with a Copy of it.

The monument of General Montgomery—May I ask what is become of it ? It has formerly been said that republicks are naturally ungrateful. The immediate resolution of Congress for erecting that monument contradicts that opinion. But the letting the monument lie eight years unpack'd, if true, seems rather a Confirmation of it.

On a review of my affairs since my return I think it proper to make some changes in the disposition of my will. Having no other copy on this side the water but that in your possession, I wish you to send it to me, which will much oblige, dear sir, your most obedient servant,

B. FRANKLIN.

GOVERNOR WILLIAM LIVINGSTON TO JAY.

ELIZABETH TOWN, 28 Aug^t, 1786.

DEAR SIR :

Are you totally discouraged from coming to Elizabeth Town by our bad luck at fishing on our last jaunt? and have you forgot the motto of *perseverando?* Pray let us try again, and I can almost assure you of better success. I wish you could come next Friday, and if not interfering with Peter's studies, to bring my little favourite with you. I need not tell you how glad all of us would be to see Mrs. Jay at the same time, if both of you can at the same time conveniently be spared from the family. I wish your answer, and if you come, I should be glad that instead of the pompous train that usually attends the great in Europe or Asia, yours were composed, amongst any others you may choose, of a few lobsters and blackfish.

> I am, Sir, Your most humble Servant,
>
> WIL: LIVINGSTON.

JAY TO THOMAS JEFFERSON.

NEW YORK, 27th October, 1786.

DEAR SIR:

The inefficacy of our government becomes daily more and more apparent. Our treasury and our credit are in a sad situation ; and it is probable that either the wisdom or the passions of the people will produce changes. A spirit of licentiousness has infected Massachusetts, which appears more formidable than some at first apprehended. Whether similar symptoms will not soon mark a like disease in several other States is very problematical.

The public papers herewith sent contain everything generally known about these matters. A reluctance to taxes, an impatience of government, a rage for property and little regard to the means of acquiring it, together with a desire of equality in all things, seem to actuate the mass of those who are uneasy in their circumstances. To these may be added the influence of ambitious adventurers, and the speculations of the many characters who prefer private to public good, and of others who expect to gain more from wrecks made by tempests than from the produce of patient and honest industry. As the knaves and fools of this world are forever in alliance, it is easy to perceive how much vigour and wisdom a government, from its construction and administration, should possess, in order to repress the evils which naturally flow from such copious sources of injustice and evil.

Much, I think, is to be feared from the sentiments which such a state of things is calculated to infuse into the minds of the rational and well-intended. In their eyes, the charms of liberty will daily fade; and in seeking for peace and security, they will too naturally turn towards systems in direct opposition to those which oppress and disquiet them.

If faction should long bear down law and government, tyranny may raise its head, or the more sober part of the people may even think of a king.

In short, my dear sir, we are in a very unpleasant situation. Changes are necessary; but what they ought to be, what they will be, and how and when to be produced, are arduous questions. I feel for the cause of liberty, and for the honour of my countrymen who have so nobly asserted it, and who, at present, so abuse its blessings. If it should not take root in this soil, little pains will be taken to cultivate it in any other.

I have the honour to be, with great respect, dear sir,
Your most obedient and very humble servant,

JOHN JAY.

JAY TO JOHN ADAMS.

OFFICE FOR FOREIGN AFFAIRS, NEW YORK,
1st November, 1786.

DEAR SIR :

My report on the answer of the British Minister to your memorial respecting our frontier posts, is under the consideration of Congress. Your ideas and mine on those subjects very nearly correspond, and I sincerely wish that you may be enabled to accommodate every difference between us and Britain, on the most liberal principles of justice and candour. The result of my inquiries into the conduct of the States relative to the treaty, is, that there has not been a single day since it took effect, on which it has not been violated in America, by one or other of the States; and this observation is just, whether the treaty be supposed to have taken effect either at the date or exchange of the provisional articles, or on the day of the date of the definitive treaty, or of the ratifications of it.

Our affairs are in a very unpleasant situation, and changes become necessary, and in some little degree probable. When government, either from defects in its construction or administration, ceases to assert its rights, or is too feeble to afford security, inspire confidence, and overawe the ambitious and licentious, the best citizens naturally grow uneasy and look to other systems.

How far the disorders of Massachusetts may extend, or how they will terminate, is problematical ; nor is it possible to decide whether the people of Rhode Island will remain much longer obedient to the very extraordinary and exceptionable laws passed,

for compelling them to embrace the doctrine of the political transubstantiation of paper into gold and silver.

I suspect that our posterity will read the history of
our last four years with much regret.

I enclose for your information a pamphlet, containing the acts of the different States granting an impost
to Congress.

You will also find enclosed a copy of an act of Congress, of 20th and 21st ult., for raising an additional
number of troops. This measure was doubtless necessary, although the difficulty of providing for the expense of it is a serious one. I flatter myself you will
be able to obviate any improper suspicions which the
minister may be led to entertain respecting the object
of this force. I have pressed the policy of deciding
on my report on the infractions of the treaty without
delay, that you may thence be furnished with conclusive arguments against the insinuations of those
who may wish to infuse and support opinions unfavourable to us on these points.

The newspapers herewith sent will give you information in detail of Indian affairs, but they will not
tell you, what however is the fact, that our people
have committed several unprovoked acts of violence
against them. These acts ought to have excited
the notice of government, and been punished in an
exemplary manner.

With great and sincere esteem and regard, I have
the honour to be, dear sir,

Your most obedient and very humble servant,

JOHN JAY.

JAY TO JOHN ADAMS.

NEW YORK, 1st November, 1786.

DEAR SIR :

Accept my thanks for your friendly letter mentioning the marriage of your daughter, and my cordial congratulations on that pleasing event. They who best know the Colonel [William S. Smith] speak of him as brave and honourable ; and strangers to the lady naturally draw the most favourable inferences from her parentage and from the attention and example of a mother whose character is very estimable. I sincerely wish, my dear friend, that you had as much reason to be pleased with your *political* as with your domestic situation. The sweets, however, of the latter must greatly soften the asperity of the former, and when public cares and considerations excite painful emotions, you doubtless enjoy the reflection that though patriots seldom rest on beds of roses, yet that your private pillow, like your conscience, is free from thorns. . . .

I am, dear sir,

Your affectionate friend and servant,

JOHN JAY.

EDWARD RUTLEDGE TO JAY.

[CHARLESTON, S. C.] Nov. 12, 1786.

MY DEAR SIR:

After a disagreeable passage and a variety of weather Tinker has at last safely landed us in Charleston, where I have resumed the character of a busy man and have a clear prospect of passing an active Winter between my professional, and political occupations. But altho' my exertions

gagement. If from our relinquishment at present, she can retain for a number of years, the exclusive navigation of the river, it is well—it will stop migration, it will concenter force, because the settlers can have no vent for the productions of that country but down the Mississippi, and, therefore, think they will not be fond of immediately inhabiting her banks. But when the time shall arrive, when the inhabitants shall be very numerous, will it not be worth the while of Spain to permit them the navigation of the river, give them the benefit of their labor, encourage in them the spirit of agriculture, and divert their minds from conquests? I should suppose it would. It will behoove Spain to consider the affair with much attention; consider too the genius as well as the interest of those western Settlers and ever carry in her remembrance that in her cession of American territory, Great Britain cherished an idea that she was sowing the seeds of discord between the States and Spain. Again, suppose at some future day Britain should set on foot, by the way of Canada and the Lakes, a negociation with the Western people, and assist them in opening not only the passage of the river, but the way to the Southern World, how is this to be counteracted? Would it not become Spain to put on the spirit of accommodation with the settlers of the distant Country and prevent by such a measure, such an injurious union? I am too little acquainted with the wisdom of that Court, to say what they will do, and after all, the changes in men and measures leave a vast field for speculation into distant ages. What is the wisdom of the most wise to-day, is depreciated into nothing to-morrow. But we must nevertheless act, and acting from the best of our judgment, endeavor to justify wisdom of her children. I am limited in time and have been repeatedly interrupted by clients since I began this letter. You shall hear from me as opportunities offer. Mrs. Rutledge has been confined to the house ever since we landed; but she is too much obliged to Mrs. Jay to forget her in any situation. We both remember her with very affectionate respect. She sends Mrs. Jay a barrel of potatoes; they are not large, but I believe they are good; size, you know, is not a characteristic of goodness. The vegetation has not as yet ceased. It will before Tinker returns, when I will send you the Fringe and Pride of India trees. I wish they may flourish. In truth I wish every thing which belongs to you may flourish; and that you may live to enjoy your family, and the fruit of your labor. Adieu, my dear Friend, and believe that I am warmly attached to your family and yourself.

Ed. Rutledge.

P. S.   Tell Peter, Henry wishes this post-script may contain affectionate remembrance.

DR. RICHARD PRICE TO JAY.

Newington Green, [England]
Nov. 25th, 1786.

Dear Sir,

I have received both the letters with which you have honoured me, and I return you many thanks for them. I know your time must be much engaged by the duties of your office, and therefore I can not but feel very sensibly your kind attention which exceeds all that I could have any reason to expect. Your civility and friendship to Mr. Curtauld deserve my particular gratitude. His mother and family are much impressed by them. . . .

I am a sad stranger to myself, if my pamphlet address'd to the United States is not an effort of well meant zeal to promote their best interests, and thro' them the happiness of mankind.[1]   Though I have given offence in some places,

---

[1] This, the most valuable of Dr. Price's pamphlets, was entitled, "Observations on the Importance of the American Revolution, and the Means of Making

I have reason to be very well satisfied on the whole with the reception it has met with. Were I to write it again I should lower some expressions in it ; for I am sensible that I have been too hasty and sanguine in my expectations. I cannot, however, despair while I know that such a person as you are, and many others of whose wisdom integrity and liberal principles I have a high opinion, are members of the United States and concerned in advising and directing them. I now see that such an improved state of society in America as I wish for must be the work of more time than I imagined ; and, perhaps, the result of severe struggles and conflicts still to be gone thro'. Affairs between this country and yours wear a dark complexion. It is unhappy for us that the coalition between L$^{d.}$ North and M$^{r.}$ Fox prevented the makers of the peace from completing it. Our councils now are under a different direction, nor is there any probability of a change. I lament continually our wretched policy. We are throwing away the trade and the friendship of a world rapidly increasing, and forcing it into the scale of France. Should the issue be a total alienation and the conversion of the extreme of love into the extreme of hatred, the fault will be chiefly ours, and we shall be the greatest sufferers. Trade is essential to *our* existence. On the contrary, the rage for trade is one of your greatest enemies ; and all events that check it may do you the greatest service. Were even all your ports shut up, you would be only rendered more independent and secure ; and in a course of years you might, with the aid of simple manners, general liberty, plenty produced by agriculture, and a *strong federal union*, become the most powerful and happy people on earth. At present your affairs, I am afraid, are far from being in this train. God forbid

it a Benefit to the World." It was published first in London in 1784, then at Philadelphia in 1785, and again at Boston in 1812, 1818, and 1820. Mirabeau translated it into French.

that, in consequence of luxery, mercantile avarice, and the feebleness of the federal government, the United States should ever become the image of our Europe.—I ask pardon, for entering into these reflexions. I did not intend them when I began this letter. I am very happy in the friendship of Mʳ· Adams. He will send better information than I can give. All (as you observe at the end of your letter) that the best men can do is to persevere in doing their duty to their country, leaving the consequences to the Disposer of all events. The happiness attending the consciousness of such conduct is the greatest any of us can enjoy. This is a happiness which I doubt not, you will enjoy. Wishing you, Dear Sir, every possible blessing I am, with great Respect, Your oblig'd humble Servᵗ

RICHᴰ PRICE.

JAY TO JACOB REED.

DEAR SIR : NEW YORK, 12th December, 1786.

Your friendly letter has long remained unanswered ; but a variety of private as well as public affairs constrained me to postpone indulging myself in the pleasure I always derive from writing to my friends. The recess (if I may so call it) of Congress gives their officers too much leisure at present ; and there is reason to fear that the members will be as long in convening this year as they were last. Business is at a stand for want of an adequate representation. The languor of the States is to be lamented ; many inconveniences have already arisen from it, and if continued, serious evils will awaken our people. Our affairs, my dear sir, are in a delicate situation, and it is much to be wished that the real patriots throughout the States would exert themselves to render it more safe and respectable. The feuds in Massachusetts are rather suspended than extinguished. What events they may ultimately produce, is uncertain ; but I should not be surprised if much trouble was to result from them. The public creditors will soon become importunate, and Congress cannot create the means of satisfying them. It is true that order usually succeeds confusion ; but it is a high price to pay for order, especially when a little virtue and good sense would procure it for us on very reasonable terms. If the best men would be prevailed upon to come forward, and take the lead in our legislatures as well as in Congress, and would unite their endeavours to rescue their country from its present condition, our affairs, both at home and abroad, would soon wear a more pleasing aspect. It is time for our people to distinguish more accurately than they seem to do between liberty and licentiousness. The late revolution would lose much of its glory, as well as utility, if our conduct should confirm the tory maxim, " That men are incapable of governing themselves."

With real esteem and regard, I am, dear sir,

Your most obedient and very humble servant,

JOHN JAY.

JAY TO THOMAS JEFFERSON.

OFFICE FOR FOREIGN AFFAIRS,
14th December, 1786.

DEAR SIR :

The situation of our captive countrymen at Algiers is much to be lamented, and the more so as their deliverance is difficult to effect. Congress cannot command money for that, nor indeed for other very important purposes ; their requisitions produce little, and government (if it may be called a government) is so inadequate to its objects, that essential alterations or essential evils must take place. If our government would draw forth the resources of the country, which, notwithstanding all appearances to the contrary, are abundant, I should prefer war to tribute, and carry our Mediterranean trade in vessels armed and manned at the public expense. I daily become more and more confirmed in the opinion, that government should be divided into executive, legislative, and judicial departments. Congress is unequal to the first, very fit for the second, and but ill calculated for the third ; and so much time is spent in deliberation, that the season for action often passes by before they decide on what should be done ; nor is there much more secrecy than expedition in their measures. These inconveniences arise, not from personal disqualifications, but from the nature and construction of the government.

If Congress had money to purchase peace of Algiers, or to redeém the captives there, it certainly would, according to their present ideas, be well to lose no time in doing both ; neither pains nor expense, if within any tolerable limits, should be spared to ransom our fellow-citizens. But the truth is, that no money is to be expected at present from hence ; nor do I think it would be right to make new loans until we have at least some prospect of paying the interest due on former ones.

Our country is fertile, abounding in useful productions, and those productions in demand and bearing a good price; yet relaxation in government and extravagance in individuals create much public and private distress, and much public and private want of good faith.

The public papers will tell you how much reason we have to apprehend an Indian war, and to suspect that Britain instigates it. In my opinion, our Indian affairs have been ill managed. Details would be tedious. Indians have been murdered by our people in cold blood, and no satisfaction given; nor are they pleased with the avidity with which we seek to acquire their lands. Would it not be wiser gradually to extend our settlements as want of room should make it necessary, than to pitch our tents through the wilderness in a great variety of places, far distant from each other, and from those advantages of education, civilization, law, and government which compact settlements and neighbourhoods afford? Shall we not fill the wilderness with white savages?—and will they not become more formidable to us than the tawny ones which now inhabit it?

As to the sums of money expected from the sale of those lands, I suspect we shall be deceived; for, at whatever price they may be sold, the collection and payment of it will not be easily accomplished.

I have the honor to be, etc.

JOHN JAY.

JAY TO WILLIAM CARMICHAEL.

DEAR SIR : New York, 4th January, 1787.

Since the 3d day of November last a sufficient number of States to do business have not been represented in Congress, and it is doubtful whether some weeks more will not elapse before that will be the case. Hence it is that I am obliged to be less particular than I should otherwise be on sundry subjects.

The public papers have informed you of commotions in Massachusetts ; they have not yet subsided, although that government have manifested great moderation, and condescended to treat the complaints of the malcontents with much respect. What may be the issue of those disturbances, or how far they will extend, is as yet far from certain.

The inefficiency of the Federal Government becomes more and more manifest, and how it is to be amended is a question that engages the serious attention of the best people in all the States. Endeavours are making to form a convention for the purpose, but it is not clear that all the States will join in that measure. On this and some other great points the public mind is fluctuating though uneasy ; perhaps a few months more may produce a greater degree of decision. The treaty with Portugal it seems meets with obstacles. I wish they may not be insuperable ; for I view a commercial connection with that nation and also with Spain as beneficial to all the parties. Our treaty with

Spain also has its difficulties; you can easily conjecture what they are. . . .

> I have the honour to be, sir,
> Your most obedient and humble servant,
>
> JOHN JAY.

JAY TO GENERAL WASHINGTON.

DEAR SIR :

NEW YORK, 7th January, 1787.

They who regard the public good with more attention and attachment than they do mere personal concerns must feel and confess the force of such sentiments as are expressed in your letter to me by Colonel Humphrey last fall. The situation of our affairs calls not only for reflection and prudence, but for exertion. What is to be done? is a common question not easy to answer.

Would the giving *any* further degree of power to Congress do the business? I am much inclined to think it would not, for among other reasons there will always be members who will find it convenient to make their seats subservient to partial and personal purposes; and they who may be able and willing to concert and promote useful and national measures will seldom be unembarrassed by the ignorance, prejudices, fears, or interested views of others.

In so large a body secrecy and despatch will be too uncommon; and foreign as well as local influence will frequently oppose and sometimes prostrate the worst measures. Large assemblies often misunderstand or neglect the obligations of character, honour, and dignity, and will collectively do or omit things which individual gentlemen in private capacities would. not approve. As the many divide blame and also divide credit, too little a portion of either falls to each man there to affect him strongly, even in cases where the whole blame or the whole credit must be national. It is not easy for those to think and feel as sovereigns who have been always accustomed to think and feel as subjects.

The executive business of sovereignty depending on so many wills, and those wills moved by such a variety of contradictory motives and inducements, will in general be but feebly done. Such a sovereignty, however theoretically responsible, cannot be effectually so in its departments and officers without adequate judicatories. I therefore promise myself nothing very desirable from any change which does not divide the sovereignty into its proper departments. Let Congress legislate—let others execute—let others judge.

Shall we have a king? Not in my opinion while other experiments remain untried. Might we not have a governor-general limited in his prerogatives and duration? Might not Congress be divided into an upper and lower house—the former appointed for life, the latter annually,—and let the governor-general (to preserve the balance), with the advice of a council, formed for that only purpose, of the great judicial officers, have a negative on their acts? Our government should in some degree be suited to our manners and circumstances, and they, you know, are not strictly democratical. What powers should be granted to the government so constituted is a question which deserves much thought. I think the more the better, the States retaining only so much as may be necessary for domestic purposes, and all their principal officers, civil and military, being commissioned and removable by the national government. These are short hints. Details would exceed the limits of a letter, and to you be superfluous.

A convention is in contemplation, and I am glad to find your name among those of its intended members. To me the policy of *such* a convention appears questionable ; their authority is to be derived from acts of the State legislatures. Are the State legislatures authorized, either by themselves or others, to alter constitutions ? I think not ; they who hold commissions can by virtue of them neither retrench nor extend the powers conveyed to them. Perhaps it is intended that this convention shall not ordain, but only recommend ; if so, there is danger that their recommendations will produce endless discussion, perhaps jealousies and party heats.

Would it not be better for Congress plainly and in strong terms to declare that the present Federal Government is inadequate to the purposes for which it was instituted ; that they forbear to point out its particular defects or to ask for an extension of any particular powers, lest improper jealousies should thence arise ; but that in their opinion it would be expedient for the people of the States without delay to appoint State conventions (in the way they choose their general assemblies), with the sole and express power of appointing deputies to a general convention who, or the majority of whom, should take into consideration the Articles of Confederation, and make such alterations, amendments, and additions thereto as to them should appear necessary and proper, and which being by them ordained and published should have the same force and obligation which all or any of the present articles now have? No alterations in the government should, I think, be made, nor if attempted will easily take place, unless deducible from the only source of just authority—*the People.*

Accept, my dear sir, my warmest and most cordial wishes for your health and happiness, and believe me to be with the greatest respect and esteem,

Your most obedient servant,

JOHN JAY.

EDWARD RUTLEDGE TO JAY.

CHARLESTON, Jan. 16th 1787.

I thank you, my dear Friend, for your letter of the 12th ulto., and for the remembrance of the commission, with which I promised to trouble you.

I have given Captain Tinker about Four Hundred dollars, which he will deliver you, and I must request you to vest them in a pair of good horses. I intend them for a very high English built coach, and they will therefore require strength, as well as size. I am attached to bays as they retain their colour in a warm climate longer than others, and in case of a loss, they are more easily matched. If you could send them by Tinker's return, they will be taken care of. You will receive by this conveyance a few of the

Pride of India, the Fringe, Tallow and Iron trees, the Yellow Jessamine, a sweet scented shrub. All but the Pride of India, are natives, (if you'll allow the expression,) of this country, and are classed with the most favoured. You will also receive some of the seed of the Pride of India; should any of them flourish and be at all acceptable to you or your friends, I will procure in the season whatever you may wish.

If reports are well founded the House of Bourbon has cut short for the present the dispute about the Mississippi. The cession of the Floridas to France will be attended with very important consequences. She is an active Nation, and will rival the Southern States in their most valuable productions. I speak from good authority when I say that the soil of the Western country is so far superior to that of the Atlantic States, as to render us contemptible by comparison. France will not only be our competitor in rice and tobacco, but she will be able to supply all the West India Islands with lumber. But how does the cession agree with her Treaty of Alliance? Perhaps you will tell me it neither agrees or exists, and put an end to this sort of speculation; could we restrain the other sort within due bounds, we might reduce things by time, into good order. But the manner of our people must undergo a very material change indeed, before the event can be expected.

Make a tender of Mrs. Rutledge's best compliments with mine, to Mrs Jay; I hope she enjoys what my female friend very much wants. She has been at the point of death since her return; and has been saved from the grave but by the greatest attention and care. I am thankful that she has recovered and that I have been shielded from an affliction that would have sunk me to the dust—Henry is perfectly well and desires to be affectionately remembered to Peter.

We have not as yet made an House of Assembly; but shall in the course of next week; and do in all probability some good and a great 'deal of mischief: or else we shall differ very much from our sister States.

Adieu, my dear friend, and believe me to be sincerely yours.

ED. RUTLEDGE.

P. S. I send you Tinker's receipt which is for more money than I thought of sending at first ; but as I wish the horses very good, I've added to the 400 dollars.

JAY TO THOMAS JEFFERSON.

NEW YORK, 9th February, 1787.

DEAR SIR :

Since my last to you of the 14th December I have been honoured with yours of the 26th September last, which, with the papers that it enclosed, has been laid before Congress ; but neither on that nor on any of your late letters have any orders as yet been made.

The annual election produces much delay in affairs ; from that time to this scarcely any thing has been done. It was not until last week that, seven States being represented, a president was elected ; the choice fell on Major-General St. Clair. They have much back business to despatch ; several reports on important subjects from the different departments are to be considered and decided upon. A form of government so constructed has inconveniences which I think will continue to operate against the public or national interest until some cause not easy to be predicted shall produce such a modification of it as that the legislative, judicial, and executive business of government may be consigned to three proper and distinct departments.

The struggles for and against the impost remain, but promise little. The States in general pay little attention to requisitions, and I fear that our debts, foreign and domestic, will not soon be provided for in a manner satisfactory to our creditors. The evils to be expected from such delays are less difficult to be foreseen than obviated. Our governments want energy, and there is reason to fear that too much has been expected from the virtue and good sense of the people.

You will receive herewith enclosed a letter from Congress to his most Christian Majesty, with a copy of it for your information. It is in answer to one received from him, and should have been of earlier date had Congress sooner convened ; be pleased to explain this circumstance to the Minister.

The public papers herewith sent contain all we at present know respecting the troubles in Massachusetts. Whether they will soon be terminated, or what events they may yet produce, is perfectly uncertain ; and the more so, as we are yet to ascertain whether and how far they may be encouraged by our neighbours.

I enclose a copy of a letter from Mr. Otto formally contradicting the report of an exchange between France and Spain for the Floridas. That report had excited attention. Our apprehensions of an Indian war still continue ; for we are at a loss to determine whether the present continuance of peace is to be ascribed to the season, or their pacific intentions.

We have not yet received the Morocco treaty; as soon as it arrives I am persuaded that Congress will take the earliest opportunity of making their acknowledgments to the friendly powers that promoted it. Mr. Lamb is still absent. He doubtless has received the order of Congress directing his return, either from you and Mr. Adams, or directly from me. Congress has not yet given any orders respecting further negotiations with the Barbary States, nor can I venture to say what their sentiments will be on that head. I am equally at a loss to judge what they will direct respecting treaties of commerce with the Emperor and other European powers. For my own part I think, and have recommended, that commissions and instructions should be sent by you and Mr. Adams for those purposes. In my opinion such treaties for short terms might be advantageous. The time is not yet come for us to expect the best. The distance of that period will however depend much on ourselves.

With very sincere esteem and regard I am, dear sir, your most obedient and humble servant,

JOHN JAY.

JAY TO JOHN ADAMS.

NEW YORK, 21st February, 1787.

DEAR SIR :

Nine States are now represented, but as yet little progress has been made in the business before them. My report on the infractions of the treaty, complained of by Britain, has been referred to a new committee, and I think a very good one ; various opinions prevail on the subject and I cannot conjecture what the ultimate decision of Congress on it will be. The insurrection in Massachusetts seems to be suppressed, and I herewith enclose the papers containing the details we have received since the 6th instant, when I wrote to you by the packet. Your sentiments on that business prove to have been just. I ought to write to you fully on many subjects, but I am not yet enabled ; when I shall be, cannot be predicted.

Our government is unequal to the task assigned it, and the people begin also to perceive its inefficiency. The convention gains ground. New York has instructed her delegates to move in Congress for a recommendation to the States to form a convention ; for this State dislikes the idea of a convention unless countenanced by Congress. I do not promise myself much further immediate good from the measure than that it will tend to approximate the public mind to the changes which ought to take place. It is hard to say what those changes should be exactly. There is one however which I think would be much for the better, viz., to distribute the federal sovereignty into its three proper departments of executive, legislative, and judicial ; for that Congress should act in these different capacities was, I think, a great mistake in our policy.

This State in their present session has greatly moderated their severities to the tories, a law having been passed to restore a very great majority of those resident here to the rights of citizens. I hope all discriminations inconsistent with the treaty of peace will gradually be abolished, as resentment gives place to reason and good faith. But, my dear sir, we labour under one sad evil—the treasury is empty though the country abounds in resources, and our people are far more unwilling than unable to pay taxes. Hence result disappointment to our creditors, disgrace to our country, and I fear disinclination in too many to any mode of government that can easily and irresistibly open their purses. Much is to be done, and the patriots must have perseverance as well as patience.

I am, dear sir,

Your affectionate friend and servant,

JOHN JAY.

JAY TO EDWARD RUTLEDGE.

NEW YORK, 25th February, 1787.

MY GOOD FRIEND:

By Captain Tinker I received your letter of the 16th of last month, together with the trees, etc., mentioned in it. I would readily have been at trouble and expense in getting them of a nurseryman, for it is agreeable to add the trees and shrubs of other climates to those of our own. But I am particularly pleased in receiving these from you. From that circumstance certain ideas, always welcome to my mind, will become associated with them, and be present whenever I prune and tend them, and watch their growth. If some of the many changes incident to this mutable scene should not interpose, I may live to enjoy under the shade of their branches a frequent retreat from noise and business; and those serene and tranquil intervals will be rendered more pleasant by the soothing reflections which recollected friendship insensibly inspires.

My inquiries for horses have been frequent and extensive; *fine, large,* and *strong,* are qualities rarely found united since the war, especially in this and the neighbouring States, from which the two armies drew great supplies, and in which a less number than formerly were bred. I could find very decent useful horses, but not of size sufficient. Some of the large Dutch horses, stout and heavy, might be had—but having no pretensions to beauty or elegance, they fall not under the description of fine.

Mr. Hunt, of Jersey, whom I employed, and who is an honest, intelligent dealer, wrote me that he did not yet know of any horses that would do. Being informed however that Mr. Hunt had a pair of clever horses, 15 hands high, I wrote to him about them. He answered that they were of that size, and stout and good, but plain. His price induced me nevertheless to suppose they must approach a good way towards fine, and as my inquiries in the upper part of the State proved fruitless, their best horses being under the size proper for your coach, I wrote to Mr. Hunt to send on his. His description of them was just, and I think them too plain to please you; they will be 7 years old this spring, and their price, 213 dollars and one 6th. They arrived two days ago, and Tinker sails the day after to-morrow, so that

there is little time for further search. I have therefore concluded to keep them for the present, and send
you mine at the price (viz. 250 dollars) which they
cost me. As I have only a light chariot, a pair of handsome, middle-sized horses will answer my purpose
and not be difficult to procure. I am not certain
that my horses will please Mrs. Rutledge. Let your
driver be sparing of his whip, and let the check reins
be loose, the curbs not too sharp, and the harness
easy, for though neither shy nor vicious, they are high-
spirited. The least and most handsome of the two
goes on the off or right-hand side. He is well broke
and to a single chair, in which way we used him often
during the last season. These horses must be about
ten years of age, but whether coming or past I cannot
say. I have no reason to think they have ever been
abused, and therefore if well kept will continue as
good as they are now for several years. I must request it as a favor that if, for any reason whatever, they
should not suit you, they may be sold on my account
and the freight charged to me, for I confess I send
these horses under an idea of their not being quite
such sedate family horses as you may prefer or want
to have. If so, let them be sold, and I will with pleasure send on others until you receive a pair to your
mind. These horses to be in proper order must be
kept high, and almost daily driven and by a driver
who understands it. From the money received by
Tinker I have taken 250 dollars. For the residue
(being the identical money he paid me) you will find
his receipt enclosed.

I also enclose a copy of a letter from Mr. Adams. On reading it you will perceive that it establishes a fact which some men, very unlike you, wish incapable of proof.

Mrs. Jay joins me in requesting the favour of you to present our best compliments to Mrs. Rutledge, to whom and to you and to yours we sincerely wish uninterrupted health and happiness.

I am, my dear sir,

Your affectionate friend and servant,

JOHN JAY.

GENERAL WASHINGTON TO JAY.

DEAR SIR: MOUNT VERNON, March 10th, 1787.

I am indebted to you for two letters. The first, introductory of Mr. Anstey, needed no apology; nor will any be necessary on future similar occasions. The other, of the 7th of January, is on a very interesting subject, deserving very particular attention.

How far the revision of the federal system, and giving more adequate powers to Congress, may be productive of an efficient government, I will not, under my present view of the matter, pretend to decide. That many inconveniences result from the present form, none can deny; those enumerated in your letter are so obvious and sensibly felt, that no logic can controvert, nor is it probable that any change of conduct will remove them; and that all attempts to alter or amend it will be like the propping of a house which is ready to fall, and which no shores can support (as many seem to think), may also be true.

But is the public mind matured for such an important change as the one you have suggested? What would be the consequence of a premature attempt?

My opinion is, that this country has yet to *feel* and *see* a little more before it can be accomplished. A thirst for power, and the bantling—I had like to have said MONSTER —sovereignty, which have taken such fast hold of the States individually, will, when joined by the many whose personal consequence in the line of State politics will in a manner be annihilated, form a strong phalanx against it ; and when to these, the few who can hold posts of honour or profit in the national government are compared with the many who will see but little prospect of being noticed, and the discontents of others who may look for appointments, the opposition would be altogether irresistible, till the mass as well as the more discerning part of the community shall see the necessity.

Among men of reflection, few will be found, I believe, who are not *beginning* to think that our system is better in theory than practice ; and that, notwithstanding the boasted virtue of America, it is more than probable we shall exhibit the last melancholy proof that mankind are not competent to their own government, without the means of coercion, in the sovereign. Yet I would try what the wisdom of the proposed Convention will suggest, and what can be effected by their counsels. It may be the last peaceable mode of essaying the practicability of the present form, without a greater lapse of time than the exigency of our affairs will admit. In strict propriety, a Convention so holden may not be legal ; Congress, however, may give it a colouring by recommendation which would fit it more to the taste, without proceeding to a definition of powers : this, however constitutionally it might be done, would not in my opinion be expedient ; for delicacy on the one hand, and jealousy on the other, would produce a mere nihil.

My name is in the delegation to this Convention ; but it was put there contrary to my desire, and remains contrary to my request. Several reasons at the time of this appointment, and which yet exist, combined to make my attendance inconvenient, perhaps improper, though a good deal urged to it. With sentiments of great regard and friendship, I have the honour to be,

Dear sir, your most obedient and

Affectionate humble servant,

GEORGE WASHINGTON.

P. S.   Since writing this letter I have seen the resolution of Congress, recommendatory of the Convention proposed to be held in Philadelphia the 2d Monday in May.

JAY TO THE PRESIDENT OF CONGRESS.

OFFICE FOR FOREIGN AFFAIRS,
11th April, 1787.

SIR:

In obedience to the order of Congress directing me to give information of the state of my negotiation with the Encargado de Negocios of Spain, I have the honour of informing your Excellency that . . . I have had several conferences with Mr. Gardoqui on the well-known points in difference between us, viz., on the navigation of the river Mississippi and on the limits.

With respect to the first point we have had repeated conversations which produced nothing but debate, and in the course of which we did not advance one single step nearer to each other.   He continued and still continues decided in refusing to admit us to navigate the river below our limits on any terms or conditions, nor will he consent to any article *declaring our rights in express terms, and stipulating to forbear the use of it for a given time.* But he did not appear to me so decidedly opposed to the same ideas in the way of *implication*, though he did not say so. I drew that inference from a number of circumstances, but yet he said nothing so unequivocal to warrant it, as to commit himself. I thought it therefore advisable to try how far he would silently yield to that idea ; and therefore drew up articles in a variety of shapes *clearly implying* the right, and expressly forbearing the use during the term of the treaty. These drafts he positively refused to admit ; and finding that arguments in support of them rather irritated than convinced him, we parted without doing any thing. Subsequent conferences took place, and he continuing inflexible in refusing the articles as they stood, we gradually but very cautiously talked of amendments. It was my business to endeavour to change the *dress* but retain the *spirit* and *sense.* Many difficulties and questions, unnecessary to detail, occurred. It was, however, finally so adjusted as in my opinion to save the *right* and only suspend the *use* during the term of the treaty, at the expiration of which this and every other article in it would become null and void. . . .

Congress will doubtless observe that the reasons assigned in this article for forbearance militate against a supposition of his Majesty's having an exclusive right ; for it does not either admit *his* right or relinquish *ours*, but, on the contrary, in order to avoid and obviate differences and questions, to suit his Majesty's system of government and policy, to meet the King's wishes, and to evince our sense of his friendship, it only stipulates *not to use*, etc.

On that and every other occasion I thought it best to be very candid with Mr. Gardoqui. I told him that he must not conclude that what I might think expedient would also be deemed so by Congress, and hoped that when he considered they were sitting in the same place with us, he would see the propriety of my observing the greatest delicacy and respect towards them.

As to the limits, I have reason from him to believe that, notwithstanding the extent of their claims, he would, in case all other matters were satisfactorily adjusted, so far recede as to give up to us all the territories not comprehended within the Floridas as ascertained by our separate and secret article with Great Britain, of which I early perceived that he was well informed.

As he could not in any manner be drawn lower down than this line, it struck me that it would be prudent to confine, if possible, all questions of limits to the land between the two lines ; and therefore hinted the expediency of settling the dispute, so limited, by Commissioners.

He expressed no reluctance to this, and I believe he has written for instructions on that point, but am not certain. He seemed very cautious of committing himself, and I cannot now say that he admitted our right to extend down to the first line, but only gave me to understand that all other things being agreed, his Majesty from motives of accommodation might be content with that limitation.

These are the facts, and so matters at present stand between him and me. A variety of circumstances and considerations which I need not mention, render this negotiation dilatory, unpleasant, and unpromising; and it is much to be wished that the United States could jointly and unanimously adopt and pursue some fixed and stable plan of policy in regard to Spain, especially during the residence of Mr. Gardoqui, who, I do verily believe, is sincerely disposed to do everything useful and acceptable to America that his instructions and the essential interests of his country, as understood by him and his master, will permit.'

I have the honour to be with great respect and esteem your Excellency's most obedient and humble servant, JOHN JAY.

JAY TO THOMAS JEFFERSON.

NEW YORK, 24th April, 1787.

DEAR SIR :

It is greatly to be regretted that communications to Congress are not kept more private; a variety of reasons which must be obvious to you oppose it, and while the federal sovereignty remains just as it is little secrecy is to be expected. These circumstances must undoubtedly be a great restraint on those public and private characters from whom you would otherwise obtain useful hints and information. I for my part have long experienced the inconvenience of it, and in some instances very sensibly.

The convention of which you have been informed will convene next month at Philadelphia. It is said that General Washington accepts his appointment to it, and will attend. I wish their councils may better our situation ; but I am not sanguine in my expectations. There is reason to fear that our errors do not proceed from want of knowledge, and therefore that reason and public spirit will require the aid of [virtue] to render their dictates effectual.

The insurrection in Massachusetts is suppressed, but the spirit of it exists and has operated powerfully in the late election. The governor, whose conduct was upright and received the approbation of the Legislature, is turned out, and Mr. Hancock is elected. Many respectable characters in both Houses are displaced, and men of other principles and views elected. Perhaps these accounts are exaggerated. Perhaps Mr. Hancock will support his former character, and that the present Legislature will be zealous to maintain the rights of government as well as respect the wishes of the people. Time alone can ascertain these matters. The language, however, of such changes is not pleasant or promising.

For your information I enclose a copy of certain resolutions of Congress relative to infractions of the treaty of peace. How they will be received or what effect they will have I know not. Some of the States have gone so far in their deviations from the treaty that I fear they will not easily be persuaded to tread back their steps, especially as the recommendations of Congress, like most of the recommendations, are seldom efficient when opposed by interest. A mere government of reason and persuasion is little adapted to the actual state of human nature in any age or country.

One of our five Indiamen, viz., an Albany sloop (?), returned a few days ago in four months from Canton, and I heard last evening that one or two vessels are preparing at Boston for a voyage to the Isle of France. The enterprise of our countrymen is inconceivable, and the number of young men daily going down to settle in the western country is a further proof of it. I fear that western country will one day give us trouble. To govern them will not be easy, and whether after two or three generations they will be fit to govern themselves is a question that merits consideration. The progress of civilization and the means of information are very tardy in special and separate settlements. I wish our differences with Spain in that quarter were well settled; but the maxim of ————(?) does not suit our southern sanguine politicians.

The English are making some important settlements on the river St. Lawrence, etc.; many of our people go there, and it is said that Vermont is not greatly inclined to be the fourteenth State. Taxes and relaxed government agree but ill.

. . . .

John Jay.

MARQUIS DE LAFAYETTE TO JAY.

Versailles, May the 1st, 1787.

My Dear Sir:

I have but a little time to write to America, and am taken up from morning until late in the night by the business of our Assembly [Notables]. I have some days ago given some account of it to Col. Hamilton to whom I refer you.

The Archbishop of Toulouse, a man of fine abilities and great honesty, has at last been put at the head of the finances. We are now collecting our ideas on the plans of economy, and measures to be taken to prevent future depredations, which the Assembly shall present to the King before we can think of advising him to new taxes. The cause of liberty will not on the whole be a looser in the bargain.

While examining the returns of the new year, the unpaid interest of the American debt has been brought before us, and as often questions have been put to me which I answered in the best way I could, but which I wish I could have answered in the manner most suitable to my feelings as an American. I cannot help observing, however, that the domestic debt, the debt to the army, is still more sacred and pressing. . . .

With mine and Madame Lafayette's most affectionate compliments to Mrs. Jay and to you,

I have the honour to be very respectfully,

Yours,

LAFAYETTE.

JAY TO JOHN ADAMS.

OFFICE FOR FOREIGN AFFAIRS,
May 12, 1787.

DEAR SIR :

I had the pleasure of writing you a few lines on the 2d of last month, since which I have received and communicated to Congress your letters of 9th, 24th, and 27th January, and 3d and 24th February last.

My health still continues much deranged, and I purpose in a few days to make an excursion into the country for about a fortnight.

A motion has lately been made in Congress to remove to Philadelphia, and the party who supported it persevere in pushing it from day to day. They are not joined by a single member from either of the Eastern States, and yet there is reason to apprehend that they will carry their point. No other motive for their strange measure is publicly assigned by them, except that Philadelphia is more central than New York. Several important affairs which ought to have been despatched have given place to this unfortunate contest, so that I can by this conveyance send you little of importance.

Accept my thanks for the book you were so kind as to send me. I have read it with pleasure and with profit.[1] I do not, however, altogether concur with you in sentiment respecting the efficiency of our great council for national purposes, whatever powers more or less may be given them. In my opinion a council *so constituted* will forever prove inadequate to the objects of its institution.

With great and sincere esteem I have the honour to be, dear sir, your most obedient and humble servant,

JOHN JAY.

P. S.—A new edition of your book is printing in this city and will be published next week. You will herewith receive the late newspapers.

---

[1] " A Defence of the Constitution of the United States against the Attack of M. Turgot," by John Adams. The work, in three volumes, was in substance " an analysis of the various free governments of ancient and modern times, with occasional summaries of their history, to illustrate the nature of the evils under which they had suffered and ultimately perished." The first volume was issued during the sitting of the Federal Convention.

JAY TO JOHN ADAMS.

OFFICE FOR FOREIGN AFFAIRS,
4th July, 1787.

DEAR SIR:

I have been honoured with your letters of the 10th, 19th, and 30th April and 1st May last. Since the sitting of the Convention, a sufficient number of States for the despatch of business have not been represented in Congress, so that it has neither been in my power officially to communicate your letters to them, nor to write on several subjects on which it is proper that Congress should make known their sentiments to you.

Your information of the attempt to counterfeit the paper of the Carolinas and the probable design of exporting base pence to this country is interesting, and shall be made proper use of.

The public attention is turned to the Convention. Their proceedings are kept secret, and it is uncertain how long they will continue to sit. It is nevertheless probable that the importance and variety of objects that must engage their attention will detain them longer than many may expect.[1] It is much to be wished that the result of their deliberations may place the United States in a better situation, for if their measures should either be inadequate or rejected, the duration of the Union will become problematical. For my own part I am convinced that a national

---

[1] In a letter to Adams of July 31st following, Jay writes: "It seems that the Convention at Philadelphia have agreed on the leading principles or great outlines of their plan, and appointed a committee to put it into form; but we know not what it is, and I believe it is best that we should not."

government, as strong as may be compatible with liberty, is necessary to give us national security and respectability.

Your book gives us many useful lessons, for, although I cannot subscribe to your chapter on Congress, yet I consider the work as a valuable one, and one that will tend greatly to recommend and establish a thorough principle of government on which alone the United States can erect any political structure worth the trouble of erecting.

The western Indians are uneasy and seem inclined to be hostile. It is not to be wondered at. Injustice is too often done them, and the aggressors escape with impunity ; in short, our governments, both particular and general, are either so impotent or so very gently administered as neither to give much terror to evil-doers nor much support and encouragement to those who do well.

I have not answered Colonel Smith's letters, but I have not forgotten him nor will I forget him. What Congress will say about your resignation or your successor I know not, for that and other matters in this department are yet to come under their consideration. The great delays which mark their proceedings on almost every interesting subject are extremely inconvenient and sometimes injurious.

With great and sincere esteem and regard, I am, dear sir,

Your affectionate and obedient servant,
JOHN JAY.

JAY TO GEORGE WASHINGTON.

DEAR SIR: NEW YORK, 25th July, 1787.

Permit me to hint whether it would not be wise and reasonable to provide a strong check to the admission of foreigners into the administration of our national government, and to declare expressly that the command-in-chief of the American army shall not be given to nor devolve on any but a natural-born citizen.

I remain, dear sir,
Your faithful friend and servant,
JOHN JAY.

JAY TO JOHN ADAMS.

MY DEAR SIR: NEW YORK, 25th July, 1787.

Your experience in affairs, your knowledge of character, and your intimate acquaintance with the concerns and interests of this country, together with other circumstances and considerations, induce me to wish that all questions between us and the Court of London, as well as other affairs in Europe, could be adjusted and arranged before you leave it. The decided manner, however, in which you mention your intention to return is decisive, and as the prospect of your doing much good here is fair and promising, perhaps it may upon the whole be best that you should be with us, especially considering the actual situation of our affairs.

You have, my dear friend, deserved well of your country, and your services and character will be truly estimated, at least by posterity, for they will know more of you than the people of this day. I have collected your public letters and despatches, and a good clerk has already recorded a large volume of them. It is common, you know, in the course of time for loose and detached papers to be lost, or mislaid, or misplaced. It is to papers in this office that future historians must recur for accurate accounts of many interesting affairs respecting the late Revolution. It is best, therefore, that they should be recorded regularly in books ; and although it will take much time and labor, which some may think unnecessary, I shall nevertheless persevere in the work.

Your book circulates, and does good. It conveys much information on a subject with which we cannot be too intimately acquainted, especially at this period, when the defects of our national government are under consideration, and when the strongest arguments are necessary to remove prejudices and to correct errors which in many instances design unites with ignorance to create, diffuse, and confirm.

If after all that we have seen and done and experienced in public life, we should yet live to see our country contentedly enjoying the sweets of peace, liberty, and safety under the protection of wise laws and a well-constructed, steady government, we shall have reason to rejoice that we have devoted so many years to her service.

Be assured of my constant esteem and attachment, and believe me to be, dear sir,

Your affectionate friend and servant,

JOHN JAY.

JAY TO THOMAS JEFFERSON.

New York, 8th September, 1787.

Dear Sir:

I had flattered myself that Chevalier Jones would have been prepared to go in the French packet which is to sail the day after to-morrow, but certain circumstances make it necessary for him to postpone his departure to some future opportunity.

On the 24th July last I had the honour of writing you that further despatches on subjects touched in your letters should soon be transmitted, and I flatter myself that the reasons which have hitherto delayed them will soon cease. Your letters of the 4th May and 21st June have since arrived and been communicated to the President of Congress. Since their arrival a quorum of the States has not been represented, so that as yet they have not been laid before Congress, and consequently have not given occasion to any acts or instructions. I read them with pleasure, for in my opinion they do honour to the writer. . .

The Convention will probably rise next week, and their proceedings will probably cause not only much consideration, but also much discussion, debate, and perhaps heat; for as *docti indoctique*, etc., so disinterested patriots and interested politicians will sit in council and in judgment, both within and without doors.[1] There is, nevertheless, a degree of intelli-

---

[1] Lafayette was as solicitous as any American. On August 4th he wrote to Jay from Paris: "With great anxiety, my dear friend, I wait for the results of the Convention. No circumstance can be more interesting to a heart that prides itself in the glory of America, and is happy of her happiness. Indeed, my dear sir, it is time for the United States to take those measures which have

gence and information in the mass of our people which affords much room for hope that by degrees our affairs will assume a more coⁿsistent and pleasing aspect. For my own part, I have long found myself in an awkward situation—so very much to be done and enabled to do very little. All we can do is to persevere, and if good results follow, our labour will not be in vain; if not, we shall have done our duty, and that reflection is valuable. With the best wishes for your health and happiness, and with very sincere esteem and regard,

I am, dear sir,

Your most obedient and humble servant

JOHN JAY.

JOHN ADAMS TO JAY.

GROSVENOR SQUARE, Septʳ· 22, 1787.

DEAR SIR:

Your private letter of the twenty-fifth of July is very friendly and obliging as usual. Give yourself no concern about my apprehensions of your want of attention. I know too well your constant and assiduous application to the duties of your public offices, as well as to the just concerns of your private friends, ever to suspect you of failing in either. I shudder when I think of your next volume of my dispatches. I shall appear before posterity in a very negligent dress and disordered air. In truth I write too much to write well, and have never time to correct any thing. Your

long been talked of by their ablest and most zealous friends. I can only pretend to be ranked among the latter, but am too deeply wounded by any circumstance that does not come up to my ideas of the future greatness, prosperity, and internal happiness of the United States, that I don't only wish them to be well, but as perfectly well as it is possible for a nation to be."

plan, however, of recording all the dispatches of the foreign ministers is indispensible. Future negotiations will often make it necessary to look back to the past, besides the importance of publick history.

The true idea of the negotiation with Holland particularly will never be formed without attending to three sorts of measures. Those taken with the Statholder and his party those taken with the aristocratical people, and those taken with the popular party. If any one of these had been omitted, that unanimity could never have been effected, without which the United States could not have been acknowledged nor their Minister admitted. By obtaining from Congress a Letter of Credence to the Prince of Orange, a measure that the patriots did not like, his party was softened; and by the inclosed letters to two very important Burgomasters in Amsterdam, his intimate friends and many others of the aristocraticks were kept steady. I had not time to transmit copies of these letters to Congress in the season of them, but they ought to be put upon the files or records of Congress. I do myself the honour to transmit you a copy for yourself and another for Congress.

Whether it would lie in my power to do most service in Europe or at home, or any at all in either situation, I know not. My determination to go home was founded in a fixed opinion that neither the honor of Congress nor my own, nor the interest of either could be promoted by the residence of a Minister here, without a British Minister at Congress; and in that opinion I am still clear.

If my book does any good I am happy. Another volume will reach you before this letter. In the calm retreat at Pens Hill I may have leisure to write another, but if I should venture to throw together my thoughts or materials on the great subject of our Confederation I should not dare to do it in such haste as the two volumes already printed have been done. The Convention at Philadelphia is composed of heroes, sages, and demigods, to be sure, who want no assistance from me in forming the best possible plan, but they may have occasion for under-labourers to make it accepted by the people, or at least to make the people unanimous in it, and contented with it. One of the underworkmen, in a cool retreat, it shall be my ambition to become. With invariable esteem and affection,

I am, dear Sir,

Your most obedient servant and real friend,

JOHN ADAMS.

JAY TO JOHN ADAMS.

OFFICE FOR FOREIGN AFFAIRS,
3d October, 1787.

DEAR SIR:

I enclose a copy of the federal government recommended by the Convention, and which has already passed from Congress to the States. What will be its fate in some of them is a little uncertain; for although generally approved, an opposition is to be expected, and in some places will certainly be made to its adoption.

There are now but nine States represented in Congress, and unless that number should continue there for some weeks, much business, and particularly in the Department of Foreign Affairs, will remain unfinished. There is much to be done, and I am apprehensive that much will be left too long undone; for the expectation of a new government will probably relax the attention and exertions of the present.

With great and sincere esteem and regard, I have the honour to be, dear sir,

Your most obedient and humble servant,

JOHN JAY.

THOMAS JEFFERSON TO JAY.

PARIS, October 8, 1787.

DEAR SIR:

The Count de Moustier, Minister Plenipotentiary from the Court of Versailles to the United States, will have the honour of delivering you this. The connection of your offices will necessarily connect you in acquaintance ; but I beg leave to present him to you on account of his personal as well as public character. You will find him open, communicative, candid, simple in his manners, and a declared enemy to ostentation and luxury. He goes with a resolution to add no aliment to it by his example, unless he finds that the disposition of his countrymen require it indispensably.— Permit me at the same time to solicit your friendly notice, and thro' you, that also of Mrs. Jay, to Madame la Marquise de B. sister-in-law to Monsieur de Moustier. She accompanies him in hopes that a change of climate may assist her feeble health, and also that she may procure a more valuable education for her son, and safer from seduction, in America than in France. I think it impossible to find a better woman, more amiable, more modest, more simple in her manners, dress and way of thinking. She will deserve the friendship of Mrs. Jay, and the way to obtain hers is to receive her and treat her without the shadow of etiquette.

The Count d' Aranda leaves us in a day or two. He desired me to recall him to your recollection and to assure you of his friendship.—In a letter which I mean as a private one, I may venture details too minute for a public one, yet not unamusing nor unsatisfactory. I may venture names too, without the danger of their getting into a newspaper. There has long been a division in the council here on the question of war and peace. M. de Montmorin and M. de Breteuil have been constantly for war. They are supported in this by the queen. The king goes for nothing : he hunts one half the day, is drunk the other, and signs whatever he is bid. The archbishop of Thoulouse desire speace. Tho' brought in by the queen he is opposed to her in this capital object, which would produce an alliance with her brother. Whether the archbishop will yield or not, I know not, but an intrigue is already begun for ousting him from his place, and it is rather probable that it will succeed. He is a good and patriotic minister for peace, and very capable in the department of finance—at least he is so in theory. I have heard his talents for execution censured.

Can I be useful here to Mrs. Jay or yourself in executing any commissions great or small? I offer you my services with great cordiality. You know whether any of the wines of this country may attract your wishes. In my tour last spring I visited the best vineyards of Burgundy, Cote-rotie, Hermitage, Lunelle, Frontignan, and white and red Bordeaux, got acquainted with all the proprietors, and can procure for you the best crops from the Vigneron himself. Mrs. Jay knows if there is anything else here in which I could be useful to her. Command me without ceremony, as it will give me real pleasure to serve you, and be assured of the sincere attachment and friendship with which I am, dear Sir, your most obedient and humble servant.

TH. JEFFERSON.

JAY TO JOHN ADAMS.

OFFICE FOR FOREIGN AFFAIRS, NEW YORK,
16th October, 1787.

DEAR SIR:

Since my last to you of the 3d inst. I have not been favoured with any letters from you.

I have at length the pleasure of transmitting to you, herewith enclosed, an act of Congress complying with your request to return, and expressing their sentiments of, and their thanks for, the important services, you have rendered your country. They have not yet come to any decision respecting a Minister or a *Chargé d'Affaires* at London, nor directed me to convey to you any instructions relative to any matters within the department of your Legation. You will also find herewith enclosed a certified copy of an act of Congress, of the 11th inst., for ratifying the contract you made on the 1st June last, together with the ratification in form. . . .

The public mind is much occupied by the plan of federal government recommended by the late Convention ; many expect much good from its institution, and others will oppose its adoption. The majority seems at present to be in its favor. For my part, I think it much better than the one we have, and therefore that we shall be gainers by the exchange, especially as there is reason to hope that experience and the good sense of the people will correct what may prove to be inexpedient in it. A compact like this, which is the result of accommodation and compromise, cannot be supposed to be perfectly consonant to the wishes and opinions of any of the parties. It corresponds a good deal with your favourite, and I think, just principles of government, whereas the present Confederation seems to have been formed without the least attention to them.

Congress have thought it best to pass a requisition for the expenses of the ensuing year, but, like most of their former ones, it will produce but little. As Mr. Jefferson's present commission will soon expire,

Congress have directed another to be prepared for him. What further arrangements they may think proper to make relative to their foreign affairs is as yet undetermined. I am inclined to think that until the fate of the new government is decided no very important measures to meliorate our national affairs will be attempted.

It is much to be wished that our friends, the Dutch, may be able to escape the evils of war in a manner consistent with their true interest and honour. I think it fortunate that neither France nor Britain are ripe for hostilities. A little republic surrounded with powerful monarchies has much to apprehend, as well from their politics as their arms. It gives me pleasure to reflect that we have no such neighbours, and that if we will but think and act for ourselves and unite, we shall have nothing to fear. I wish it may be convenient to you to return in some vessel bound to this port, that I may have the pleasure of taking you by the hand and personally assuring you of the sincere esteem and regard with which I am, dear sir,

Your most obedient and humble servant,

JOHN JAY.

JAY TO THOMAS JEFFERSON.

OFFICE FOR FOREIGN AFFAIRS, NEW YORK,
3d November, 1787.

DEAR SIR:

Since the date of my last, which was the 24th ult., Congress have been pleased to pass an act, of which the enclosed is a copy. It contains instructions to you relative to the demands of the United States against the Court of Denmark. As they are express and particular, remarks upon them would be unnecessary. I am persuaded that the manner in which the business will be conducted and concluded will evince the propriety of its being committed to your direction.

Advices from Georgia represent that State as much distressed by the Indians. It is said that the apprehensions of the people there are so greatly alarmed that they are even fortifying Savannah. There doubtless is reason to fear that their frontier settlements will be ravaged. The Indians are numerous and they are exasperated, and will probably be put to no difficulties on account of military stores. The embarrassments result from want of a proper government to guard good faith and punish violations of it. With very sincere esteem and regard I have the honour to be, dear sir,

> Your most obedient and humble servant,
>
> JOHN JAY.

FEDERALIST PAPERS.[1]

NO. II.

TO THE PEOPLE OF THE STATE OF NEW YORK:

When the people of America reflect that they are now called upon to decide a question which, in its consequences, must prove one of the most important that ever engaged their attention, the propriety of

---

[1] Of the eighty-five papers which make up the *Federalist*, Jay wrote Nos. II., III., IV., V., and LXIII., the original drafts of which, No. II. excepted,

their taking a very comprehensive, as well as a very serious, view of it will be evident.

Nothing is more certain than the indispensable necessity of government, and it is equally undeniable that, whenever and however it is instituted, the people must cede to it some of their natural rights, in order to vest it with requisite powers. It is well worthy of consideration, therefore, whether it would conduce more to the interest of the people of America, that they should, to all general purposes, be one nation, under one federal government, or that they should divide themselves into separate confederacies, and give to the head of each the same kind of powers which they are advised to place in one national government.

It has until lately been a received and uncontradicted opinion, that the prosperity of the people of America depended on their continuing firmly united, and the wishes, prayers, and efforts of our best and wisest citizens have been constantly directed to that object. But politicians now appear, who insist that this opinion is erroneous, and that instead of looking for safety and happiness in union, we ought to seek it in a division of the States into distinct confederacies or sovereignties. However extraordinary this new doctrine may appear, it nevertheless has its advocates ; and certain characters who were much opposed to it formerly, are at present of the number. Whatever

are known to be preserved. Jay was interrupted in his contributions by the wound he received in the "Doctor's Mob" in New York City, April, 1788.

may be the arguments or inducements which have wrought this change in the sentiments and declarations of these gentlemen, it certainly would not be wise in the people at large to adopt these new political tenets without being fully convinced that they are founded in truth and sound policy.

It has often given me pleasure to observe, that independent America was not composed of detached and distant territories, but that one connected, fertile, wide-spreading country was the portion of our western sons of liberty. Providence has in a particular manner blessed it with a variety of soils and productions, and watered it with innumerable streams, for the delight and accommodation of its inhabitants. A succession of navigable waters forms a kind of chain round its borders, as if to bind it together; while the most noble rivers in the world, running at convenient distances, present them with highways for the easy communication of friendly aids, and the mutual transportation and exchange of their various commodities.

With equal pleasure I have as often taken notice, that Providence has been pleased to give this one connected country to one united people; a people descended from the same ancestors, speaking the same language, professing the same religion, attached to the same principles of government, very similar in their manners and customs, and who, by their joint counsels, arms, and efforts, fighting side by side throughout a long and bloody war, have nobly established their general liberty and independence.

This country and this people seem to have been made for each other, and it appears as if it was the design of Providence, that an inheritance so proper and convenient for a band of brethren, united to each other by the strongest ties, should never be split into a number of unsocial, jealous, and alien sovereignties.

Similar sentiments have hitherto prevailed among all orders and denominations of men among us. To all general purposes we have uniformly been one people ; each individual citizen everywhere enjoying the same national rights, privileges, and protection. As a nation we have made peace and war ; as a nation we have vanquished our common enemies ; as a nation we have formed alliances and made treaties and entered into various compacts and conventions with foreign states.

A strong sense of the value and blessings of union induced the people, at a very early period, to institute a federal government to preserve and perpetuate it. They formed it almost as soon as they had a political existence ; nay, at a time, when their habitations were in flames ; when many of their citizens were bleeding, and when the progress of hostility and desolation left little room for those calm and mature inquiries and reflections which must ever precede the formation of a wise and well-balanced government for a free people. It is not to be wondered at, that a government instituted in times so inauspicious should on experiment be found greatly deficient and inadequate to the purpose it was intended to answer.

This intelligent people perceived and regretted these defects. Still continuing no less attached to union, than enamoured of liberty, they observed the danger, which immediately threatened the former and more remotely the latter ; and being persuaded that ample security for both could only be found in a national government more wisely framed, they, as with one voice, convened the late Convention at Philadelphia, to take that important subject under consideration.

This Convention, composed of men who possessed the confidence of the people, and many of whom had become highly distinguished by their patriotism, virtue, and wisdom in times which tried the minds and hearts of men, undertook the arduous task. In the mild season of peace, with minds unoccupied by other subjects, they passed many months in cool, uninterrupted, and daily consultations ; and finally, without having been awed by power, or influenced by any passions except love for their Country, they presented and recommended to the people the plan produced by their joint and very unanimous councils.

Admit, for so is the fact, that this plan is only *recommended*, not imposed, yet let it be remembered, that it is neither recommended to *blind* approbation nor to *blind* reprobation, but to that sedate and candid consideration which the magnitude and importance of the subject demand, and which it certainly ought to receive. But this (as was remarked in the foregoing number of this Paper) is more to be wished than expected, that it may be so considered and examined. Experience on a former occasion teaches us not to be too sanguine in such hopes. It is not yet forgotten, that well grounded apprehensions of imminent danger induced the people of America to form the memorable Congress of 1774. That body recommended certain measures to their constituents, and the event proved their wisdom; yet it is fresh in our memories how soon the press began to teem with pamphlets and weekly papers against those very measures. Not only many of the officers of government who obeyed the dictates of personal interest, but others, from a mistaken estimate of consequences, or the undue influence of former attachments, or whose ambition aimed at objects which did not correspond with the public good, were indefatigable in their endeavors to persuade the people to reject the advice of that patriotic Congress. Many indeed were deceived and deluded, but the great majority of the people reasoned and decided judiciously; and happy they are in reflecting that they did so.

They considered that the Congress was composed of many wise and experienced men. That being convened from different parts of the country, they brought with them and communicated to each other a variety of useful information. That in the course of the time they passed together in inquiring into and discussing the true interests of their country, they must have acquired very accurate knowledge on that head. That they were individually interested in the public liberty and prosperity, and therefore that it was not less their inclination than their duty, to recommend only such measures as after the most mature deliberation they really thought prudent and desirable.

These and similar considerations then induced the people to rely greatly on the judgment and integrity of the Congress; and they took their advice, notwithstanding the various arts and endeavors used to deter and dissuade them from it. But if the people at large had reason to confide in the men of that Congress, few of whom had then been fully tried or generally known, still greater reason have they now to respect the judgment and advice of the Convention, for it is well known that some of the most distinguished members of that Congress, who have been since tried and justly approved for patriotism and abilities, and who have grown old in acquiring political information, were also members of this Convention, and carried into it their accumulated knowledge and experience.

It is worthy of remark, that not only the first but every succeeding Congress, as well as the late Convention, have invariably joined with the people in thinking that the prosperity of America depended on its Union. To preserve and perpetuate it was the great object of the people in forming that Convention, and it is also the great object of the plan which the Convention has advised them to adopt. With what propriety, therefore, or for what good purposes, are attempts at this particular period, made by some men, to depreciate the importance of the Union? Or why is it suggested that three or four confedera-

cies would be better than one? I am persuaded in
my own mind, that the people have always thought
right on this subject, and that their universal and uniform attachment to the cause of the Union rests on
great and weighty reasons, which I shall endeavor to
develop and explain in some ensuing papers. They
who promote the idea of substituting a number of distinct confederacies in the room of the plan of the Convention, seem clearly to foresee that the rejection of
it would put the continuance of the Union in the utmost jeopardy : that certainly would be the case, and
I sincerely wish that it may be as clearly foreseen by
every good citizen, that whenever the dissolution of
the Union arrives, America will have reason to ex-
claim in the words of the poet, " FAREWELL ! A LONG
FAREWELL, TO ALL MY GREATNESS."

PUBLIUS.

FEDERALIST PAPERS.

NO. III.

TO THE PEOPLE OF THE STATE OF NEW YORK :

It is not a new observation that the people of any
country (if, like the Americans, intelligent and well-
informed) seldom adopt, and steadily persevere for
many years in an erroneous opinion respecting their
interests. That consideration naturally tends to create
great respect for the high opinion which the people of
America have so long and uniformly entertained of
the importance of their continuing firmly united under

one federal government, vested with sufficient powers for all general and national purposes.

The more attentively I consider and investigate the reasons which appear to have given birth to this opinion, the more I become convinced that they are cogent and conclusive.

Among the many objects to which a wise and free people find it necessary to direct their attention, that of providing for their *safety* seems to be the first. The *safety* of the people doubtless has relation to a great variety of circumstances and considerations, and consequently affords great latitude to those who wish to define it precisely and comprehensively.

At present I mean only to consider it as it respects security for the preservation of peace and tranquillity, as well against dangers from *foreign arms and influence*, as from dangers of the *like kind* arising from domestic causes. As the former of these comes first in order, it is proper it should be the first discussed. Let us therefore proceed to examine whether the people are not right in their opinion, that a cordial Union under an efficient national government, affords them the best security that can be devised against *hostilities* from abroad.

The number of wars which have happened or will happen in the world will always be found to be in proportion to the number and weight of the causes, whether *real* or *pretended*, which *provoke* or *invite* them. If this remark be just, it becomes useful to inquire, whether so many *just* causes of war are likely to be given by *united America* as by *disunited* America ; for if it should turn out that united America will probably give the fewest, then it will follow, that in this respect the Union tends most to preserve the people in a state of peace with other nations.

The *just* causes of war for the most part arise either from violations of treaties, or from direct violence. America has already formed treaties with no less than six foreign nations, and all of them, except Prussia, are maritime, and therefore able to annoy and injure us. She has also extensive commerce with Portugal, Spain, and Britain, and, with respect to the two latter, has, in addition, the circumstance of neighborhood to attend to.

It is of high importance to the peace of America, that she observe the laws of nations towards all these Powers, and to me it appears evident that this will be more perfectly and punctually done by one national government than it could be either by thirteen separate States, or by three or four distinct confederacies.

Because when once an efficient national government is established, the best men in the country will not only consent to serve, but also will generally be appointed to manage it ; for although town or country, or other contracted influence, may place men in State assemblies, or senates, or courts of justice, or executive departments, yet more general and extensive reputation for talents and other qualifications will be necessary to recommend men to offices under the national government,—especially, as it will have the widest field for choice, and never experience that want of proper persons which is not uncommon in some of the States. Hence it will result, that the administration, the political counsels, and the judicial decisions of the national government will be more wise, systematical, and judicious than those of individual States, and consequently more satisfactory with respect to other nations, as well as more *safe* with respect to us.

Because, under the national government, treaties and articles of treaties, as well as the laws of nations, will always be expounded in one sense, and executed in the same manner,—whereas adjudications on the same points and questions, in thirteen States, or in three or four confederacies, will not always accord or be consistent; and that, as well from the variety of independent courts and judges appointed by different and independent governments, as from the different local laws and interests which may affect and influence them. The wisdom of the Convention, in committing such questions to the jurisdiction and judgment of courts appointed by, and responsible only to, one national government, cannot be too much commended.

Because the prospect of present loss or advantage may often tempt the governing party in one or two States to swerve from good faith and justice; but those temptations not reaching the other States, and consequently having little or no influence on the national government, the temptation will be fruitless, and good faith and justice be preserved. The case of the treaty of peace with Great Britain adds great weight to this reasoning.

Because even if the governing party in a State should be disposed to resist such temptations, yet as such temptations may, and commonly do, result from circumstances peculiar to the State, and may affect a great number of the inhabitants, the governing party may not always be able, if willing, to prevent the injustice meditated, or to punish the aggressors. But the national government, not being affected by those local circumstances, will neither be induced to commit the wrong themselves, nor want power or inclination to prevent or punish its commission by others.

So far therefore as either designed or accidental violations of treaties and the laws of nations afford *just* causes of war, they are less to be apprehended under one general government than under several lesser ones, and in that respect the former most favors the *safety* of the people.

As to those just causes of war which proceed from direct and unlawful violence, it appears equally clear to me, that one good national government affords vastly more security against dangers of that sort than can be derived from any other quarter.

Because such violences are more frequently caused by the passions and interests of a part than of the whole ; of one or two States than of the Union. Not a single Indian war has yet been occasioned by aggressions of the present Federal Government, feeble as it is ; but there are several instances of Indian hostilities having been provoked by the improper conduct of individual States, who, either unable or unwilling to restrain or punish offences, have given occasion to the slaughter of many innocent inhabitants.

The neighbourhood of Spanish and British territories, bordering on some States and not on others, naturally confines the causes of quarrel more immediately to the borderers. The bordering States, if any, will be those who, under the impulse of sudden irritation, and a quick sense of apparent interest or injury, will be most likely, by direct violence, to excite war with those nations; and nothing can so effectually obviate that danger as a national government, whose wisdom and prudence will not be diminished by the passions which actuate the parties immediately interested.

But not only fewer just causes of war will be given by the national government, but it will also be more in their power to accommodate and settle them amicably. They will be more temperate and cool, and in that respect, as well as in others, will be more in capacity to act advisedly than the offending State. The pride of States, as well as of men, naturally disposes them to justify all their actions, and opposes their acknowledging, correcting, or repairing their errors and offences. The national government, in such cases, will not be affected by this pride, but will proceed with moderation and candor to consider and decide on the means most proper to extricate them from the difficulties which threaten them.

Besides it is well known that acknowledgments, explanations, and compensations are often accepted as satisfactory from a strong united nation, which would be rejected as unsatisfactory if offered by a State or Confederacy of little consideration or power.

In the year 1685 the State of Genoa, having offended Louis XIV., endeavored to appease him. He demanded that they should send their *Doge*, or chief magistrate, accompanied by four of their Senators, to *France*, to ask his pardon and receive his terms. They were obliged to submit to it for the sake of peace. Would he on any occasion either have demanded, or have received, the like humiliation from Spain, or Britain, or any other *powerful* nation?

PUBLIUS.

FEDERALIST PAPERS.

NO. IV.

TO THE PEOPLE OF THE STATE OF NEW YORK:

My last Paper assigned several reasons why the safety of the people would be best secured by Union, against the danger it may be exposed to by *just* causes of war given to other nations; and those reasons show that such causes would not only be more rarely given, but would also be more easily accommodated by a national government, than either by the State governments, or the proposed little confederacies.

But the safety of the people of America against dangers from *foreign* force depends not only on their forbearing to give *just* causes for war to other nations, but also on their placing and continuing themselves in such a situation as not to *invite* hostility or insult; for it need not be observed, that there are *pretended* as well as just causes of war.

It is too true, however disgraceful it may be to human nature, that nations in general will make war whenever they have a prospect of getting anything by it; nay, that absolute monarchs will often make war when their nations are to get nothing by it, but for purposes and objects merely personal, such as a thirst for military glory, revenge for personal affronts, ambition, or private compacts to aggrandize or support their particular families or partisans. These, and a variety of motives, which affect only the mind of the Sovereign, often lead him to engage in wars not sanctified by justice, or the voice and interests of his people. But, independent of these inducements to war, which are more prevalent in absolute monarchies, but which well deserve our attention, there are others which affect nations as often as kings; and some of them will on examination be found to grow out of our relative situation and circumstances.

With France and with Britain, we are rivals in the fisheries, and can supply their markets cheaper than they can themselves, notwithstanding any efforts to prevent it by bounties on their own, or duties on foreign fish.

With them and with most other European nations, we are rivals in navigation and the carrying trade; and we shall deceive ourselves, if we suppose that any of them will rejoice to see it flourish : for as our carrying trade cannot increase, without in some degree diminishing theirs, it is more their interest, and will be more their policy, to restrain than to promote it.

In the trade to China and India, we interfere with more than one nation, inasmuch as it enables us to partake in advantages which they had in a manner monopolized, and as we thereby supply ourselves with commodities which we used to purchase from them.

The extension of our own commerce in our own vessels cannot give pleasure to any nations who possess territories on or near this continent, because the cheapness and excellence of our productions, added to the circumstance of vicinity, and the enterprise and address of our merchants and navigators, will give us a greater share in the advantages which those territories afford, than consists with the wishes or policy of their respective Sovereigns.

Spain thinks it convenient to shut the Mississippi against us on the one side, and Britain excludes us from the Saint Lawrence on the other ; nor will either of them permit the other waters, which are between them and us, to become the means of mutual intercourse and traffic.

From these and such like considerations, which might, if consistent with prudence, be more amplified and detailed, it is easy to see that jealousies and uneasinesses may gradually slide into the minds and cabinets of other nations ; and that we are not to expect they should regard our advancement in union, in power and consequence by land and by sea, with an eye of indifference and composure.

The people of America are aware that inducements to war may arise out of these circumstances, as well as from others not so obvious at present; and that whenever such inducements may find fit time and opportunity for operation, pretences to color and justify them will not be wanting. Wisely therefore do they consider Union and a good national government as necessary to put and keep them in *such a situation* as, instead of *inviting* war, will tend to repress and discourage it. That situation consists in the best possible state of defence, and necessarily depends on the Government, the arms, and the resources of the country.

As the safety of the whole is the interest of the whole, and cannot be provided for without government, either one or more or many, let us inquire whether one good government is not, relative to the object in question, more competent than any other given number whatever.

One government can collect and avail itself of the talents and experience of the ablest men, in whatever part of the Union they may be found. It can move on uniform principles of policy. It can harmonize, assimilate, and protect the several parts and members, and extend the benefit of its foresight and precautions to each. In the formation of treaties it will regard the interest of the whole, and the particular interests of the parts as connected with that of the whole. It can apply the resources and power of the whole to the defence of any particular part, and that more easily and expeditiously than State governments, or separate confederacies can possibly do, for want of concert and unity of system. It can place the militia under one plan of discipline, and, by putting their officers in a proper line of subordination to the Chief Magistrate, will, as it were, consolidate them into one corps, and thereby render them more efficient than if divided into thirteen or into three or four distinct independent bodies.

What would the militia of Britain be, if the English militia obeyed the Government of England, if the Scotch militia obeyed the Government of Scotland, and if the Welsh militia obeyed the Government of Wales? Suppose an invasion: would those three governments (if they agreed at all) be able, with all their respective forces, to operate against the enemy so effectually as the single Government of Great Britain would?

We have heard much of the fleets of Britain, and the time may come, if we are wise, when the fleets of America may engage attention. But if one national government had not so regulated the navigation of Britain as to make it a nursery for seamen—if one national government had not called forth all the national means and materials for forming fleets, their prowess and their thunder would never have been celebrated. Let England have its navigation and fleet—let Scotland have its navigation and fleet— let Wales have its navigation and fleet—let Ireland have its navigation and fleet—let those four of the constituent parts of the British Empire be under four independent governments, and it is easy to perceive how soon they would each dwindle into comparative insignificance.

Apply these facts to our own case. Leave America divided into thirteen, or if you please into three or four, independent governments, what armies could they raise and pay, what fleets could they ever hope to have? If one was attacked, would the others fly to its succor, and spend their blood and money in its defence. Would there be no danger of their being flattered into neutrality by specious promises, or seduced by a too great fondness for peace to decline hazarding their tranquillity and present safety for the sake of neighbors, of whom perhaps they have been jealous, and whose importance they are content to see diminished? Although such conduct would not be wise, it would nevertheless be natural. The history of the states of Greece, and of other countries, abounds with such instances; and it is not improbable, that what has so often happened would, under similar circumstances, happen again.

But admit that they might be willing to help the invaded State or Confederacy. How, and when, and in what proportion shall aids of men and money be afforded? Who shall command the allied armies, and from which of them shall he receive his orders? Who shall settle the terms of peace, and in case of disputes what umpire shall decide between them, and compel acquiescence? Various difficulties and inconveniences would be inseparable from such a situation ; whereas one government, watching over the general and common interests, and combining and directing the powers and resources of the whole, would be free from all these embarrassments, and conduce far more to the safety of the people.

But whatever may be our situation, whether firmly united under one national government, or split into a number of confederacies, certain it is, that foreign nations will know and view it exactly as it is ; and they will act towards us accordingly. If they see that our national government is efficient and well administered—our trade prudently regulated—our militia properly organized and disciplined—our resources and finances discreetly managed—our credit re-established —our people free, contented, and united, they will be much more disposed to cultivate our friendship than provoke our resentment. If, on the other hand, they find us either destitute of an effectual government, (each State doing right or wrong, as to its rulers may seem convenient,) or split into three or four independent and probably discordant republics or confederacies, one inclining to Britain, another to France, and a third to Spain, and perhaps played off against each other by the three, what a poor, pitiful figure will America make in their eyes ! How liable would she become not only to their contempt, but to their outrage ; and how soon would dear-bought experience proclaim that when a people or family so divide, it never fails to be against themselves.

PUBLIUS.

FEDERALIST PAPERS.

NO. V.

To the People of the State of New York:

Queen Anne, in her letter of the 1st July, 1706, to the Scotch Parliament, makes some observations on the importance of the *Union* then forming between England and Scotland, which merit our attention. I shall present the public with one or two extracts from it. "An entire and perfect Union will be the solid foundation of lasting peace : It will secure your religion, liberty, and property, remove the animosities amongst yourselves, and the jealousies and differences betwixt our two kingdoms. It must increase your strength, riches, and trade; and by this Union the whole Island, being joined in affection and free from all apprehensions of different interest, will be *enabled to resist all its enemies*." "We most earnestly recommend to you calmness and unanimity in this great and weighty affair, that the Union may be brought to a happy conclusion, being the only *effectual* way to secure our present and future happiness ; and disappoint the designs of our and your enemies, who will doubtless, on this occasion, *use their utmost endeavors to prevent or delay this Union*."

It was remarked in the preceding Paper, that weakness and divisions at home would invite dangers from abroad, and that nothing would tend more to secure us from them than Union, strength, and good government within ourselves. This subject is copious and cannot easily be exhausted.

The history of Great Britain is the one with which we are in general the best acquainted, and it gives us many useful lessons. We may profit by their experience, without paying the price which it cost them. Although it seems obvious to common-sense, that the people of such an island should be but one nation, yet we find that they were for ages divided into three, and that those three were almost constantly embroiled in quarrels and wars with one another. Notwithstanding their true interest, with respect to the continental nations, was really the same, yet by the arts and policy and practices of those nations, their mutual jealousies were perpetually kept inflamed, and for a long series of years they were far more inconvenient and troublesome than they were useful and assisting to each other.

Should the people of America divide themselves into three or four nations, would not the same thing happen? Would not similar jealousies arise; and be in like manner cherished? Instead of their being " joined in affection, and free from all apprehension of different interests," envy and jealousy would soon extinguish confidence and affection, and the partial interests of each confederacy, instead of the general interests of all America, would be the only objects of their policy and pursuits. Hence, like most other *bordering* nations, they would always be either involved in disputes and war, or live in the constant apprehension of them.

The most sanguine advocates for three or four confederacies cannot reasonably suppose that they would long remain exactly on an equal footing in point of strength, even if it was possible to form them so at first; but admitting that to be practicable, yet what human contrivance can secure the continuance of such equality? Independent of those local circumstances which tend to beget and increase power in one part, and to impede its progress in another, we must advert to the effects of that superior policy and good management which would probably distinguish the government of one above the rest, and by which their relative equality in strength and consideration would be destroyed. For it cannot be presumed that the same degree of sound policy, prudence, and foresight would uniformly be observed by each of these confederacies for a long succession of years.

Whenever, and from whatever causes, it might happen, and happen it would, that any one of these nations or confederacies should rise on the scale of political importance much above the degree of her neighbors, that moment would those neighbors behold her with envy and with fear. Both those passions would lead them to countenance, if not to promote, whatever might promise to diminish her importance, and would also restrain them from measures calculated to advance or even to secure her prosperity. Much time would not be necessary to enable her to discern these unfriendly dispositions. She would soon begin, not only to lose confidence in her neighbors, but also to feel a disposition equally unfavorable to them. Distrust naturally creates distrust, and by nothing is good will and kind conduct more speedily changed than by invidious jealousies and uncandid imputations, whether expressed or implied.

The North is generally the region of strength, and many local circumstances render it probable, that the most Northern of the proposed confederacies would, at a period not very distant, be unquestionably more formidable than any of the others. No sooner would this become evident, than the *Northern Hive* would excite the same ideas and sensations in the more Southern parts of America which it formerly did in the Southern parts of Europe. Nor does it appear to be a rash conjecture, that its young swarms might often be tempted to gather honey in the more blooming fields and milder air of their luxurious and more delicate neighbors.

They who well consider the history of similar divisions and confederacies, will find abundant reason to apprehend, that those in contemplation would in no other sense be neighbors than as they would be borderers ; that they would neither love nor trust one another, but on the contrary would be a prey to discord, jealousy, and mutual injuries ; in short, that they would place us exactly in the situations in which some nations doubtless wish to see us, viz., *formidable only to each other.*

From these considerations it appears that those gentlemen are greatly mistaken who suppose that alliances offensive and defensive might be formed between these confederacies, and would produce that combination and union of wills, of arms, and of resources, which would be necessary to put and keep them in a formidable state of defence against foreign enemies.

When did the independent states, into which Britain and Spain were formerly divided, combine in such alliances, or unite their forces against a foreign enemy? The proposed confederacies will be *distinct nations.* Each of them would have its commerce with foreigners to regulate by distinct treaties; and as their productions and commodities are different, and proper for different markets, so would those treaties be essentially different. Different commercial concerns must create different interests, and of course different degrees of political attachment to, and connection with, different foreign nations. Hence it might and probably would happen, that the foreign nation with whom the *Southern* confederacy might be at war would be the one with whom the *Northern* confederacy would be the most desirous of preserving peace and friendship. An alliance so contrary to their immediate interest would not therefore be easy to form, nor, if formed, would it be observed and fulfilled with perfect good faith.

Nay, it is far more probable that in America, as in Europe, neighboring nations, acting under the impulse of opposite interests and unfriendly passions, would frequently be found taking different sides. Considering our distance from Europe, it would be more natural for these confederacies to apprehend danger from one another than from distant nations, and therefore that each of them should be more desirous to guard against the others, by the aid of foreign alliances, than to guard against foreign dangers by alliances between themselves.   And here let us not forget how much more easy it is to receive foreign fleets into our ports, and foreign armies into our country, than it is to persuade or compel them to depart.   How many conquests did the Romans and others make in the character of allies, and what innovations did they, under the same character, introduce into the governments of those whom they pretended to protect.

Let candid men judge, then, whether the division of America into any given number of independent sovereignties would tend to secure us against the hostilities and improper interference of foreign nations.

PUBLIUS.

FEDERALIST PAPERS.

NO. LXIII.

TO THE PEOPLE OF THE STATE OF NEW YORK:

It is a just and not a new observation, that enemies to particular persons, and opponents to particular measures, seldom confine their censures to such things only in either as are worthy of blame.   Unless on this principle, it is difficult to explain the motives of their conduct, who condemn the proposed Constitution in the aggregate, and treat with severity some of the most unexceptionable articles in it.

The second section gives power to the President, "*by and with the advice and consent of the Senate, to make treaties*, PROVIDED TWO THIRDS OF THE SENATORS PRESENT CONCUR."

The power of making treaties is an important one, especially as it relates to war, peace, and commerce ; and it should not be delegated but in such a mode, and with such precautions, as will afford the highest security, that it will be exercised by men the best qualified for the purpose, and in the manner most conducive to the public good. The Convention appears to have been attentive to both these points ; they have directed the President to be chosen by select bodies of electors, to be deputed by the people for that express purpose; and they have committed the appointment of Senators to the State Legislatures. This mode has, in such cases, vastly the advantage of elections by the people in their collective capacity, where the activity of party zeal, taking advantage of the supineness, the ignorance, and the hopes and fears of the unwary and interested, often places men in office by the votes of a small proportion of the electors.

As the select Assemblies for choosing the President, as well as the State Legislatures who appoint the Senators, will in general be composed of the most enlightened and respectable citizens, there is reason to presume, that their attention and their votes will be directed to those men only who have become the most distinguished by their abilities and virtue, and in whom the people perceive just grounds for confidence.

The Constitution manifests very particular attention to this object. By excluding men under thirty-five from the first office, and those under thirty from the second, it confines the electors to men of whom the people have had time to form a judgment, and with respect to whom they will not be liable to be deceived by those brilliant appearances of genius and patriotism, which, like transient meteors, sometimes mislead as well as dazzle. If the observation be well founded, that wise kings will always be served by able ministers, it is fair to argue, that as an assembly of select electors possesses, in a greater degree than kings the means of extensive and accurate information relative to men and characters, so will their appointments bear at least equal marks of discretion and discernment. The inference which naturally results from these considerations is this, that the President and Senators so chosen will always be of the number of those who best understand our national interests, whether considered in relation to the several States or to foreign nations, who are best able to promote those interests, and whose reputation for integrity inspires and merits confidence. With such men the power of making treaties may be safely lodged.

Although the absolute necessity of system in the conduct of any business is universally known and acknowledged, yet the high importance of it in national affairs has not yet become sufficiently impressed on the public mind. They who wish to commit the power under consideration to a popular assembly, composed of members constantly coming and going in quick succession, seem not to recollect, that such a body must necessarily be inadequate to the attainment of those great objects which require to be steadily contemplated in all their relations and circumstances, and which can only be approached and achieved by measures which not only talents, but also exact information, and often much time, are necessary to concert and to execute. It was wise, therefore, in the Convention to provide, not only that the power of making treaties should be committed to able and honest men, but also that they should continue in place a sufficient time to become perfectly acquainted with our national concerns, and to form and introduce a system for the management of them. The duration prescribed is such as will give them an opportunity of greatly extending their political information, and of rendering their accumulating experience more and more beneficial to their country. Nor has the Convention discovered less prudence, in providing for the frequent elections of Senators in such a way as to obviate the inconvenience of periodically transferring those great affairs entirely to new men ; for by leaving a considerable residue of the old ones in place, uniformity and order, as well as a constant succession of official information, will be preserved.

There are few who will not admit, that the affairs of trade and navigation should be regulated by a system cautiously formed and steadily pursued, and that both our treaties and our laws should correspond with and be made to promote it. It is of much consequence that this correspondence and conformity be carefully maintained; and they who assent to the truth of this position will see and confess, that it is well provided for by making concurrence of the Senate necessary, both to treaties and to laws.

It seldom happens in the negotiation of treaties, of whatever nature, but that perfect *secrecy* and immediate *despatch* are sometimes requisite. There are cases where the most useful intelligence may be obtained, if the persons possessing it can be relieved from apprehensions of discovery. Those apprehensions will operate on those persons, whether they are actuated by mercenary or friendly motives; and there doubtless are many of both descriptions, who would rely on the secrecy of the President, but who would not confide in that of the Senate, and still less in that of a large popular Assembly. The Convention have done well, therefore, in so disposing of the power of making treaties, that although the President must, in forming them, act by the advice and consent of the Senate, yet he will be able to manage the business of intelligence in such a manner as prudence may suggest.

They who have turned their attention to the affairs of men must have perceived that there are tides in them; tides very irregular in their duration, strength, and direction, and seldom found to run twice exactly in the same manner or measure. To discern and to profit by these tides in national affairs is the business of those who preside over them; and they who have had much experience on this head inform us, that there frequently are occasions when days, nay, even when hours, are precious. The loss of a battle, the death of a prince, the removal of a minister, or other circumstances intervening to change the present posture and aspect of affairs, may turn the most favorable tide into a course opposite to our wishes. As in the field, so in the cabinet, there are moments to be seized as they pass, and they who preside in either should be left in capacity to improve them. So often and so essentially have we heretofore suffered from the want of secrecy and despatch, that the Constitution would have been inexcusably defective if no attention had been paid to those objects. Those matters which in negotiations usually require the most secrecy and the most despatch are those preparatory and auxiliary measures which are no otherwise important in a national view, than as they tend to facilitate the attainment of the objects of the negotiation. For these, the President will find no difficulty to provide ; and should any circumstance occur, which requires the advice and consent of the Senate, he may at any time convene them. Thus we see, that the Constitution provides that our negotiations for treaties shall have every advantage which can be derived from talents, information, integrity, and deliberate investigations, on the one hand, and from secrecy and despatch, on the other.

But to this plan, as to most others that have ever appeared, objections are contrived and urged.

Some are displeased with it, not on account of any errors or defects in it, but because, as the treaties, when made, are to have the force of laws, they should be made only by men invested with legislative authority. These gentlemen seem not to consider that the judgments of our courts, and the commissions constitutionally given by our Governor, are as valid and as binding on all persons whom they concern, as the laws passed by our Legislature. All constitutional acts of power, whether in the executive or in the judicial department, have as much legal validity and obligation as if they proceeded from the Legislature; and therefore, whatever name be given to the power of making treaties, or however obligatory they may be when made, certain it is, that the people may, with much propriety, commit the power to a distinct body from the Legislature, the Executive, or the Judicial. It surely does not follow, that because they have given the power of making laws to the Legislature, that therefore they should likewise give them power to do every other act of sovereignty by which the citizens are to be bound and affected.

Others, though content that treaties should be made in the mode proposed, are averse to their being the *supreme* laws of the land. They insist, and profess to believe, that treaties, like Acts of Assembly, should be repealable at pleasure. This idea seems to be new and peculiar to this country; but new errors, as well as new truths, often appear. These gentlemen would do well to reflect, that a treaty is only another name for a bargain; and that it would be impossible to find a Nation who would make any bargain with us, which should be binding on them *absolutely*, but on us only so long and so far as we may think proper to be bound by it. They who make laws may, without doubt, amend or repeal them ; and it will not be disputed that they who make treaties may alter or cancel them : but still let us not forget that treaties are made, not by only one of the contracting parties, but by both ; and consequently, that as the consent of both was essential to their formation at first, so must it ever afterwards be to alter or cancel them. The proposed Constitution, therefore, has not in the least extended the obligation of treaties. They are just as binding, and just as far beyond the lawful reach of Legislative acts now, as they will be at any future period, or under any form of government.

However useful jealousy may be in republics, yet when like bile in the natural, it abounds too much in the body politic, the eyes of both become very liable to be deceived by the delusive appearances which that malady casts on surrounding objects. From this cause, probably, proceed the fears and apprehensions of some, that the President and Senate may make treaties without an equal eye to the interests of all the States. Others suspect, that two thirds will oppress the remaining third, and ask, whether those gentlemen are made sufficiently responsible for their conduct ; whether, if they act corruptly, they can be punished ; and if they make disadvantageous treaties, how are we to get rid of those treaties ?

As all the States are equally represented in the Senate, and by men the most able and the most willing to promote the interests of their constituents, they will all have an equal degree of influence in that body, especially while they continue to be careful in appointing proper persons, and to insist on their punctual attendance. In proportion as the United States assume a national form, and a national character, so will the good of the whole be more and more an object of attention ; and the government must be a weak one indeed, if it should forget, that the good of the whole can only be promoted by advancing the good of each of the parts or members which compose the whole. It will not be in the power of the President and Senate to make any treaties by which they and their families and estates, will not be equally bound and affected with the rest of the community ; and having no private interests distinct from that of the Nation, they will be under no temptations to neglect the latter.

As to corruption, the case is not supposable. He must either have been very unfortunate in his intercourse with the world, or possess a heart very susceptible of such impressions, who can think it probable, that the President and two thirds of the Senate will ever be capable of such unworthy conduct. The idea is too gross, and too invidious, to be entertained. But in such a case, if it should ever happen, the treaty so obtained from us would, like all other fraudulent contracts, be null and void by the law of nations.

With respect to their responsibility, it is difficult to conceive how it could be increased. Every consideration that can influence the human mind, such as honor, oaths, reputations, conscience, the love of country, and family affections and attachments, afford security for their fidelity. In short, as the Constitution has taken the utmost care that they shall be men of talents and integrity, we have reason to be persuaded, that the treaties they make will be as advantageous as, all circumstances considered, could be made ; and so far as the fear of punishment and disgrace can operate, that motive to good behavior is amply afforded by the Article on the subject of impeachments.   Publius.

AN ADDRESS TO THE PEOPLE OF THE STATE OF NEW YORK.[1]

Friends and Fellow-Citizens :

There are times and seasons when *general evils* spread general alarm and uneasiness, and yet arise from causes too complicated and too little understood by many to produce a unanimity of opinions respecting their remedies. Hence it is that on such occasions the conflict of arguments too often excites a conflict of passions, and introduces a degree of discord and animosity which, by agitating the public mind, dispose it to precipitation and extravagance. They who on the ocean have been unexpectedly enveloped with tempests, or suddenly entangled

---

[1] The authorship of this paper, which appeared anonymously, in the spring of 1788, was readily traced to Jay. The library of the New York Historical Society contains a copy of the original pamphlet, which was published under the title, " An Address to the People of the State of New York, On the Subject of the Constitution, Agreed upon at Philadelphia, the 17th of September, 1787. New York : Printed by Samuel and John Loudon, Printers to the State."

among rocks and shoals, know the value of that serene self-possession and presence of mind to which in such cases they owed their preservation ; nor will the heroes who have given us victory and peace hesitate to acknowledge that we are as much indebted for those blessings to the calm prevision and cool intrepidity which planned and conducted our military measures, as to the glowing animation with which they were executed.

While reason retains her rule, while men are as ready to receive as to give advice, and as willing to be convinced themselves as to convince others, there are few political evils from which a free and enlightened people cannot deliver themselves. It is unquestionably true that the great body of the people love their country, and with it prosperity ; and this observation is particularly applicable to the people of a *free* country, for they have more and stronger reasons for loving it than others. It is not, therefore, to vicious motives that the unhappy divisions which sometime prevail among them are to be imputed ; the people at large always mean well, and although they may on certain occasions be misled by the counsels or injured by the efforts of the few who expect more advantage from the wreck than from the preservation of national prosperity, yet the motives of these few are by no means to be confounded with those of the community in general.

That such seeds of discord and danger have been disseminated and begin to take root in America as, unless eradicated, will soon poison our gardens and our fields, is a truth much to be lamented; and the more so as their growth rapidly increases while we are wasting the season in honestly but imprudently disputing, not whether they shall be pulled up, but by whom, in what manner, and with what instruments the work shall be done.

When the King of Great Britain, misguided by men who did not merit his confidence, asserted the unjust claim of binding us in all cases whatsoever, and prepared to obtain our submission by force, the object which engrossed our attention, however important, was nevertheless plain and simple. "What shall be done?" was the question; the people answered, "Let us unite our counsels and our arms." They sent delegates to Congress and soldiers to the field. Confiding in the probity and wisdom of Congress, they received their recommendations as if they had been laws; and that ready acquiescence in their advice enabled those patriots to save their country. Then there was little leisure or disposition for controversy respecting the expediency of measures; hostile fleets soon filled our ports, and hostile armies spread desolation on our shores. Union was then considered as the most essential of human means, and we almost worshipped it with as much fervor as pagans in distress implored the protection of their tutelar deities. That Union was the child of wisdom. Heaven blessed it and wrought out our political salvation.

That glorious war was succeeded by an advantageous peace. When danger disappeared, ease,

.tranquillity, and a sense of security loosened the bonds of union ; and Congress and soldiers and good faith depreciated with their apparent importance. Recommendations lost their influence, and requisitions were rendered nugatory, not by their want of propriety, but by their want of power. The spirit of private gain expelled the spirit of public good, and men became more intent on the means of enriching and aggrandizing themselves than of enriching and aggrandizing their country. Hence the war-worn veteran, whose reward for toil and wounds existed in written promises, found Congress without the means, and too many States without the disposition, to do him justice. Hard necessity compelled him, and others under similar circumstances, to sell their honest claims on the public for a little bread ; and thus unmerited misfortunes and patriotic distresses became articles of speculation and commerce.

These and many other evils, too well known to require enumeration, imperceptibly stole in upon us, and acquired an unhappy influence on our public affairs. But such evils, like the worst of weeds, will naturally spring up in so rich a soil ; and a good government is as necessary to subdue the one, as an attentive gardener or husbandman is to destroy the other. Even the garden of Paradise required to be dressed, and while men continue to be constantly impelled to error and to wrong by innumerable circumstances and temptations, so long will society experience the increasing necessity of government.

It is a pity that the expectations which actuated

the authors of the existing Confederation neither have nor can be realized. Accustomed to see and admire the glorious spirit which moved all ranks of people in the most gloomy moments of the war, observing their steadfast attachment to union, and the wisdom they so often manifested both in choosing and confiding in their rulers, these gentlemen were led to flatter themselves that the people of America only required to know what ought to be done, to do it. This amiable mistake induced them to institute a national government in such a manner as, though very fit to give advice, was yet destitute of power, and so constructed as to be very unfit to be trusted with it. They seem not to have been sensible that mere advice is a bad substitute for laws; nor to have recollected that the advice even of the all-wise and best of Beings has been always disregarded by a great majority of all the men that ever lived.

Experience is a severe preceptor, but it teaches useful truths, and, however harsh, is always honest. Be calm and dispassionate and listen to what it tells us.

Prior to the revolution we had little occasion to inquire or know much about national affairs, for although they existed and were managed, yet they were managed *for* us and not *by* us. Intent on our domestic concerns, our internal legislative business, our agriculture, and our buying and selling, we were seldom anxious about what passed or was doing in foreign courts. As we had nothing to do with the department of policy, so the affairs of it were not detailed to us, and we took as little pains to inform ourselves as others did to inform us of them. War and peace, alliances and treaties, and commerce and navigation were conducted and regulated without our advice or control. While we had liberty and justice, and in security enjoyed the fruits of our "vine and fig-tree," we were in general too content and too much occupied to be at the trouble of investigating the various political combinations in this department, or to examine and perceive how exceedingly important they often were to the advancement and protection of our prosperity. This habit and turn of thinking affords one reason why so much more care was taken, and so much more wisdom displayed, in forming our State governments than in forming our Federal or national one.

By the Confederation as it now stands, the direction of general and national affairs is committed to a single body of men—viz., the Congress. They may make war, but they are not empowered to raise men or money to carry it on. They may make peace, but without the means to see the terms of it observed. They may form alliances, but without ability to comply with the stipulations on their part. They may enter into treaties of commerce, but without power to enforce them at home or abroad. They may borrow money, but without having the means of repayment. They may partly regulate commerce, but without authority to execute their ordinances. They may appoint ministers and other officers of trust, but without power to try or punish them for misdemeanors.

They may resolve, but cannot execute either with despatch or with secrecy. In short, they may consult, and deliberate, and recommend, and make requisitions, and they who please may regard them.

From this new and wonderful system of government it has come to pass that almost every national object of every kind is at this day unprovided for ; and other nations, taking the advantage of its imbecility, are daily multiplying commercial restraints upon us. Our fur trade is gone to Canada, and British garrisons keep the keys of it. Our ship-yards have almost ceased to disturb the repose of the neighbourhood by the noise of the axe and the hammer ; and while foreign flags fly triumphantly above our highest houses, the American stars seldom do more than shed a few feeble rays about the humbler masts of river sloops and coasting schooners. The greater part of our hardy seamen are ploughing the ocean in foreign pay, and not a few of our ingenious shipwrights are now building vessels on alien shores. Although our increasing agriculture and industry extend and multiply our productions, yet they constantly diminish in value ; and although we permit all nations to fill our country with their merchandises, yet their best markets are shut against us. Is there an English, or a French, or a Spanish island or port in the West Indies to which an American vessel can carry a cargo of flour for sale ? Not one. The Algerines exclude us from the Mediterranean and adjacent countries ; and we are neither able to purchase nor to command the free use of those seas. Can our little towns or larger cities consume the immense productions of our fertile country? or will they without trade be able to pay a good price for the proportion which they do consume? The last season gave a very unequivocal answer to those questions. What numbers of fine cattle have returned from this city to the country for want of buyers? What great quantities of salted and other provisions still lie useless in the stores? To how much below the former price is our corn, and wheat, and flour, and lumber rapidly falling? Our debts remain undiminished, and the interest on them accumulating; our credit abroad is nearly extinguished, and at home unrestored; they who had money have sent it beyond the reach of our laws, and scarcely any man can borrow of his neighbour. Nay, does not experience also tell us that it is as difficult to pay as to borrow; that even our houses and lands cannot command money; that law-suits and usurious contracts abound; that our farms fall on executions for less than half their value; and that distress in various forms and in various ways is approaching fast to the doors of our best citizens?

These things have been gradually coming upon us ever since the peace; they have been perceived and proclaimed, but the universal rage and pursuit of private gain conspired, with other causes, to prevent any proper efforts being made to meliorate our condition by due attention to our national affairs, until the late Convention was convened for that purpose. From the result of their deliberations, the States expected to derive much good, and should they be disappointed, it will probably be not less their misfortune than their fault. That Convention was in general composed of excellent and tried men—men who had become conspicuous for their wisdom and public services, and whose names and characters will be venerated by posterity. Generous and candid minds cannot perceive without pain the illiberal manner in which some have taken the liberty to treat them, nor forbear to impute it to impure and improper motives. Zeal for public good, like zeal for religion, may sometimes carry men beyond the bounds of reason, but it is not conceivable that on this occasion it should find means so to inebriate any *candid* American as to make him forget what he owed to truth and to decency, or induce him either to believe or to say that the almost unanimous advice of the Convention proceeded from a wicked combination and conspiracy against the liberties of their country. This is not the temper with which we should receive and consider their recommendations, nor the treatment that would be worthy either of us or of them. Let us continue careful, therefore, that facts do not warrant historians to tell future generations that envy, malice, and uncharitableness pursued our patriotic benefactors to their graves, and that not even pre-eminence in virtue, nor lives devoted to the public, could shield them from obloquy and detraction. On the contrary, let our bosoms always retain a sufficient degree of honest indignation to disappoint and discourage those who expect our thanks or applause for calumniating our most faithful and meritorious friends. The Convention concurred in opinion with the people, that a national government, competent to every national object, was indispensably necessary ; and it was as plain to them as it now is to all America, that the present Confederation does not provide for such a government. These points being agreed, they proceeded to consider how and in what manner such a government could be formed, as, on the one hand, should be sufficienty energetic to raise us from our prostrate and distressed situation, and, on the other, be perfectly consistent with the liberties of the people of every State. Like men to whom the experience of other ages and countries had taught wisdom, they not only determined that it should be erected by, and depend on, the people, but, remembering the many instances in which governments vested solely in one man, or one body of men, had degenerated into tyrannies, they judged it most prudent that the three great branches of power should be committed to different hands, and therefore that the executive should be separated from the legislative, and the judicial from both. Thus far the propriety of their work is easily seen and understood, and therefore is thus far almost universally approved ; for no one man or thing under the sun ever yet pleased everybody.

The next question was, what particular powers should be given to these three branches. Here the different views and interests of the different States, as well as the different abstract opinions of their members on such points, interposed many difficulties.

Here the business became complicated, and presented a wide field for investigation—too wide for every eye to take a quick and comprehensive view of it.

It is said that " in a multitude of counsellors there is safety," because, in the first place, there is greater security for probity ; and in the next, if every member cast in only his mite of information and argument, their joint stock of both will thereby be greater than the stock possessed by any one single man out-of-doors. Gentlemen out-of-doors, therefore, should not be hasty in condemning a system which probably rests on more good reasons than they are aware of, especially when formed under such advantages, and recommended by so many men of distinguished worth and abilities.

The difficulties before mentioned occupied the Convention a long time ; and it was not without mutual concessions that they were at last surmounted. These concessions serve to explain to us the reason why some parts of the system please in some States which displease in others, and why many of the objections which have been made to it are so contradictory and inconsistent with one another. It does great credit to the temper and talents of the Convention that they were able so to reconcile the different views and interests of the different States, and the clashing opinions of their members, as to unite with such singular and almost perfect unanimity in any plan whatever on a subject so intricate and perplexed. It shows that it must have been thoroughly discussed and understood ; and probably if the com-

munity at large had the same lights and reasons
before them they would, if equally candid and uninfluenced, be equally unanimous.

It would be arduous, and indeed impossible, to com-
prise within the limits of this address a full discussion
of every part of the plan. Such a task would require
a volume ; and few men have leisure or inclination to
read volumes on any subject. The objections made
to it are almost without number, and many of them
without reason. Some of them are real and honest,
and others merely ostensible. There are friends to
union and a national government who have serious
doubts, who wish to be informed and to be convinced ;
and there are others who, neither wishing for union
nor any national government at all, will oppose and
object to any plan that can be contrived.

We are told, among other strange things, that the
liberty of the press is left insecure by the proposed
Constitution ; and yet that Constitution says neither
more nor less about it than the constitution of the
State of New York does. We are told that it deprives us of trial by jury ; whereas the fact is, that it
expressly secures it in certain cases, and takes it away
in none. It is absurd to construe the silence of this,
or of our own constitution, relative to a great number of our rights, into a total extinction of them.
Silence and blank paper neither grant nor take
away anything. Complaints are also made that the
proposed Constitution is not accompanied by a bill
of rights ; and yet they who make the complaints
know, and are content, that no bill of rights accom-

panied the constitution of this State. In days and centuries when monarchs and their subjects were frequently disputing about prerogative and privileges, the latter then found it necessary, as it were, to run out the line between them, and oblige the former to admit, by solemn acts, called bills of rights, that certain enumerated rights belonged to the people, and were not comprehended in the royal prerogative. But, thank God, we have no such disputes ; we have no monarchs to contend with or demand admissions from. The proposed government is to be the government of the people ; all its officers are to be their officers, and to exercise no rights but such as the people commit to them. The Constitution serves only to point out that part of the people's business which they think proper by it to refer to the management of persons therein designated ; those persons are to receive that business to manage, not for themselves and as their own, but as agents and overseers for the people, to whom they are constantly responsible, and by whom only they are to be appointed.

But the design of this address is not to investigate the merits of the plan, nor of the objections made to it. They who seriously contemplate the present state of our affairs will be convinced that other considerations, of at least equal importance demand their attention. Let it be admitted that this plan, like everything else devised by man, has its imperfections. That it does not please everybody, is certain ; and there is little reason to expect one that will. It is a question of great moment to you, whether the probability of our being able seasonably to obtain a better, is such as to render it prudent or desirable to reject this and run the risk. Candidly to consider this question, is the design of this address.

As the importance of this question must be obvious to every man, whatever his private opinions may be, it becomes us all to treat it in that calm and temperate manner which a subject so deeply interesting to the future welfare of our country and propriety requires. Let us therefore, as much as possible, repress and compose that irritation in our minds which too warm disputes about it may have excited. Let us endeavour to forget that this or that man is on this or that side ; and that we ourselves, perhaps without sufficient reflection, have classed ourselves with one or the other party. Let us remember that this is not a matter that only touches our local parties, but as one so great, so general, and so extensive, in its future consequence to America, that, for our deciding upon it according to the best of our unbiased judgment, we must be highly responsible both here and hereafter.

The question now before us naturally leads to three inquiries :

1. Whether it is probable that a better plan can be obtained.

2. Whether, if attainable, it is likely to be in season.

3. What would be our situation if, after rejecting this, all our efforts to obtain a better should prove fruitless.

The men who formed this plan are Americans, who

had long deserved and enjoyed our confidence, and who are as much interested in having a good government as any of us are or can be. They were appointed to that business at a time when the States had become very sensible of the derangement of our national affairs and of the impossibility of retrieving them under the existing Confederation. Although well persuaded that nothing but a good national government could oppose and divert the tide of evils that were flowing in upon us, yet those gentlemen met in Convention with minds perfectly unprejudiced in favor of any particular plan. The minds of their constituents were at that time equally cool and dispassionate. All agreed in the necessity of doing something; but no one ventured to say decidedly what precisely ought to be done. Opinions were then fluctuating and unfixed; and whatever might have been the wishes of a few individuals, yet while the Convention deliberated the people remained in quiet suspense. Neither wedded to favorite systems of their own, nor influenced by popular ones abroad, the members were more desirous to receive light from, than to impress their private sentiments on, one another.

These circumstances naturally opened the door to that spirit of candour, of calm inquiry, of mutual accommodation, and mutual respect which entered into the Convention with them and regulated their debates and proceedings.

The impossibility of agreeing upon any plan, that would exactly quadrate with the local policy and objects of every State, soon became evident; and they wisely thought it better mutually to coincide and accommodate, and in that way to fashion their system as much as possible by the circumstances and wishes of the different States, than by pertinaciously adhering each to his own ideas, oblige the Convention to rise without doing anything. They were sensible that obstacles, arising from local circumstances, would not cease while those circumstances continued to exist; and, so far as those circumstances depended on differences of climate, productions, and commerce, that no change was to be expected. They were likewise sensible that, on a subject so comprehensive and involving such a variety of points and questions, the most able, the most candid, and the most honest men will differ in opinion. The same proposition seldom strikes many minds in exactly the same point of light. Different habits of thinking, different degrees and modes of education, different prejudices and opinions, early formed and long entertained, conspire, with a multitude of other circumstances, to produce among men a diversity and contrariety of opinions on questions of difficulty. Liberality, therefore, as well as prudence, induced them to treat each other's opinions with tenderness, to argue without asperity, and to endeavour to convince the judgment without hurting the feelings of each other. Although many weeks were passed in these discussions, some points remained on which a unison of opinions could not be effected. Here, again, that same happy disposition to unite and conciliate induced them to meet each other ; and enabled them, by mutual concessions, finally to complete and agree to the plan they have recommended, and that, too, with a degree of unanimity which, considering the variety of discordant views and ideas they had to reconcile, is really astonishing.

They tell us, very honestly, that this plan is the result of accommodation. They do not hold it up as the best of all possible ones, but only as the best which they could unite in and agree to. If such men, appointed and meeting under such auspicious circumstances, and so sincerely disposed to conciliation, could go no farther in their endeavours to please every State and every body, what reason have we, at present, to expect any system that would give more general satisfaction ?

Suppose this plan to be rejected, what measures would you propose for obtaining a better ? Some will answer : " Let us appoint another Convention ; and, as everything has been said and written that can well be said and written on the subject, they will be better informed than the former one was, and consequently be better able to make and agree upon a more eligible one."

This reasoning is fair, and, as far as it goes, has weight ; but it nevertheless takes one thing for granted which appears very doubtful ; for, although the new Convention might have more information, and perhaps equal abilities, yet it does not from thence follow that they would be equally disposed to agree. The contrary of this position is most probable. You must have observed that the same temper and equanimity which prevailed among the people on former occasions no longer exist. We have unhappily become divided into parties, and this important subject has been handled with such indiscreet and offensive acrimony, and with so many little unhandsome artifices and misrepresentations, that pernicious heats and animosities have been kindled, and spread their flames far and wide among us. When, therefore, it becomes a question who shall be deputed to the new Convention, we cannot flatter ourselves that the talents and integrity of the candidates will determine who shall be elected. Federal electors will vote for federal deputies, and anti-federal electors for anti-federal ones. Nor will either party prefer the most moderate of their adherents ; for, as the most staunch and active partisans will be the most popular, so the men most willing and able to carry points, to oppose and divide and embarrass their opponents, will be chosen. A Convention formed at such a season, and of such men, would be too exact an epitome of the great body that named them. The same party views, the same propensity to opposition, the same distrusts and jealousies, and the same unaccommodating spirit which prevail without, would be concentrated and ferment with still greater violence within. Each deputy would recollect who sent him, and why he was sent, and be too apt to consider himself bound in honour to contend and act vigorously under the standard of his party, and not to hazard their displeasure by preferring compromise to victory. As vice does not sow the seed of virtue, so neither does passion cultivate the fruits of reason. Suspicion and resentment create no disposition to conciliate, nor do they infuse a desire of making partial and personal objects bend to general union and common good. The utmost efforts of that excellent disposition were necessary to enable the late Convention to perform their task ; and although contrary causes sometimes operate similar effects, yet to expect that discord and animosity should produce the fruits of confidence and agreement, is to expect " grapes from thorns and figs from thistles."

The States of Georgia, Delaware, Jersey, and Connecticut have adopted the present plan with unexampled unanimity. They are content with it as it is ; and consequently their deputies, being apprised of the sentiments of their constituents, will be little inclined to make alterations, and cannot be otherwise than averse to changes which they have no reason to think would be acceptable to their people. Some other States, though less unanimous, have nevertheless adopted it by very respectable majorities, and for reasons so evidently cogent that even the minority in one of them have nobly pledged themselves for its promotion and support. From these circumstances the new Convention would derive and experience difficulties unknown to the former. Nor are these the only additional difficulties they would have to encounter. Few are ignorant that there has lately sprung up a set of politicians who teach, and profess to believe, that the extent of our nation is too

with their policy or interests, cannot fail to wish that we may continue a weak and a divided people.

These considerations merit much attention ; and candid men will judge how far they render it probable that a new Convention would be able either to agree in a better plan, or, with tolerable unanimity, in any plan at all. Any plan, forcibly carried by a slender majority, must expect numerous opponents among the people, who, especially in their present temper, would be more inclined to reject than adopt any system so made and carried. We should, in such a case, again see the press teeming with publications for and against it ; for, as the minority would take pains to justify their dissent, so would the majority be industrious to display the wisdom of their proceeding. Hence new divisions, new parties, and new distractions would ensue ; and no one can foresee or conjecture when or how they would terminate.

Let those who are sanguine in their expectations of a better plan from a new Convention, also reflect on the delays and risks to which it would expose us. Let them consider whether we ought, by continuing much longer in our present humiliating condition, to give other nations further time to perfect their restrictive systems of commerce, reconcile their own people to them, and to fence, and guard, and strengthen them by all those regulations and contrivances in which a jealous policy is ever fruitful. Let them consider whether we ought to give further opportunities to discord to alienate the hearts of our citizens from one another, and thereby encourage

new Cromwells to bold exploits. Are we certain that
our foreign creditors will continue patient, and ready
to proportion their forbearance to our delays? Are
we sure that our distresses, dissensions, and weakness
will neither invite hostility nor insult? If they should,
how ill prepared shall we be for defence, without
union, without government, without money, and without credit!

It seems necessary to remind you that some time
must yet elapse before all the States will have decided
on the present plan. If they reject it, some time
must also pass before the measure of a new Convention can be brought about and generally agreed to.
A further space of time will then be requisite to elect
their deputies, and send them on to Convention.
What time they may expend, when met, cannot be
divined; and it is equally uncertain how much time
the several States may take to deliberate and decide
on any plan they may recommend. If adopted, still
a further space of time will be necessary to organize
and set it in motion. In the meantime, our affairs
are daily going from bad to worse; and it is not rash
to say that our distresses are accumulating like com-
pound interest.

But if, for reasons already mentioned, and others
that we cannot now perceive, the new Convention,
instead of producing a better plan, should give us
only a history of our disputes, or should offer us one
still less pleasing than the present, where should we
be? Then the old Confederation has done its best,
and cannot help us; and is now so relaxed and feeble,

that, in all probability, it would not survive so violent a shock.

Then "To your tents, O Israel!" would be the word. Then every band of union would be severed. Then every State would be a little nation, jealous of its neighbour, and anxious to strengthen itself, by foreign alliances, against its former friends. Then farewell to fraternal affection, unsuspecting intercourse, and mutual participation in commerce, navigation, and citizenship. Then would rise mutual restrictions and fears, mutual garrisons and standing armies, and all those dreadful evils which for so many ages plagued England, Scotland, Wales, and Ireland, while they continued disunited, and were played off against each other.

Consider, my fellow-citizens, what you are about before it is too late ; consider what in such an event would be your particular case. You know the geography of your State, and the consequences of your local position. Jersey and Connecticut, to whom your impost laws have been unkind—Jersey and Connecticut, who have adopted the present plan and expect much good from it, will impute its miscarriage and all the consequent evils to you. They now consider your opposition as dictated more by your fondness for your impost, than for those rights to which they have never been behind you in attachment. They cannot, they will not, love you ; they border upon you and are your neighbours, but you will soon cease to regard their neighbourhood as a blessing. You have but one port or outlet to your commerce, and how you are to keep that outlet free and uninterrupted merits consideration. What advantages Vermont, in combination with others, might take of you, may easily be conjectured; nor will you be at a loss to perceive how much reason the people of Long Island, whom you cannot protect, have to deprecate being constantly exposed to the depredations of every invader.

These are short hints; they ought not to be more developed; you can easily in your own minds dilate and trace them through all their relative circumstances and connections. Pause then for a moment and reflect whether the matters you are disputing about are of sufficient moment to justify your running such extravagant risks. Reflect that the present plan comes recommended to you by men and fellow-citizens who have given you the highest proofs that men can give, of their justice, their love of liberty and their country, of their prudence, of their application, and of their talents. They tell you it is the best that they could form, and that in their opinion, it is necessary to redeem you from those calamities which already begin to be heavy upon us all. You find that not only those men, but others of similar characters, and of whom you have also had very ample experience, advise you to adopt it. You find that whole States concur in the sentiment, and among them are your next neighbours, both of whom have shed much blood in the cause of liberty, and have manifested as strong and constant a predilection for a free republican government as any States in the Union, and perhaps in the world. They perceive not those latent mischiefs in it with which some double-sighted politicians endeavour to alarm you. You cannot but be sensible that this plan or Constitution will always be in the hands and power of the people, and that if on experiment it should be found defective or incompetent, they may either remedy its defects, or substitute another in its room. The objectionable parts of it are certainly very questionable, for otherwise there would not be such a contrariety of opinions about them. Experience will better determine such questions than theoretical arguments, and so far as the danger of abuses is urged against the institution of a government, remember that a power to do good always involves a power to do harm. We must, in the business of government as well as in all other business, have some degree of confidence, as well as a great degree of caution. Who, on a sick-bed, would refuse medicines from a physician merely because it is as much in his power to administer deadly poisons as salutary remedies?

You cannot be certain that by rejecting the proposed plan you would not place yourselves in a very awkward situation. Suppose nine States should nevertheless adopt it, would you not in that case be obliged either to separate from the Union or rescind your dissent? The first would not be eligible, nor could the latter be pleasant. A mere hint is sufficient on this topic. You cannot but be aware of the consequences.

Consider, then, how weighty and how many considerations advise and persuade the people of America to remain in the safe and easy path of union; to continue to move and act, as they hitherto have done, as a band of brothers ; and to have confidence in themselves and in one another ; and, since all cannot see with the same eyes, at least to give the proposed Constitution a fair trial, and to mend it as time, occasion, and experience may dictate. It would little become us to verify the predictions of those who ventured to prophesy that peace, instead of blessing us with happiness and tranquillity, would serve only as the signal for factions, discord, and civil contentions to rage in our land, and overwhelm it with misery and distress.

Let us all be mindful that the cause of freedom depends on the use we make of the singular opportunities we enjoy of governing ourselves wisely ; for, if the event should prove that the people of this country either cannot or will not govern themselves, who will hereafter be advocates for systems which, however charming in theory and prospect, are not reducible to practice ? If the people of our nation, instead of consenting to be governed by laws of their own making and rulers of their own choosing, should let licentiousness, disorder, and confusion reign over them, the minds of men everywhere will insensibly become alienated from republican forms, and prepared to prefer and acquiesce in governments which, though less friendly to liberty, afford more peace and security.

Receive this address with the same candour with which it is written ; and may the spirit of wisdom and patriotism direct and distinguish your councils and your conduct.

A CITIZEN OF NEW YORK.

GENERAL WASHINGTON TO JAY.

MOUNT VERNON, Jan. 20th, 1788.

DEAR SIR:

Your goodness upon a former occasion, accompanied with assurances of forwarding any dispatches I might have for Europe in future, is the cause of my troubling you with the letters herewith sent.

The one for the Marquis de la Fayette contains a vocabulary of the Delaware and Shawanese languages, for the Empress of Russia. I beg leave therefore to recommend it to your particular care. To send it by post from Havre I am informed would be expensive. To trust it to chance might be still worse. I leave it therefore to your own judgment to convey it and the other letters in such a manner as you shall think it best and least expensive.

We are locked fast in ice, expecting, as soon as the weather breaks, to hear that the Conventions of Connecticut and Massachusetts have resolved on with respect to the proposed Government.—The decisions of New York and Virginia on this important subject are more problematical than any others; yet, with respect to the latter, little doubt remains in my mind of the adoption of it. In this however I may be mistaken, for going seldom from home and seeing few, except travellers, my conjectures may be erroneous. North Carolina it seems has fixed a late period for the meeting of its Convention; hence, it is not unfair to infer, they mean to take the tone from this State.—With much concern I have heard that Mrs. Jay and you have been indisposed. I hope both of you are perfectly restored. The best wishes, and affectionate regards of Mrs. Washington and myself are presented, and I am, Dear Sir, with much truth and sincerity,

Your most obedient and most humble Servant,

G. WASHINGTON.

WILLIAM BINGHAM TO JAY.

PHILADELPHIA, Jan. 29, 1788.

DEAR SIR:

I have seen various detached numbers of a periodical publication under the title of the *Federalist*, which have much pleased me, as the author has treated the subject in a strong masterly manner.

I have heard that it is about to be republished in the form of a pamphlet, in which case I shall be much indebted to you for a copy.

The opposition to the new Government in this State, which was confined to a few factious characters, is daily growing weaker, and it is evident little impression has been made in favor of their views, by all their laborious productions.

The friends to the Federal Constitution are much alarmed at a report that your Legislature are averse to calling a Convention of the people, to ratify it.

I am happy to find that a Minister has arrived from the Court of Versailles and that he has brought several of his family. If they can be reconciled to our simple Republican manners, they may prove valuable accessions to your society at New York.

Mrs. Bingham joins me in respectful compliments to Mrs. Jay. Believe me to be with sincere esteem,

Dear Sir,

Yours,

WM. BINGHAM.

JAY TO GENERAL WASHINGTON.

NEW YORK, 3 February, 1788.

DER SIR:

An English gentleman having been so obliging as to procure for me some rhubarb seed, which from the account he gives of it there is reason to believe it of the best kind, I take the liberty of sending you a little parcel of it. If the seed proves good, you will soon be able to determine whether it will flourish in your climate, and in what soil and situation best. . . .

Our Legislature has agreed to call a Convention. The opponents to the proposed Constitution are nevertheless numerous and indefatigable, but as the balance of abilities and property is against them, it is reasonable to expect that they will lose ground as the people become better informed.

I am therefore inclined to think that the Constitution will be adopted in this State, especially if our eastern neighbours should generally come into the measure. Our accounts, or rather calculations from Massachusetts are favourable but not decisive.

Your favour of the 20th ult. was delivered to me this morning. The letters which accompanied it shall be conveyed by the most early and proper opportunities that may offer. Are you apprised that all American letters, indeed most others, which pass through the French post-office are opened ? It is the fact ; while in that country I never received a single one from the office which did not bear marks of inspection.

The influence of Massachusetts on the one hand and of Virginia on the other render their conduct on the present occasion very interesting. I am happy that we have as yet no reason to despair of either. Connecticut has decided, and the gazettes tell us that Georgia has done the same.

A few months more will decide all questions respecting the adoption of the proposed Constitution. I sincerely wish it may take place, though less from an idea that it will fully realize the sanguine expectations of many of its friends, than because it establishes some great points, and smooths the way for a system more adequate to our national objects. Its reputation and success will I think greatly depend on the manner in which it may first be organized and administered, but on this head we have no reason to despond. Mrs. Jay's health, which was a little deranged by her too kind attendance on me while sick, is again pretty well established. For my own part I have much reason to be thankful, for although a constant pain in my left side continues to give me some but no great trouble, yet I am happy that my long and severe illness has left me nothing more to complain of. We are both obliged by your kind attention and assure you and Mrs. Washington of our best wishes. I am, with the greatest respect and esteem, dear sir, your affectionate and humble servant,

JOHN JAY.

GENERAL WASHINGTON TO JAY.

MOUNT VERNON, March 3d. 1788.

DEAR SIR:

In acknowledging the receipt of your obliging favor of the 3d ult. permit me to thank you for the rhubarb seed which accompanied it; to the growth of which, if good, a fair trial shall be given.

I was not unapprised of the treatment of letters in the Post Office of France; but am not less obliged by the friendly hint you have given me respecting this matter.   Mine contain nothing which will be injurious to the receiver, if the contents of them are inspected.

The decision of Massachusetts would have been more influencial had the majority been greater, and the ratification unaccompanied by the recommendatory Act.   As it stands however, the blow is severely felt by the anti-federalists in the equivocal States.   This adoption added to the five States which have gone before it and to the favorable decision of the three which is likely to follow next, will (as there can be little doubt of Rhode Island following the example of her eastern brethren) be too powerful, I conceive, for locality and sophistry to combat.

On this day our elections of delegates to the Convention of this State, commences.—They will progress as our court days in this month shall arrive, and form an interesting epoch in our annals.

After the choice is made, the probable decision on the proposed Constitution (from the character of the members) can with more ease be conjectured; for myself I have never entertained much doubt of its adoption, tho' I am incompetent to judge, never having been six miles beyond the limits of my own farm since my return from Philadelphia, and receive information of the sentiments of the people from visitors only.[1]

It gives me much pleasure to hear that Mrs. Jay's health is restored, and that you have the slight remains only of your long and painful indisposition.   A little time and more moderate weather (if it should ever arrive, for at present there is no appearance of it) will, it is to be hoped, set you quite right again.   In wishes for this purpose, and in offer

---

[1] Speaking for New York, Jay wrote briefly, April 20th, in reply to the above from Washington: "The Constitution still continues to cause great party zeal and ferment among us, and the opposition is yet so formidable that the issue appears problematical."   This was before the State convention met.

ing compliments to Mrs. Jay, I am joined by Mrs. Washington. With sentiments of the highest esteem and regard,
I am, Dear Sir,
Yr. most obedient and affectionate Servant,
G. WASHINGTON.

JAY TO WILLIAM BINGHAM.

NEW YORK, 24 March, 1788.

DEAR SIR:

Agreable to your request and my promise, I have now the pleasure of sending you herewith enclosed the first volume of the *Fœderalist ;* as soon as the other is published it shall also be forwarded to you. The people of this State are turning their attention to the election of persons to represent them in the ensuing Convention ; they continue much divided in sentiment respecting the proposed Constitution, and it is probable that these elections will be the most contested of any we have had since the Revolution. Be pleased to present Mrs. Jay's and my compliments to Mrs. Bingham and believe me to be, dear sir, your affectionate and humble servant, JOHN JAY.

GENERAL WASHINGTON TO JAY.

MOUNT VERNON, April 15th, 1788.

DEAR SIR:

Your card of the 24th ult. and first vol. of the *Fœderalist* came safe, for which I pray you to accept my thanks, and assurances of the sincere esteem and regard with which I am,
Dear Sir,
Your most obedient and affectionate humble Servant,
G. WASHINGTON.

JAY TO THOMAS JEFFERSON.

New York, 24th April, 1788.

Dear Sir :

Since the 3d November last I have been honoured with your favours of the 19th, 22d, and 24th September, 8th and 27th October, 3d and 7th November, 21st and 31st December, and 5th February last, all of which have been laid before Congress ; but they have given me no orders respecting the subjects of them.

The state of my health was for a long time such as to oblige me to omit some good opportunities of writing to you fully. It is not yet perfectly re-established but I am nevertheless so far recovered as to have reason to hope that the approaching season will moderate, if not wholly remove any remaining complaints. Since the rising of the late convention at Philadelphia Congress has done but little business, and I apprehend that will continue to be the case while the fate of the proposed Constitution remains undecided. You will perceive from the public papers that it has given occasion to heats and parties in several of the States.

The late commercial arrangements of France relative to the United States will tend to render the connection between the two countries more intimate. They bear marks of wisdom and liberality and cannot fail of being very acceptable. It is to be regretted that the mercantile people in France oppose a system which certainly is calculated to bind the two nations together, and from which both would eventually derive commercial as well as political advantages. It appears to me that France has not a single ally in Europe on which she can fully depend, and it doubtless would be wise in her to endeavour so to blend her interests with ours as if possible to render them indissoluble. This in my opinion can only be done by giving us all the privileges of Frenchmen, and accepting in return all the privileges of Americans. If they could bring themselves to adopt this idea, their schemes of policy respecting us would be greatly simplified. But the spirit of monopoly and exclusion has prevailed in Europe too long to be done away with at once, and however enlightened the present age may appear when compared with former ones, yet whenever ancient prejudices are touched we find that we only have light enough to see our want of more. Toleration in commerce like toleration in religion gains ground, it is true; but I am not sanguine in my expectations that either will soon take place in their due extent.

I have the honour to be with great respect and esteem, dear sir,

Your most obedient and very humble servant,

JOHN JAY.

JAY TO THE MARQUIS DE LAFAYETTE.

NEW YORK, 26th April, 1788.

DEAR SIR:

Since last fall I have enjoyed so little health that it has not been in my power to be as punctual in my correspondences as I wished. I have had the pleasure of receiving and communicating to Congress your favour of the 15th October last. The apprehensions you then entertained have been removed by the subsequent estrangements between France and Britain. For my part I wish they may continue at peace, as well because war always brings distress upon great numbers as because the present state of our affairs is not accommodated to the circumstances and consequences which such a war would produce. You have doubtless seen the plan of government recommended by the late convention at Philadelphia. Six States have adopted it; what the others will do is not certain. It is the subject of animated discussions among the people. In this State the opposition is considerable. A few months more will decide the great question.

The late commercial regulations of France relative to this country are certainly very acceptable, but my private opinion is that much more is yet to be done before the interests of France and America will be properly provided for. I fear the prejudices and partial views of your people will restrain the court from going all the lengths which true policy seems to dictate; nor can I answer for opinions on this side of the water. I will tell you very candidly what I think on the subject; it is this—that your people should have all the commercial privileges of American citizens, and our people all the commercial privileges of French subjects. I have not at present health or leisure to explain the reasons on which this opinion rests, nor is it necessary, for I am persuaded

that few of them will escape your observation.   Mr.
Jefferson's letters mention your constant attention
and attachment to the interests of this country, and
how much he and we are indebted to your friendly
aid and exertions.

With very sincere esteem and regard, I have the
honour to be, dear sir, your most obedient and humble servant,   JOHN JAY.

GRANVILLE SHARP TO THE PRESIDENT,[1] VICE-PRESIDENT,
AND TREASURER OF THE SOCIETY ESTABLISHED IN
NEW YORK FOR THE MANUMISSION OF SLAVES.

LONDON, May 1, 1788.

GENTLEMEN:

We received your favour of the 28th of Feby. last which
afforded us much satisfaction, and we have now the pleasure
of informing you that our cause is daily gaining ground in
this Country.   Our opponents have long urged the supposed incapacity of the black people to enjoy the blessings
of freedom and civilization, as a plea for Slavery; but they
now seem to be sensible of its futility.—Their Arguments,
or rather insinuations, have lately been more particularly
confined to the impolicy of abolishing the Slave trade, on
which they would have it believed that the existance of the
Plantations and the consequent revenue of this Kingdom
essentially depends.   On the other hand it is contended,
and we trust on much better authority, that neither injury
to the Plantations nor defalcation of revenue would eventually ensue.—

To the doubts industriously suggested by some who are
interested in favouring the former Opinion we may partly

[1] To Jay as President of the Society.   See his letters to the French Society,
June, 1788, and to Lafayette and Sharp, September 1st following.

attribute the prayers of some of the numerous petitions which have already been presented to the House of Commons requesting the mere regulation of a Commerce which no possible modification can rectify. But we are enclined to believe that many of them were so expressed from inadvertance, or the want of a thorough knowledge of the subject.

Remembering the declarations of the American Congress so frequently repeated during the contention with Britain we could not but flatter ourselves that the late Convention would have produced more unequivocal proofs of a regard to consistency of character than an absolute prohibition of Federal Government from complying with the acknowledged obligations of humanity and justice, for the term of twenty-one years.

What may be the event of the Parliamentary discussion of this important business is yet uncertain at present; the prospect is encouraging and though we are aware how liable those expectations are to fail, which depend upon simple and honest principles when opposed by the intrigues of wealth and power, yet we can scarcely avoid flattering ourselves with the hope arising from the number and respectability of the patrons of this undertaking that it will at length be successful.—Our adversaries, who had till lately, been remarkably quiet, probably because they held our endeavours in contempt, have now taken the alarm, and use every artifice of Sophistry and misrepresentation to defeat our purpose. One of their most plausible Allegations is that, if the British Nation should lay down the trade, other Nations will take it up; and therefore that the situation of the Africans would not be improved, though England would sustain a considerable loss. The reply is obvious; that this Nation ought to do what is right, let others do as they please; and we have a strong persuasion that, on the whole, the African Trade is a losing one to this

Country. It is however our fervent wish, that an Appeal might be made to the humanity of other Countries and Governments; and for this purpose we some time ago commenced a Correspondence in France. A Society is now forming there, whose object it will be to diffuse the knowledge of this traffic and shew it in its true colours.—It may perhaps be in your power to assist our views in thus extending the sphere of action. The Privy Council is now engaged in enquiries into the Slave Trade, and the Colonial Slavery; and we expect the Subject will shortly be investigated in Parliament. The University of Cambridge has expressed its sense of it, in a very forcible Petition to the House of Commons, and the Clergy of the established Church in many other parts have equally testified their zeal in the Common Cause. Many Counties, Cities, and Towns have sent up Petitions. Amongst the Cities we have the satisfaction to enumerate Bristol, one capital Seat of the African Trade. The Presbyterians, Independants, and Baptists have petitioned collectively; and the religious Society called Quakers have repeated their applications on the occasion. More petitions are expected from various quarters. The attempt to retrieve the National Character and assert the common rights of our Nature has awakened the attention, and excited the good wishes of people of all descriptions. It was only necessary that the torch of truth should be lighted to flash conviction in the face of humanity. But Avarice is wilfully blind. One solitary petition is come up against us from the town of *Liverpool;* yet we are not without well wishers and even Advocates in that Summary of Slave traders. We shall herewith send you some copies of this committee's report to our Society at large, as also such other of the tracts lately published here on the Subject as we can collect; some of these you may think it proper to republish and we shall be obliged by any returns of the same kind you may be able to make. Referring you to our report for further information respecting our proceeedings we have only to repeat our sincere wishes that yours may meet with the success they deserve. I am, with great respect, Gentlemen,

Your most obedient and most humble Servant,

GRANVILLE SHARP,

Chairman of the Committee.

GENERAL WASHINGTON TO JAY.

MOUNT VERNON, May 17th, 1788.

DEAR SIR:

I am indebted to you for your favors of the 20th and 24th ult. and thank you for your care of my foreign letters. —I do the same for the pamphlet you were so obliging as to send me.—The good sense, forceable observations, temper and moderation with which it is written cannot fail, I should think, of making a serious impression even upon the antifœderal mind where it is not under the influence of such local views as will yield to no arguments—no proofs.

Could you conveniently, furnish me with another of these pamphlets I would thank you, having sent the last to a friend of mine.

Since the elections in this State little doubt is entertained of the adoption of the proposed Constitution with us (if no mistake has been made with respect to the sentiments of the Kentucky members).—The opponents to it I am informed are *now* also of this opinion.—Their grand manœuvres were exhibited at the elections, and some of them, if report be true, were not much to their credit.—Failing in their attempt to exclude the friends to the new Government from the Convention, and baffled in their exertions to effect an adjournment in Maryland, they have become more passive *of late.* Should South Carolina (now in session) decide favourably, and the government thereby (nine States having acceded) get in motion, I can scarcely conceive that any one of the remainder, or all of them together, were they to converse for the purpose of deliberation, would (separated from each other as they then would be in a geographical point of view) incline to withdraw from the union with the other nine.

Mrs. Washington unites with me in compliments and good wishes for you and Mrs. Jay, and with sentiments of very great esteem and regard

      I am, Dear Sir,

   Yr. most obedient and affectionate servant,

                G. WASHINGTON.

JAY TO TENCH COXE.

NEWYORK, 18th May, 1788.

SIR:

Your favour of the 8th instant was delivered to me this morning.

It is much to the honour of Pennsylvania that the cause of humanity has in so many instances been patronized and asserted by her citizens. The situation of our unfortunate countrymen in captivity at Algiers is greatly to be lamented. Congress has not been unmindful of them. Everything has been done and is doing that circumstances would permit. That business is now under the direction of Mr. Jefferson who is very able as well as willing to conduct it properly. There is reason to fear that every measure that may now be taken *publicly* for their redemption will enhance the price of it, and increase the difficulties which at present exist. In my opinion nothing better can be done than to leave the matter entirely to Mr. Jefferson, and *privately* to remit to him whatever monies may be raised for the purpose of their relief or redemption. You will find enclosed a state of the facts you request. The impost you suggest is a measure that merits attention; a good national government may do that and many other things of essential benefit to the United States.

I have read with pleasure the late act you allude to, and wish similar measures for the restraint and abolition of slavery were passed in all the States.

I have the honour to be, sir,

Your most obedient and humble servant,

JOHN JAY.

JAY TO GENERAL WASHINGTON.

NEW YORK, 29th May, 1788.

DEAR SIR:

I was two days ago favoured with yours of the 15th inst. It gives me pleasure to find that the probability of Virginia's adopting the proposed Constitution rather increases; such an event would undoubtedly disarm the opposition. It appears by recent advices from Charleston, that we may count on South Carolina; and the New-Hampshire delegates assure me that their State will come into the measure. There is much reason to believe that the majority of the Convention of this State will be composed of anti-federal characters; but it is doubtful whether the leaders will be able to govern the party. Many in opposition are friends to union, and mean well; but their principal leaders are very far from being solicitous about the fate of the Union; they wish and mean, if possible, to reject the Constitution with as little debate and as much speed as may be. It is not, however, certain that the greater part of their party will be equally decided, or rather equally desperate.

An idea has taken air that the southern part of the State will at all events, adhere to the Union; and, if necessary to that end, seek a separation from the northern. This idea has influence on the fears of the party. I cannot find that they have as yet so looked forward to contingent events, or even to those the most probable, as to have united in or formed any system adapted to them.

With perfect respect and esteem, I am, dear sir, your affectionate and humble servant,

JOHN JAY.

JOHN VAUGHAN TO JAY.

June, 1788.

DEAR SIR:

I have perused with singular pleasure some thoughts on the Constitution addressed to the State of New York. I was expressing my sentiments to our good friend Dr. Franklin—who observed that if you was the author (as said) he thought it incumbent upon you to put your name to it—to give it additional weight at this awful crisis. I call it awful because a rejection in your State would be productive of infinite mischief. Virginia will I believe adopt. Randolph has declared highly for it in the present situation of affairs; my intelligence comes from a member of Virginia.

Let me request, Sir, that you will attend to the observation of our venerable friend. Could I presume, I could with propriety intrude my own opinion upon the occasion, I would urge it from myself, being actuated not by intemperate zeal—but by a strong impression and persuasion that you will by it add one more to the many signal services you have rendered this Country.

I remain, Dear Sir,

Your friend and adviser,

JNO. VAUGHAN.

GENERAL WASHINGTON TO JAY.

MOUNT VERNON, June 8th, 1788.

DEAR SIR:

By the last mail, I had the pleasure to receive your letter of the 29th of May, and have now the satisfaction to congratulate you on the adoption of the Constitution by the Convention of South Carolina.

I am sorry to learn there is a probability that the majority of members in the New York Convention will be anti-federalists. Still I hope that some event will turn up before they assemble, which may give a new complexion to the business. If this State should, in the intermediate time, make the ninth that shall have ratified the proposed Government, it will, I flatter myself, have its due weight. To shew that this event is now more to be expected than heretofore, I will give you a few particulars which I have from good authority and which you might not, perhaps, immediately obtain through any public channel of conveyance.

On the day appointed for the meeting of the Convention, a large proportion of the members assembled and unani_mously placed Mr. Pendleton in the chair.—Having on that and the subsequent day chosen the rest of their officers and fixed upon the mode of conducting the business, it was moved by some one of those opposed to the Constitution to debate the whole by paragraphs, without taking any question until the investigation should be completed. This was as unexpected as acceptable to the Federalists; and their ready acquiescence seems to have somewhat startled the opposition for fear they had committed themselves.

Mr. Nicholas opened the business by very ably advocating the system of representation. Mr. Henry in answer went more vaguely into the discussion of the Constitution, intimating that the Fœderal Convention had exceeded their powers and that we had been, and might be happy under the old Confederation with a few alterations. This called up Governor Randolph, who is reported to have spoken with great pathos in reply and who declared, that, since so many of the States had adopted the proposed Constitution he considered the sense of America to be already taken and that he should give his vote in favor of it without insisting previously upon amendments. Mr. Mason rose in opposition and Mr. Madison reserved himself to obviate the objections of Mr. Henry and Col. Mason the next day. Thus the matter rested when the last accounts came away.

Upon the whole, the following inferences seem to have been drawn—that Mr. Randolph's declarations will have considerable effect with those who have hitherto been wavering.

Mr. Henry and Colonel Mason took different and awkward ground, and by no means equalled the public expectations in their speeches; the former has, probably, receeded somewhat from his violent measures to coalesce with the latter, and the leaders of the opposition appear rather chagreened and hardly to be decided as to their mode of opposition.—

The *sanguine* friends to the Constitution counted upon a majority of twenty at their first meeting which number they imagine will be greatly increased; while those equally strong but more temperate in their habits of thinking speak less confidently of the greatness of the majority and express apprehensions of the arts that may yet be practised to excite alarms, particularly with the members from the western District (Kentucke). All, however, agree that the beginning has been as auspicious as could possibly have been expected. A few days will now ascertain us of the result.

With sentiments of the highest esteem and regard,

I am, Dear Sir,

Your most obedient and affectionate, humble servant,

G. WASHINGTON.

JAY TO THOMAS JEFFERSON.

OFFICE OF FOREIGN AFFAIRS,
9th June, 1788.

DEAR SIR:

By the newspapers herewith sent, you will perceive that South Carolina has adopted the proposed Constitution. The convention of this State will convene on Tuesday at Poughkeepsie, and as this city and county have elected me one of their deputies to it, I shall be absent from hence until it rises.[1] There is reason to believe that the majority of the convention are decidedly opposed to the Constitution; so that whether they will venture to reject it, or whether they will adjourn and postpone a decision on it, is uncertain.

Accounts from Virginia and New Hampshire render it probable that those States will adopt it; and, if so, it may be presumed that North Carolina and even this State will follow the example. Being exceedingly engaged in despatching a variety of matters preparatory to my going out of town, I must post-

---

[1] Jay and Hamilton were two of the six delegates elected to represent New York City and County at the State Constitutional Convention, Jay receiving all but 98 out of 2,833 votes cast.

pone the pleasure of writing more by this opportunity. With great and sincere esteem and regard, I am, dear sir,

Your most obedient and humble servant,

JOHN JAY.

EDWARD RUTLEDGE TO JAY.

[CHARLESTON] June 20, 1788.

MY DEAR FRIEND:

A gentleman for whom I have a considerable share of esteem has informed that he is on the wing for New York, and tho' I am much indisposed with a large share of fatigue that public and professional business have oppressed me with from day to day since the 12th of the last Month, I could not forgo his requesting being made known to one whose character he very much respects. He is himself a gentleman, and a Man of much worth. I shall be obliged to you for any attention you may shew him.

I hope the Friends of Federal Government may be as successful in New York, as they have been in South Carolina. We had a tedious but trifling opposition to contend with. We had prejudices to contend with and sacrifices to make. Yet they were worth making for the good old cause.— People become more and more satisfied with the adoption, and if well administered, and administered with moderation they will cherish and bless those who have offered them a Constitution which will secure to them all the Advantages that flow from good government.

Mrs. Rutledge joins me in best respects to Mrs. Jay and Henry to his young friends. I am, long have been, and ever shall be, my dear Friend,

Affectionally yours,

ED. RUTLEDGE.

JAY TO MRS. JAY.

My Dear Sally: POUGHKEEPSIE, 21 June, 1788.

A gentleman now in town, and who will set out for New York in about an hour, gives me an opportunity of writing you a few lines. The convention assembled with unusual punctuality. There are not more than two members that I recollect absent, and the house has entered on the business with great assiduity and regularity. As yet, these proceedings and debates have been temperate and inoffensive to either party. The opposition to the proposed Constitution appears formidable, though more so from numbers than other considerations. What the event will be is uncertain. For my part I do not despair on the one hand, although I see much room for apprehension on the other.

It would give me great pleasure to hear that your health has been mended by the leisure, air, and exercise which your present situation affords. Mine continues in the state it was when we parted. As Peter omitted to take leave of me, I hope he will think it but right to make amends by the number of his letters. Remember me affectionately to all the family. Adieu, my dear Sally.   Yours very sincerely,

JOHN JAY.

JAY TO THE ENGLISH ANTI-SLAVERY SOCIETY.[1]

Gentlemen :

Our society has been favoured with your letter of the 1st of May last, and are happy that efforts so

---

[1] In 1788 a society in France, and another in England, formed for promoting the abolition of slavery, opened a correspondence with the New York society

honourable to the nation are making in your country to promote the cause of justice and humanity relative to the Africans. That they who know the value of liberty, and are blessed with the enjoyment of it, ought not to subject others to slavery, is, like most other moral precepts, more generally admitted in theory than observed in practice. This will continue to be too much the case while men are impelled to action by their passions rather than their reason, and while they are more solicitous to acquire wealth than to do as they would be done by. Hence it is that India and Africa experience unmerited oppression from nations which have been long distinguished by their attachment to their civil and religious liberties, but who have expended not much less blood and treasure in violating the rights of others than in defending their own. The United States are far from being irreproachable in this respect. It undoubtedly is very inconsistent with their declarations on the subject of human rights to permit a single slave to be found within their jurisdiction, and we confess the justice of your strictures on that head.

Permit us, however, to observe, that although consequences ought not to deter us from doing what is right, yet that it is not easy to persuade men in general to act on that magnanimous and disinterested principle. It is well known that errors, either in opinion or practice, long entertained or indulged, are difficult to eradicate, and particularly so when they have become, as it were, incorporated in the

---

through its president. The above letter to the English society was from Jay's pen. See letter from Granville Sharp, May 1, 1788.

civil institutions and domestic economy of a whole people.

Prior to the great revolution, the great majority or rather the great body of our people had been so long accustomed to the practice and convenience of having slaves, that very few among them even doubted the propriety and rectitude of it. Some liberal and conscientious men had, indeed, by their conduct and writings, drawn the lawfulness of slavery into question, and they made converts to that opinion ; but the number of those converts compared with the people at large was then very inconsiderable. Their doctrines prevailed by almost insensible degrees, and was like the little lump of leaven which was put into three measures of meal : even at this day, the whole mass is far from being leavened, though we have good reason to hope and to believe that if the natural operations of truth are constantly watched and assisted, but not forced and precipitated, that end we all aim at will finally be attained in this country.

The Convention which formed and recommended the new Constitution had an arduous task to perform, especially as local interests, and in some measure local prejudices, were to be accommodated. Several of the States conceived that restraints on slavery might be too rapid to consist with their particular circumstances ; and the importance of union rendered it necessary that their wishes on that head should, in some degree, be gratified.

It gives us pleasure to inform you, that a disposition favourable to our views and wishes prevails more and more, and that it has already had an influence on our laws. When it is considered how many of the legislators in the different States are proprietors of slaves, and what opinions and prejudices they have imbibed on the subject from their infancy, a sudden and total stop to this species of oppression is not to be expected.

We will cheerfully co-operate with you in endeavouring to procure advocates for the same cause in other countries, and perfectly approve and commend your establishing a correspondence in France. It appears to have produced the desired effect; for Mons. De Varville, the secretary of a society for the like benevolent purpose at Paris, is now here, and comes instructed to establish a correspondence with us, and to collect such information as may promote our common views. He delivered to our society an extract from the minutes of your proceedings, dated 8th of April last, recommending him to our attention, and upon that occasion they passed the resolutions of which the enclosed are copies.

We are much obliged by the pamphlets enclosed with your letter, and shall constantly make such communications to you as may appear to us interesting.

By a report of the committee for superintending the school we have established in this city for the education of negro children, we find that proper attention is paid to it, and that —— scholars are now taught in it. By the laws of this State, masters may now liberate healthy slaves of a proper age without giving security that they shall not become a parish charge; and the exportation as well as importation of them is prohibited. The State has also manumitted such as became its property by confiscation ; and we have reason to expect that the maxim, that every man, of whatever colour, is to be presumed to be free until the contrary be shown, will prevail in our courts of justice. Manumissions daily become more common among us ; and the treatment which slaves in general meet with in this State is very little different from that of other servants.

I have the honour to be, gentlemen,

Your humble servant,

JOHN JAY,

President of the Society for Promoting the Manumission of Slaves.

JAY TO THE SOCIETY AT PARIS FOR THE MANUMIS-
SION OF SLAVES.

NEW YORK, June (?), 1788.

GENTLEMEN :

The society established here for promoting the manumission of slaves, etc., have lately received from Monsr. Brissot de Varville the letter which you did them the honour to write on the 29th of April last. We have their orders to assure you that the institution of a society at Paris for purposes so benevolent gives them very sincere satisfaction, and that they will most cheerfully co-operate with you in every measure that may be deemed conducive to those important ends. You will perceive from the enclosed extracts from their journal that Monsr. de Varville may expect from them all the attention and aid which is due to your recommendation and his personal character, as well as to the interesting objects of his voyage. As a further mark of respect for you and for him they have admitted him as an honorary member of the society, and we flatter ourselves you will soon receive from him such information respecting our views, proceedings, and prospects as to preclude the necessity of such detail at present.[1]

We are happy to find that a correspondence subsists between your society and the one in London ; and it gives us pleasure to reflect that the cause of humanity cannot fail to derive very essential advantages from the patronage and exertions of the enlightened and respectable characters in both kingdoms who at present advocate it.

JAY TO GENERAL WASHINGTON.

POUGHKEEPSIE, June [30th ?], 1788.

DEAR SIR :

Your obliging letter of the 8th instant found me at this place. I thank you for the interesting circumstances mentioned in it. The completion of our

---

[1] M. Jean Pierre Brissot de Varville, secretary of the Paris Manumission Society, was introduced to the members of the New York Society in the communication of April 29th, as a gentleman " who, by his Sentiments of humanity, his talents, and his unremitted zeal, has principally contributed to the institution and progress of our Society, and has now undertaken a voyage to North America. In the course of this voyage he proposes to acquire all the information possible, respecting the condition of the negroes in that part of the world, the measures taken either to manumit them or prevent their importation, the result of those measures in relation both to the cultivation of the land, and the moral character of the negroes, and in general, whatever may concern that unfortunate but interesting class of men, and may conduce to incline Governments and individuals in their favor."

convention is such as was expected. They have hitherto proceeded with singular temper and moderation, but there is no reason to think that either party has made much impression on the other. The leaders in opposition seem to have more extensive views than their adherents, and until the latter perceive that circumstance they will probably continue combined. The greater number are, I believe, averse to a vote of rejection. Some would be content with recommendatory amendments; others wish for explanatory ones to settle constructions which they think doubtful; others would not be satisfied with less than absolute and previous amendments; and I am mistaken if there be not a few who prefer a separation from the Union to any national government whatever. They suggest hints of the importance of this State, of its capacity to command terms, of the policy of its taking its own time, and fixing its own price, etc. They hint that an adjournment may be expedient, and that it might be best to see the operation of the new government before they receive it. The people, however, are gradually coming right, notwithstanding the singular pains taken to prevent it. The accession of New Hampshire does good, and that of Virginia would do more. With the greatest respect and esteem

I am, dear sir,

Your affectionate and obedient servant,

JOHN JAY.

JAY TO JOHN ADAMS.

POUGHKEEPSIE, 4th July, 1788.

I congratulate you, my dear sir, most cordially on your return to your native country, and am greatly pleased with the reception you have met with. You deserved well of your country, and I am happy to find that the acknowledgment of your services is not left solely to posterity.

Our convention is still sitting. The opposers to the Constitution have proposed many amendments. As yet we proceed with much temper and moderation. I am not without hopes of an accommodation, although my expectations of it are not very sanguine. Be pleased to present my compliments and congratulations to Mrs. Adams, and believe me to be with sincere esteem and regard,

Dear sir,

Your affectionate friend and servant,

JOHN JAY.

JAY TO MRS. JAY.

POUGHKEEPSIE, July 5, 1788.

MY DEAR SALLY:

Col. W. S. Livingston, who brought us the news of the adoption of the Constitution by Virginia, is about setting out, and I will not let him go without a few lines for you. Yesterday was a day of festivity, and both the parties united in celebrating it. Two tables, but in different houses, were spread for the convention, and the two parties mingled at each table, and the toasts (of which each had copies) were communicated by the sound of drum and accompanied by the discharge of cannon.

We shall probably be here another week. The weather has not yet become settled, and I have had but little exercise. My health, however, continues as usual, and I shall be well content if it remains as it is. I wrote to you a few days ago.

Adieu.

Yours very affectionately,

JOHN JAY.

JAY TO MRS. JAY.

POUGHKEEPSIE, 16th July, 1788.

MY DEAR SALLY:

I was yesterday favoured with your kind letter of the 7th instant. You mention having written me a letter by the preceding post, enclosing one from Peter; as yet I have received but one letter from Peter. It gives me pleasure to hear that he continues constantly employed. I hope my letter to him, in one for you, has come to hand.

Our business here goes on heavily. The issue is yet uncertain. Nor can I tell you how long we may yet remain here. The season of the year makes many of the members impatient to return. Before the end of the week it is probable that some important question will be decided.

Last night my sorrel mare was taken out of the stable, and I think it very doubtful whether I shall see her again. I am much obliged to the thief for

momentous question of a general government was to come before the people. I have seen no good apology, not even in Mr. Hazard's publication, for deviation from the old custom of permitting printers to exchange their papers by the mail. That practice was a great public convenience and gratification. If the priviledge was not from convention an original right, it had from prescription strong pretensions for continuance; especially at so interesting a period. The interruption in that mode of conveyance has not only given great concern to the friends of the Constitution, who wished the public to be possessed of every thing that might be printed on both sides of the question, but it has afforded its enemies very plausible pretext for dealing out their scandals and exciting jealousies, by inducing a belief that the suppression of intelligence at that critical juncture was a wicked trick of policy, contrived by an aristocratic junto. Now, if the Postmaster General (with whose character I am unacquainted, and therefore would not be understood to form an unfavorable opinion of his motives) has any candid advisers who conceive that he merits the public employment, they ought to counsel him to wipe away the aspersion he has incautiously brought upon a good cause. If he is unworthy of the office he holds, it would be well that the ground of a complaint, apparently so general, should be enquired into, and, if founded, redressed through the medium of a better appointment. It is a matter, in my judgement, of primary importance that the public mind should be relieved from inquietude on this subject. I know it is said that the irregularity or defect has happened accidently, in consequence of the contract for transporting the mail on horseback, instead of having it carried in the *stages*, but I must confess, I could never account, upon any satisfactory principles, for the inveterate enmity with which the Postmaster General is asserted to be actuated against that valuable institution. It has often been understood by wise politicians and enlightened patriots that giving a facility to the means of travelling for strangers and of intercourse for Citizens, was an object of Legislative concern and a circumstance highly beneficial to any Country. In England, I am told, they consider the Mail coaches as a great modern improvement in their Post Office regulations. I trust we are not too old or too proud to profit by the experience of others. In this article the materials are amply within our reach. I am taught to imagine that the horses, the vehicles, and the accomodations in America (with very little encouragement) might in a short period become as good as the same articles are to be found in any Country of Europe, and at the same time I am sorry to learn that the line of stages is at present interrupted in some parts of New England and totaly discontinued at the southward.

I mention these suggestions only as my particular thoughts on an Establishment which I had conceived to be of great importance. Your proximity to the person in question and connection with the characters in power, will enable you to decide better than I can on the validity of the allegations; and in that case, to weigh the expediency of dropping such hints as may serve to give satisfaction to the public. With sentiments of the highest consideration and regard

I am, dear Sir,

Your most obedient, affectionate, humble Servant,

G. WASHINGTON.

P. S. Since writing this letter, I have been favoured with the one which you began on the 4th and finished on the 8th instant from Poughkeepsie and thank you for the information contained therein. A little time will I hope bring the agreeable account of the ratification by your State unfettered with *previous* amendments.

Yours, &c.,

G. W———N.

GENERAL WASHINGTON TO JAY.

MOUNT VERNON, Augt. 3^d, 1788.

DEAR SIR,

The letters which you did me the favor of writing to me on the 17th and 23^d of last month from Poughkeepsie, came duly to hand and claim my particular acknowledgements.

With peculiar pleasure I now congratulate you on the success of your labours to obtain an unconditional ratification of the proposed Constitution in the Convention of your State the account of which was brought to us by the mail of yesterday. Although I could hardly conceive it possible, after ten States had adopted the Constitution, that New York, separated as it is from the remaining three, and so peculiarly divided in sentiment as it is, would withdraw herself from the Union; yet, considering the great majority which appeared to cling together in the Convention, and the decided temper of the leaders in the opposition I did not, I confess, see the means by which it was to be avoided. The exertions of those who were able to effect this great work, must have been equally arduous and meritorious. It is to be hoped that the State of North Carolina will not spend much time in deciding on this question and as to Rhode Island, its conduct hitherto has so far baffled all calculation that few are disposed to hazard a conjecture thereon.

With sentiments of the sincerest esteem and regard

I am, Dear Sir,

Your most Obedient and affectionate Servant,

G. WASHINGTON.

CIRCULAR LETTER FROM THE CONVENTION OF THE STATE OF NEW YORK, TO THE EXECUTIVES OF THE DIFFERENT STATES, TO BE LAID BEFORE THEIR RESPECTIVE LEGISLATURES.

BY JOHN JAY.[1]

SIR :

We, the members of the convention of this State, have deliberately and maturely considered the Constitution proposed for the United States.

Several articles in it appear so exceptionable to a majority of us, that nothing but the fullest confidence of obtaining a revision of them by a general convention, and an invincible reluctance to separating from our sister States, could have prevailed upon a sufficient number to ratify it, without stipulating for previous amendments.

We all unite in opinion that such a revision will be necessary to recommend it to the approbation and support of a numerous body of our constituents.

We observe that amendments have been proposed, and are anxiously desired by several of the States as well as by this, and we think it of great importance that effectual measures be immediately taken for calling a convention to meet at a period not far remote ; for we are convinced, that the apprehensions and discontents which those articles occasion cannot be removed or allowed, unless an act to provide for it be among the first that shall be passed by the new Congress.

---

[1] See " Life of Jay," vol. i., pp. 269, 270, where the authorship of this paper is credited to Jay. It was published in the New York *Daily Advertiser*, August 8, 1788.

As it is essential that an application for the purpose should be made to them by two thirds of the States, we earnestly exhort and request the legislature of your State (or Commonwealth) to take the earliest opportunity of making it. We are persuaded that a similar one will be made by our legislature at their next session; and we ardently wish and desire that the other States may concur in adopting and promoting the measure.

It cannot be necessary to observe that no government, however constructed, can operate well unless it possesses the confidence and good-will of the great body of the people; and as we desire nothing more than that the amendments proposed by this or other States be submitted to the consideration and decision of a general convention, we flatter ourselves that motives of mutual affection and conciliation will conspire with the obvious dictates of sound policy, to induce even such of the States as may be content with every article in the Constitution to gratify the reasonable desires of that numerous class of American citizens who are anxious to obtain amendments of some of them.

Our amendments will manifest that none of them originated in local views, as they are such as if acceded to must equally affect every State in the Union.

Our attachment to our sister States, and the confidence we repose in them, cannot be more forcibly demonstrated than by acceding to a government which many of us think imperfect, and devolving the power of determining whether that government shall be rendered perpetual in its present form, or altered agreeable to our wishes or a minority of the States with whom we unite.

We request the favour of your Excellency to lay this letter before the legislature of your State (or Commonwealth), and we are persuaded that your regard for our national harmony and good government will induce you to promote a measure which we are unanimous in thinking very conducive to those interesting objects.

We have the honour to be, with the highest respect, your excellency's most obedient servants.

By the unanimous order of the convention,

GEO. CLINTON, President.

JAY TO THE CHEVALIER DE BOURGOING.

DEAR SIR :   August 29, 1788.

. . . The Constitution of our country is about to assume a new form, and there is reason to hope that it will gradually be made to operate in such a manner as to give a greater degree of stability and efficiency to our national government than it has hitherto experienced. While a people continue blessed with opportunities of deliberating without interruption, and of deciding without being injured by any influence except that of reason and argument, they may flatter themselves that their civil institutions will become more and more perfect in proportion as their knowledge and experience increases.

Advices from your country lead us to expect some important changes in government will likewise take place there. It is to be hoped that neither party will extend their views too far, and that an undue desire of innovation may not make them forget that the prerogatives of the crown and the rights of the people may and ought to be so defined and confirmed, as that instead of being hostile to each other they may conspire in promoting the glory and happiness of the kingdom.

With the best wishes for your health and prosperity I have the honor to be, dear sir,

Your most obedient, humble servant,

JOHN JAY.

JAY TO THE MARQUIS DE LAFAYETTE.

NEW YORK, 1st September, 1788.

DEAR SIR :

The society in this city for promoting the manumission of slaves, etc., were much pleased to find you were a member of a similar one at Paris. They have admitted you an honourary member of theirs, and sincerely wish that your generous exertions in the cause of freedom and humanity may continue to be crowned with success.

With sentiments of real esteem and attachment, I am, dear sir,

Your affectionate and humble servant,

JOHN JAY,
President.

JAY TO GRANVILLE SHARPE.

NEW YORK, 1st September, 1788.

SIR :

The society established in this city for promoting the manumission of slaves did at their last meeting admit you an honourary member of it, and I have now the pleasure of transmitting to you herewith enclosed a certified extract from their minutes on the subject. Be pleased, sir, to consider this as a mark of the esteem and respect with which your exertions in the cause of humanity have inspired them, and permit me to assure you that, with similar sentiments, I have the honour, to be, sir,

Your most obedient and humble servant,

JOHN JAY.

JAY TO WILLIAM CARMICHAEL.

OFFICE FOR FOREIGN AFFAIRS,
9th September, 1788.

SIR :

You will receive herewith enclosed a certified copy of an act of Georgia of the 30th January last, and of a letter from Governor de Lespidos dated the 12th of December, 1787. These papers I have the honor of transmitting to you by order of Congress. They respect the inconveniences which the States bordering on the Floridas experience from the asylum afforded to their fugitive slaves in those provinces of her Catholic Majesty. Although this is a practice not consistent with good neighbourhood, yet it seems from the letter of Governor Lespidos that without instructions from her court it will not be in his power to prevent it. It is the pleasure of Congress, therefore, that you make to her Catholic Majesty the representations and appearances specified in the before-mentioned act; and it will be useful that they be informed as speedily and precisely as possible of the answer that may be given to you. It certainly is of much importance to both countries, that the harmony at present subsisting between them be preserved, and that their conduct towards each other give no cause of disgust or complaint to either.

I have the honour to be, sir,

Your most obedient and humble servant,

JOHN JAY.

JAY TO THE PRESIDENT OF CONGRESS.

OFFICE FOR FOREIGN AFFAIRS,
12th September, 1788.

SIR :

On the 12th of October last Congress was pleased, on a report from the Board of Treasury, to resolve that the balance of the appropriation from the Barbary treaties of the 14th of November, 1785, not then applied to that object, be constituted a fund for *redeeming* the American captives at Algiers, and that the same be *for that* purpose subject to the direction of the Minister of the United States at the Court of Versailles. As neither this act nor any other that I recollect provides for the subsistence of these captives, whose situation claims from their country such aids and supplies as may be necessary to render their condition as comfortable as the pains and rigors of slavery may permit, I take the liberty of submitting to Congress the propriety of directing their Minister at Versailles, out of the before-mentioned fund, to make such provision for the maintenance and comfortable subsistence of the American captives at Algiers, and to give such orders touching the same, as shall to him appear right and proper. Mr. Jefferson indeed instructed Mr. Lamb to supply as well as to redeem them ; but Mr. Lamb is now in this country, and Mr. Jefferson observes in his letter that his giving such instructions "must rest for *justification* on the emergency of the case"; and that "it would be a comfort to know that Congress does not disapprove of this step." On this letter I reported (viz., 11 May, 1786) a resolution suggesting such approbation ; but I am not informed that it was ever agreed to.

Mr. Jefferson has found it necessary, in order to facilitate their redemption, to let it be reported and believed at Algiers, that Congress would not redeem them. That intelligence has greatly added to their distress ; but it would not be expedient that they should at present be undeceived.

Little supplies may, however, be conveyed in so indirect a manner as not to be traced either by them or by the Algerines, and would tend greatly to the comfort of these unhappy people.

I have the honour to be, etc.

JOHN JAY.

JAY TO GENERAL WASHINGTON.

DEAR: SIR   NEW YORK, 21st September, 1788.

I am not sure that the new government will be found to rest on principles sufficiently stable to produce a uniform adherence to what justice, dignity, and liberal policy may require; for however proper such conduct may be, none but great minds will always deem it expedient. Men in general are guided more by conveniences than by principles; this idea accompanies all my reflections on the new Constitution, and induced me to remark to our late convention at Poughkeepsie, that some of the most unpopular and strong parts of it appeared to me to be the most unexceptionable. Government without liberty is a curse; but, on the other hand, liberty without government is far from being a blessing.

The opponents in this State to the Constitution decrease and grow temperate. Many of them seem to look forward to another convention, rather as a measure that will justify their opposition, than produce all the effects they pretended to expect from it. I wish that measure may be adopted with a good grace, and without delay or hesitation. So many good reasons can be assigned for postponing the *session* of such a convention for three or four years, that I really believe the great majority of its advocates would be satisfied with that delay; after which I think we should not have much danger to apprehend from it, especially if the new government should in the meantime recommend itself to the people by the wisdom of their proceedings, which I flatter myself will be the case. The division of the powers of government into three departments is a great and valuable point gained, and will give the people the best opportunity of bringing the question, whether they can govern themselves, to a decision in their favour.

I remain, dear sir,
Your faithful friend and obedient servant,
JOHN JAY.

SAMUEL VAUGHAN, JR., TO JAY.

HAMSTEAD, JAMAICA, 10th Oct., 1788.

DEAR SIR:

By the date of this letter you will perceive that I have met with unexpected disappointments in this Island, since I told you that my return was to be in June last. Indeed they are the inducements of my troubling you at present; for as I am not able personally to take care of my interest I am under the necessity of requesting a little attention to it on the part of my friends, among whom, from your uniform conduct ever since I had the honor of your acquaintance, I may reckon yourself; and upon every other occasion but the present I should add Mrs. Jay, to whom I beg my particular respects. . . .

The adoption of the New Constitution must have afforded you great satisfaction, as the execution of it will give the first polish to the noble statue formed by the late glorious Revolution. There is no doubt that time will finish it, but the present event gives us reason to expect that the period of its perfection is not so far distant. The progress of reason may be infinitely more rapid than even the increase of money capitals, as represented by your friend Dr. Price's and Mr. Richard's calculations. If so, although we have been till this period in gaining the height we have yet attained, our future improvements must be far beyond our wildest imaginations.

I hope Mrs. Jay and yourself enjoy a better state of health than when I had the pleasure of seeing you last. With perfect respect, I remain, Dear Sir,

Your very obedient humble Servant,

SAMUEL VAUGHAN, JUNᴿ.

JAY TO EDWARD RUTLEDGE.

NEW YORK, 15th October, 1788.

MY DEAR SIR:

I thank you for your friendly letter. . . .

You have seen from the public papers that the new Constitution was with difficulty adopted in this State. The opposition which was violent has daily become more moderate, and the minds of the people will gradually be reconciled to it in proportion as they see the government administered in the manner you mention. The measure of a new convention to consider and decide on the proposed amendments will, I think, be expedient to terminate all questions on the subject. If immediately carried, its friends will be satisfied, and if convened three years hence, little danger, perhaps some good, will attend it. Mrs. Jay and my little family are well. I wish we were near neighbours. Henry would, I think, derive advantages from this climate. If the new Congress should call you here, might it not be well to bring him with you? We have now good schools, and he would lose no time. Assure Mrs. Rutledge of our best wishes, and believe me to be,

Your sincere and affectionate friend,

JOHN JAY.

JAY TO MAJOR PIERCE.

New York, 3d January, 1789.

Dear Sir :

It is as yet exceedingly uncertain who will be senators for this State, and consequently it cannot be even conjectured by what leading .motives they will probably be influenced in their appointments.   Whoever they may be, I shall not omit to apprize them of your services and character.   This I take to be the precise extent of your request, and thus far my desire of serving you may, I think, be gratified.   You are aware, my dear sir, that my official station prescribes a degree of delicacy and reserve relative to other departments, which, though sometimes unpleasant, is always proper.   It gives me pleasure to be persuaded that on this head our sentiments correspond, and that you prefer a uniform adherence to propriety, to any friendly efforts beyond its limits.

I am, dear sir,

Your most obedient and humble servant,

John Jay.

JAY TO JOHN ADAMS.

New York, 16th January, 1789.

Dear Sir :

.You will receive this at Braintree, where you will again find yourself surrounded by your amiable family —a pleasing circumstance, and I congratulate you on the occasion.   We are much obliged to Mrs. Adams for having honoured us, though for a little while, with her company ; it has confirmed that esteem which her character has inspired.   If wishes were not vain, I should wish you all well settled in our neighbourhood, but I am not without hopes that we may yet pass much time together. I forbear saying anything of public affairs, because our friends will tell you as much about them as I can. They do not wear a bright aspect in this or some other States; but we have seen darker days, and have been too much accustomed to political navigation to despair of seeing the ship survive much harder weather. Adieu, my friend, may you long continue to do good and be happy.

Yours affectionately,
JOHN JAY.

MRS. ADAMS TO MRS. JAY.

BRAINTREE, February 20th, 1789.

MY DEAR MADAM,

When I left your hospitable Mansion, I did not design so many days should have elapsed, before I had expressed to you the pleasing sense I entertained of your kindness and friendship; they have left a double impression upon my mind, and an ardent desire to cultivate them in future.

I reached home ten days after I left New York; we had an agreeable journey, good roads, fine weather and tolerable accommodations; our mush and lemon brandy were of great service to us, and we never failed to toast the donor, whilst our hearts were warmed by the recollection. I hope, my dear Madam, that your health is better than when I left you, and this not for your own sake only, but for that of your worthy partner, who I am sure sympathised so much with you, that he never really breakfasted the whole time I was with you. My best regards attend him. I hope both he and you will one day do me the honour of visiting Braintree, where I would do all within my power to render the fireside as social and as pleasing as I found Broadway.

If Miss Livingston is still with you pray present my regards to her; my love to Master Peter, the grave Maud and the sprightly little French girl; compliments to Lady Kitty, and to all the other ladies from whom I received particular attentions whilst at New York, and do me the favour to let me hear from you by the first opportunity.

This letter will be delivered to you by Mr. Ames, the Suffolk Representative, a young Gentleman of an amiable character and very good abilities. He was so good as to offer to take charge of any letters I might have for New York. I have embraced this opportunity to present my little friend Maud with a brooch which I hope may be pleasing and usefull to her.

Mr. Adams joins me in affectionate regards to Mr. Jay and best wishes for your health and happiness. Be assured I am, my dear Madam, with Sentiments of esteem and Regard,

Your Friend and Humble Servant

ABIGAIL ADAMS.

JAY TO THOMAS JEFFERSON.

OFFICE FOR FOREIGN AFFAIRS,
9th March, 1789.

DEAR SIR:

Since the thirteenth day of September nine States have not been represented in Congress, and since the —— day of October last a sufficient number for ordinary business have not convened. No progress therefore could be made in the affairs of the department, and such will continue to be the case unless the government shall be organized.

Many members of the new Congress are now here, but not a sufficient number of both houses to form quorums. There is, nevertheless, reason to expect that both houses will be in capacity next week to open the ballots for President and Vice-President. It is generally supposed, and indeed known, that General Washington is chosen for the first and Mr. Adams for the second.

. . . The reasons assigned for your wishing to make a short visit to America are in my opinion sufficient to justify you in asking leave, and myself in granting it ; but, my dear sir, there is no Congress sitting, nor have any of their servants authority to interfere. As soon as the President shall be in office I will, without delay, communicate your letters to him, and urge the business with all the despatch in my power. To this I shall be prompted not only by official duty, but by that personal esteem and regard with which I am, dear sir,

Your most obedient and humble servant,

JOHN JAY.

JAY TO GENERAL WASHINGTON.

DEAR SIR : NEW YORK, 14th April, 1789.

On my return last evening from a fortnight's absence in the country, I was informed that proper arrangements for your immediate accommodation were not yet made. Permit me, therefore, to take the liberty of requesting the favour of you to be with me in the meantime ; and if Mrs. Washington should accompany you, we should be still more happy. As the measures that were in contemplation on this subject would have given an earlier invitation the appearance of a mere compliment, it was omitted. Considering all circumstances, I really think you would experience at least as few inconveniences with me as in any other situation here. Your reluctance to give trouble will doubtless suggest objections ; apprised of this, we shall be particularly careful to preserve such a degree of simplicity in our domestic management as will render you easy on that head. In a word, you shall be received and entertained exactly in the way which, if in your place, I should prefer, viz., with plain and friendly hospitality.

You will soon want a secretary, and it would be convenient to have him near you. Let me therefore add that I have a room very much at his service, and which may as well be occupied by him as remain as it now is, empty.

I cannot conclude this letter without thanking you as an American for generously complying with the wishes of our country at this interesting period. Personal considerations strongly recommend retirement, and none but public and national ones would draw you from it. The people at large seem sensible of this, and do you justice ; and I am glad of it for their sake as well as yours, for the more justice they do you, the more good you will be able to do them. With the most perfect esteem and regard, I am, dear sir,

Your affectionate and obedient servant,

JOHN JAY.

EDWARD RUTLEDGE TO JAY.

CHARLESTON, May 21, 1789.

MY DEAR FRIEND:

. . . I rejoice to find that we are likely to have something which resembles a government. But with all the fair appearances there must be a considerable lapse of time before an efficient one is firmly established.

In this State two causes contributed very much to impede the operation of government: one was the importance which a considerable number of individuals assumed for the services which they had rendered whilst the enemy were in the country. The state of things in this part of the continent rendered it necessary to act, not a little, without control. We had here too many Commanders in Chief, and they found it very difficult to fall back in the ranks. The other cause was, the immense debt which was owing from all descriptions of men; and this made it extremely inconvenient to most people to submit to a regular government. If in Republics the general sense of the community, I mean the sense of feeling, is against the operation of laws, it is almost impossible to coerce obedience; and I am as convinced as I am of my existence that if we are to preserve the tranquility of our States we must devise some method to prevent our people from running into debt. It is to little purpose to tell us, that credit will be the life of commerce. With us it has been a monster that has shaken the foundations of government and blighted the honor of our citizens. Nor will the opening, as it is called, of the courts of justice ever so wide afford the expected relief. There is no body of military men in existence to enforce an obedience to the laws; and to suppose that neighbors and fellow debtors will execute the laws for the benefit of creditors, is to imagine a vain thing. It is the duty therefore of wise men, to prevent the evil; and this can only be done by some regular, uniform system. I sincerely pray it may be in our day, for I believe we both wish much for peace and honor for our country.

Mrs. Rutledge desires me to present her affectionate compliments to Mrs. Jay and yourself, and I am, my dear friend, as ever your affectionate and obliged,

Ed. Rutledge.

PRESIDENT WASHINGTON TO JAY.

New York, June, 1789.

Sir:

Although, in the present unsettled state of the Executive Departments under the Government of the Union, I do not conceive it expedient to call upon you for information officially, yet I have supposed that some informal communications from the office of Secretary for Foreign Affairs might neither be improper or unprofitable. For finding myself, at this moment, less occupied with the duties of my office, than I shall probably be at almost any time hereafter, I am desirous of employing myself in obtaining an acquaintance with the real situation of the several great Departments at the period of my acceding to the administration of the general Government. For this purpose, I wish to receive in writing such a clear account of the Department at the head of which you have been, as may be sufficient without overburdening or confusing a mind which has very many objects to claim its attention at the same instant, to impress me with a full, precise and distinct *general idea* of the United States, so far as they are comprehended in, or connected with that Department.

As I am now at leisure to inspect such papers and documents, as may be necessary to be acted upon hereafter, or as may be calculated to give me an insight into the business and duties of that Department, I have thought fit to address this notification to you accordingly. I am with due consideration, Sir, Your most humble servant,

G. Washington.

GOUVERNEUR MORRIS TO JAY.

Paris, 1st July, 1789.

My Dear Sir:

I am too much occupied to find time for the use of a cipher, and in effect, the government here is so much occupied with their own affairs, that in transmitting to you a

Vol. III—24

letter under an envelope, there is no risk. This, however, I am pretty certain will go safe. The States-general have now been a long time in session, and have done nothing hitherto. They have been engaged in a dispute, whether they shall form one body or three. The commons, who are represented by a number equal to both the others, and who besides have at least one-half the representatives of the clergy, insist on forming a single house. They have succeeded. But the nobles deeply feel their situation. The king, after siding with them, was frightened into an abandonment of them. He acts now from terror only. The soldiery in this city, particularly the French guards, declare they will not act against the people. They are now treated by the mobility, and parade about the streets drunk, huzzaing for the *Tiers*. Some of them have, in consequence, been confined, not by the force, but by the adroitness of authority. Last night this circumstance became known, and immediately a mob repaired to the prison. The soldiers on guard unfixed their bayonets, and joined the assailants. A party of dragoons, ordered on duty to disperse the riot, thought it better to drink with the rioters, and return back to their quarters. The soldiers, with others confined in the same prison, were then paraded in triumph to the Palais Royal, which is now the liberty pole of this city, and there they celebrated, as usual, their joy. Probably this evening some other prisons will be opened, for " Liberté " is now the general cry, and " autorite " is a name, not a real existence.

The court are about to form a camp in the neighbourhood of Paris, of 25,000 men, under the command of the Marechal de Broglio. I do not know him personally, therefore cannot judge what may be expected from his talents ; but all my information goes to the point, that he will never bring his army to act against the people. The Guard du Corps are as warm adherents (in general) to the Tiers as anybody else, strange as that may seem ; so that in effect the sword has slipped out of the monarch's hands, without his perceiving a tittle of the matter. All these things in a nation not yet fitted by education and habit for the enjoyment of freedom, gives one frequent suspicions that they will indeed greatly overshoot their mark, if indeed they have not already done it. Already some people talk of limiting the king's negative upon the laws. And as they have hitherto felt severely the authority exercised in the name of their princes, every limitation of that authority seems to them desirable. Never having felt the evils of too weak an executive, the disorders to be apprehended from anarchy make, as yet, no impression.

The provincial assemblies or administrations, in other words, the *popular executive* of the provinces, which Turgot had imagined as a means of moderating the *regal legislative* of the court, is now insisted on as a counter security against the monarch, when they shall have established a *democratical legislative*, for you will observe that the noble and clerical orders are henceforth to be vox et præterea nihil. The king is to be limited to the exact sum needful for his personal expenses. The management of the public debt, and revenues to provide for it, will be taken entirely out of his hands, and the subsistence of the army is to depend on temporary grants. Hence it must follow, that his negative, in whatever form reserved, will be of little avail. These are the outlines of the proposed constitution, by which at the same time lettres de cachet are to be abrogated, and the liberty of the press established.

My private opinion is, that the king, to get fairly out of the scrape in which he finds himself, would subscribe to any thing; and truly from him little is to be expected in any way. The queen, hated, humbled, mortified, feels, and feigns, and intrigues to save some shattered remnants of the royal authority; but to know that she favours a measure is the certain means to frustrate its success. The Count

D'Artois, alike hated, is equally busy, but has neither sense to counsel himself, nor choose counsellors for himself, much less to counsel others. The nobles look up to him for support, and lean on what they know to be a broken reed, for want of some more solid dependence. In their anguish, they curse Neckar, who is, in fact, less the cause than the instrument of their sufferings. His popularity depends now more on the opposition he meets with from one party, than any serious regard of the other. It is the attempt to throw him down which saves him from falling. He has no longer the preponderating weight in council, which a fortnight ago decided every thing. If they were not afraid of consequences, he would be dismissed; and, on the same principle, the king has refused to accept his resignation. If his abilities were equal to his genius, and he were as much supported by firmness as he is swayed by ambition, he would have had the exalted honour of giving a free constitution to above twenty millions of his fellow-creatures, and would have reigned long in their hearts, and received the unanimous applause of posterity. But, as it is, he must soon fall. Whether his exit will be physical or moral, must depend on events which I cannot foresee. The best chance that royalty has is, that popular excesses may alarm. At the rate in which things are now going, the king of France must soon be one of the most limited monarchs in Europe. Adieu.

I am yours,
GOUVERNEUR MORRIS.

JAY TO CHARLES PETTIT.

DEAR SIR: NEW YORK, 14th July, 1789.

Your obliging letter of the 5th instant was delivered to me last week.

You know it is important that confidence and cordiality subsist between the heads of the departments, that they may, when necessary, unite their efforts to promote their respective operations for the public good.   To this end much delicacy and candour should be observed towards each other, and all unnecessary interference avoided.   It is likewise important that harmony and confidence subsist between the principal and other officers of each department, that no personal jealousies or discontents may embarrass the business of it.   These and all other prudential considerations will doubtless have their due degree of weight with the President, in all his nominations; and I mention them, merely because they lead me to think it would be improper for me to *recommend* to the President any person for a place in any other department than the one in which I may hold the first. All that I could do, therefore, in the present case was, to inform the President that it would give you pleasure to serve the public in the place you mention. This I have done; nor could details be necessary. You are far from being a stranger to the public; you have enjoyed strong marks of their confidence, and have long been personally known to the President.

I have the honour to be, dear sir,

Your most obedient and humble servant,

JOHN JAY.

GOVERNOR LIVINGSTON TO JAY.

ELIZABETH TOWN, 30th July, 1789.

DEAR SIR:

I find it attended with loss to shop it in New York with Jersey money at the unconscionable discount which your brokers and merchants exact; and it is as damnifying to deal with our merchants here in that currency, since they proportionably advance the price of their commodities. For this reason it is much to my interest, till times shall grow better in this respect, to collect what New York money I may want to lay out in your metropolis from debts due to me in your State. I have the promise of more than I shall this year have occasion for; but as I do not altogether rely upon the performance of it, I shall be obliged to you for intimating to the ——— that it would gratify me much if they would, by the first of October, pay fifty pounds upon their bond. I am

Your most humble servant,

WIL: LIVINGSTON.

D. HARTLEY TO JAY.

LONDON, August, 1789.

DEAR SIR:

It has given me much pleasure to have received a letter from you, and to hear that yourself and Mrs. Jay are well. I hope this will find Mrs. Jay perfectly recovered from her indisposition.

I sincerely rejoice in the prosperity of your Country; that is to say, in the return of prosperity by the abatement of the war. I think America was equally free to every effect of prosperity before her declared independence as since. The British claims of taxation and legislation did disturb the prospect for a time, but those claims being relinquished, all future life is now freely opened before you. You must not expect to find it otherwise than checquered with good and ill, such as is the lot of human life. To be *as happy as any people in the world* is a lot that you must not expect to exceed. You will doubtless have heard of the Revolution in France. The rights of mankind which have been withheld for many centuries from the subjects of that kingdom, have been claimed, ceded and confirmed by the King in a trice of time, not exceeding a few days. Whatever may be the result in the end, as to detail, the principle of unlimited monarchy is abolished for ever. We must all rejoice in this example for the future benefit of all future ages. The indelible principle is written by Providence in the heart's core of his creatures. Other kingdoms will soon catch the example and spread universal liberty over the face of the earth, with peace and good will among men.

All memory of hostilities is abated in this country towards America. I hope and trust the same in yours. I beg to be kindly remembered to yourself and family and to all the friends and inheritors of liberty in your country.

I am ever, Dear Sir,

Your sincere and affectionate friend,

D. HARTLEY.

I thank you for your kindness to Mr. Upton; He is a very worthy young man and will soon return to your country.

D. HARTLEY TO JAY.

LONDON, August, 1789.

DEAR SIR:

A thought has just occured to me, to subjoin a postscript to my letter which you will receive by Mr. Johnston.

The object of this postscript is to you as a private gentleman, not as Secretary of State for your Country. Altho' it is a public thought—you know how much I wish amity and Concord between our two Countries. I assure you there is no hostility in this Country towards yours, tho' I fear in America it is thought otherwise. Perhaps, too, we may suspect that your country is not favourable to us, and thus jealosies may create what they suggest. I think it would have a benevolent effect to receive from your Country some token of returning charity. You know the unhappy infirmity under which our Sovereign in this Country was for some months afflicted, and from which by the favour of Heaven he has been happily relieved and re-established.

Would not a word of affectionate congratulation on such an event to a king once yours and still the Sovereign of the country from which you are derived, and to which you are once more restored in Amity and Peace—would not such a word from your Country do honour to humanity and to yourselves as holding forth an example of true and dignified magnanimity in the oblivion of past resentments and the return of goodwill?

But! you have no minister. Let not a punctilio obstruct the exercise and display of the first of human virtues. Let it be your ambition to take the first step to universal peace and charity amongst men. Such an act of respectfull attention and benevolence to your parent state (for such we must always remain) and to its sovereign will make every British heart glow with sympathetic humanity in the reception and reciprocity. Our present age will be reunited, and future ages will be cemented in consanguinity and future sympathy of affections.—Let not a punctilio obstruct. If you have no minister you may find a friend thro' whom you might drop the sweet words of peace. *Amicitiæ sempiternæ inimicitiæ placabiles.* Let me hear from you and your Country. You know me to be a sincere friend to both our Countries,

And ever yours,

D. HARTLEY.

THOMAS JEFFERSON TO JAY.

PARIS, Sept. 17, 1789.

DEAR SIR,

I have sent from this place, together with my own baggage, two hampers and two boxes, which when arrived at Havre I have taken the liberty to order to be separated from my baggage and sent by the first vessel to New York to your address. The marks and contents are as follows.

T I. No. 30 } These are hampers containing samples of the
T I. No. 31 } best wines of this country, which I beg leave to present to the President and yourself, in order that you

may decide whether you would wish to have any, and which of them for your own tables hereafter, and to offer my service in procuring them for you. The kinds are, 1—Monraché (the best kind of white Burgundy.) 2—Champagne non mousseux (i. e. still) much preferred here to the sparkling, which goes all to foreign countries. 3—Sauterne (a white Bordeaux). 4—Rochegude (from the neighborhood of Avignon, somewhat of the Madeira quality). 5. Frontignan. I have bought all of these from the Vignerons who made them, the 1st, 2d and 5th when on the spots myself, the 3d and 4th by writing to them. The Vigneron never adulterates his wine, but on the contrary gives it the most perfect and pure possible. But when once a wine has been into a merchant's hands, it never comes out unmixed. This being the basis of their trade, no degree of honesty, of personal friendship, or of kindred prevents it. I must beg the favor of you to deliver one hamper to the President with my offer of service, and the preceding explanation.

T. I. No. 32—A box containing two busts in plaister of Admiral Jones, who has desired me to present them on his part to yourself and General Irvine.

T. I. No. 36—A box containing 6 officers fusils, for the war office which I have explained in a letter to General Knox, a duplicate of which I will take the liberty of putting under the cover of my first public letter to you.

I send the present letter to the person at Havre to whom I have consigned the packages, desiring him to forward it with them and to enclose to you the bill of lading. Hoping they may come safely to hand, I beg leave to assure you of the sentiments of sincere esteem and respect with which I am, Dear Sir,

Your most obedient and most humble servant,

THOS. JEFFERSON.

P. S. Every bottle is marked (with a diamond) with the initial letter of the wine it contains.

PRESIDENT WASHINGTON TO JAY.

NEW YORK, 5th October, 1789.

SIR,

It is with singular pleasure that I address you as Chief Justice of the Supreme Court of the United States, for which office your commission is enclosed.

In nominating you for the important Station, which you now fill, I not only acted in conformity to my best judgment, but I trust I did a grateful thing to the good citizens of these United States; and I have a full Confidence that the love which you bear to our country, and a desire to promote the general happiness, will not suffer you to hesitate a moment to bring into action the talents, knowledge, and integrity which are so necessary to be exercised at the head of that department which must be considered as the keystone of our political fabric.

I have the honor to be, with high consideration and sentiments of esteem, &c.,

GEO. WASHINGTON.

JAY TO PRESIDENT WASHINGTON.

NEW YORK, October 6, 1789.

SIR :

When distinguished discernment and patriotism unite in selecting men for stations of trust and dignity, they derive honour not only from their offices, but from the hand which confers them.

With a mind and a heart impressed with these reflections, and their correspondent sensations, I assure you that the sentiments expressed in your letter of yesterday and implied by the commission it enclosed, will never cease to excite my best endeavours to fulfil the duties imposed by the latter, and as far as may be in my power, to realize the expectations which your nominations, especially to important places, must naturally create.

With the most perfect respect, esteem, and attachment I have the honour to be, sir,

Your most obedient and humble servant,

JOHN JAY.

JAY TO FISHER AMES.

NEW YORK, 27th November, 1789.

DEAR SIR:

I have this moment been favoured with your letter of the tenth of this month. Mr. Sedgwick has given me the same character of Mr. Tucker that you do. There are at present several candidates for the place in question,[1] and probably the number will be increased before the appointment takes place. As it should be the result of mutual information and joint consultation between the judges, it appears to me proper that I should in the meantime remain free from engagements, express or implied, to or for any gentleman, however well recommended. The reserve which this consideration imposes will not permit me to enlarge upon this subject; but I know of no consideration which should restrain me from assuring you very explicitly of the esteem with which I am, dear sir,

Your most obedient and humble servant,

JOHN JAY.

[1] Clerk of the Supreme Court.

PRESIDENT WASHINGTON TO JAY.

The President of the United States presents his best compliments to the Chief Justice of the United States and his lady, and encloses them tickets for the theatre this evening.

As this is the last night the President proposes visiting the theatre for the season, he cannot deny himself the gratification of requesting the company of the Chief Justice and his Lady; altho' he begs at the same time that they will consider this invitation in such a point of view as not to feel themselves embarrassed, in the smallest degree, upon the occasion, if they have any reluctance to visiting the theatre; for the President presents the tickets as to his friends who will act as most agreeable to their feelings, knowing thereby that they will meet the wishes of the person who invites them.

Monday, November 30th, 1789.

JAY TO PRESIDENT WASHINGTON.

The Chief Justice of the United States and Mrs. Jay esteem themselves honoured and obliged by the President's invitation, which they accept with pleasure, and by his delicate attention to their embarrassment, which he had reason to think probable, but which ceased with all questions between government and the theatre.

30th November, 1789.

JAY TO THOMAS JEFFERSON.

Dear Sir: New York, 12th December, 1789.

It gives me great pleasure to address a letter to you in our own country. Being informed of your having sailed, the storm a few weeks ago rendered us apprehensive that you might be at least embarrassed on the coast. I congratulate you very sincerely on your arrival, and join in the general wish that you may consent to remain among us in the station to which, during your absence and without your knowledge, you have been appointed.[1] The changes in our government will enable you to employ in that department your talents and information in a manner as useful to the public and honorable to yourself as you have done during your legation in France.

The young gentlemen in the office (who are the only ones I have employed in it) are solicitous that I should mention them to you in such terms as I conceive they merit. Their conduct has given me entire satisfaction, and therefore I think it my duty to give you this information.

With great esteem and regard I have the honour to be, dear sir,

Your most obedient and humble servant,

JOHN JAY.

PRESIDENT WASHINGTON TO JAY.

The President of the United States presents his Compliments to Mr. Jay, and informs him that the harness of the President's Carriage was so much injured in coming from Jersey that he will not be able to use it to-day. If Mr. Jay should propose going to Church this morning the President would be obliged to him for a seat in his Carriage.

Sunday Morn'g, [Dec. 13 (?), 1789.]

---

[1] Secretary of State.

JAY TO D. HARTLEY.

NEW YORK, 14th December, 1789.

DEAR SIR :

I have had the pleasure of receiving your letter of the —— day of August last.

Whether the United States will be more or less happy than other nations, God only knows ; I am inclined to think they will be, because in my opinion more light and knowledge are diffused through the mass of the people of this country than of any other. The Revolution in France certainly promises much, and I sincerely wish it may perform what it promises. The general expectations of its influence on other kingdoms seem to me to be rather sanguine ; there are many nations not yet ripe for liberty, and I fear that even France has some lessons to learn, and, perhaps, to *pay for* on the subject of free government.

It gives me pleasure to be informed by *you* that "all memory of hostilities is abated in your country towards America" ; there is reason therefore to hope that all questions between them will be settled liberally and satisfactorily.

When that takes place the present causes of diffidence and distrust will cease, and I can discern no rational ground for future ones.

The trust conveyed in your postscript perfectly corresponds with my sentiments as to the propriety of the measure you recommend ; but I confess very frankly that, however proper in general, I doubt its expediency in this particular instance. Liberal and benevolent actions are always meritorious and in that sense proper; but their *expediency* is questionable whenever circumstances afford popular and plausible reasons for them to other and less worthy motives. The recovery of the king gives me real pleasure, both on his own account, and on account of the nation; and if there was no danger that the congratulations of the United States on the occasion would by too many and too publicly be ascribed rather to interest than generous consideration, my feelings as a man and as an American would prompt me to promote the measure.

I am persuaded that you wish prosperity to my country. Your friendly attentions to me when in England are and will remain fresh in my memory, and I shall always be happy in opportunities of evincing the esteem and attachment with which I am, dear sir,

Your affectionate humble servant,

JOHN JAY.

JAY TO GOVERNOR LIVINGSTON.[1]

NEW YORK, 25th January, 1790.

DEAR SIR:

The last list of the *Saratoga's* officers and men was carefully examined by Mr. Remsen this morning. It is dated the 20th December, 1780, and noted to have

---

[1] Among the younger officers lost in the Continental man-of-war *Saratoga* was midshipman John L. Livingston, son of Governor Livingston, Jay's father-in-law. The report reaching the Governor, through the sailors named above, that his son was alive, a prisoner in Algiers, he requested Jay to have the matter investigated. In the latter's reply, we have the first account of the probable manner in which that vessel foundered. See vol. i., p. 376.

been received in the office the 9th of February, 1781. There are no such names as Reynolds and Minor in it.

The *Saratoga* is with great probability supposed to have been lost on the 18th of March, 1781, about four o'clock in the afternoon of that day. One of the lieutenants, who had been put into a prize, parted from her a little before that time, and left her in full chase of a sail, the wind coming on so exceeding violent that the prize before mentioned was obliged to take in her sails. The lieutenant, I am told, is persuaded that the *Saratoga*, whose captain was venturous and full of ardour, was then lost.

Besides it would be very extraordinary, indeed, that a young gentleman of talents should be for years working in Algiers, and that openly on the fortifications, and there meet with this Blinckhorn, and Reynolds, and Minor, and yet never be able to convey intelligence of himself to any of the Christian consuls or captives, or to the regency of the country. He knew I was in Spain, that we had ministers also at courts at peace with Algiers, and must soon have learned that among other friendly nations the French had a consul there.

I will nevertheless cause copies of your letter to be transmitted to the French and English consuls at Algiers, for although Blinckhorn's story appears to me to deserve no credit, yet in cases of this kind no pains should be spared to remove doubts.

JAY TO JOHN DUMONT.

NEW YORK, 27th February, 1790.

DEAR SIR:

I was favoured with yours of the 28th ultimo as I was preparing to go out of town. It was not until last evening that I returned, or I should have taken an earlier opportunity of answering your letter.

Accept my thanks for your friendly congratulations. I believe them sincere, and value them accordingly. It would give me great pleasure to see your situation more comfortable. On these occasions it is best to be very explicit ; it would neither be friendly nor candid to excite delusory expectations, or to make promises without a good prospect of performing them. There is not a single office in my gift ; nor do I recollect that there is more than one in the appointment of the court, I mean their clerk. As to offices in the gift of other departments, I think it my duty not to interfere, nor to ask favours, it being improper for a judge to put himself under such obligations.

I am sincerely disposed to serve my friends, and you among others ; but it can only be in a way perfectly consistent with the duties and proprieties of my public station. These considerations will, I am persuaded, have their due weight with you, and rather increase than diminish the esteem and attachment you have always expressed and manifested for me. I regret that on this occasion I cannot say things more consonant with your wishes ; but sincerity, though not always pleasing, is preferable to mere civility.

Be assured of my constant regard, and that I remain

Your friend,

JOHN JAY.

JAY TO MR. GRAND.

NEW YORK, 1st March, 1790.

DEAR SIR :

I had this morning the pleasure of receiving your obliging letter of the 30th of November last, and thank you for your attention to mine of the preceding December. As the sum is small, the difference of exchange is not important ; and I am perfectly persuaded that it was not in your power to make the remittance on better terms.

The people of this country ardently wish success to the revolution in France, and that they may speedily enjoy all the blessings of peace, plenty, and good government. The natural propensity in mankind of passing from one extreme too far towards the opposite one sometimes leads me to apprehend that may be the case with your national assembly.

Affairs in this country have a promising aspect, and we have reason to flatter ourselves that our new government will realize to us many of the advantages which the revolution placed within our reach.

Mr. Jefferson is now Secretary of State, so that there is at present no probability of his returning to France. Who will succeed him is as yet uncertain.

I am glad my friend Morris is frequently with you. I
shall be mistaken if he is not as much pleased with
you as you are with him. Be so good as to present
Mrs. Jay's and my compliments to your admirable
family, and believe me to be, with great and sincere
esteem and regard, dear sir,

Your most obedient and humble servant,

JOHN JAY.

CHARGE TO GRAND JURIES BY CHIEF-JUSTICE JAY.[1]

Whether any people can long govern themselves
in an equal, uniform, and orderly manner, is a question which the advocates for free government justly
consider as being exceedingly important to the cause
of liberty. This question, like others whose solution
depends on facts, can only be determined by experience. It is a question on which many think some
room for doubt still remains. Men have had very
few fair opportunities of making the experiment; and
this is one reason why less progress has been made in
the science of government than in almost any other.
The far greater number of the constitutions and governments of which we are informed have originated in
force or in fraud, having been either imposed by improper exertions of power, or introduced by the arts
of designing individuals, whose apparent zeal for

---

[1] This document is endorsed: " The charges of Chief Justice Jay to the
Grand Juries on the Eastern circuit at the circuit Courts held in the Districts of
New York on the 4th, of Connecticut on the 22d days of April, of Massachu-
setts on the 4th, and of New Hampshire on the 20th days of May, 1790."

liberty and the public good enabled them to take advantage of the credulity and misplaced confidence of their fellow-citizens.

Providence has been pleased to bless the people of this country with more perfect opportunities of choosing, and more effectual means of establishing their own government, than any other nation has hitherto enjoyed ; and for the use we may make of these opportunities and of these means we shall be highly responsible to that Providence, as well as to mankind in general, and to our own posterity in particular. Our deliberations and proceedings being unawed and uninfluenced by power or corruption, domestic or foreign, are perfectly free ; our citizens are generally and greatly enlightened, and our country is so extensive that the personal influence of popular individuals can rarely embrace large portions of it. The institution of general and State governments, their respective conveniences and defects in practice, and the subsequent alterations made in some of them, have operated as useful experiments, and conspired to promote our advancement in this interesting science. It is pleasing to observe that the present national government already affords advantages which the preceding one proved too feeble and ill-constructed to produce. How far it may be still distant from the degree of perfection to which it may possibly be carried, time only can decide. It is a consolation to reflect that the good-sense of the people will be enabled by experience to discover and correct its imperfections, especially while they continue to retain a proper confidence in themselves, and avoid those jealousies and dissensions which, often springing from the worst designs, frequently frustrate the best measures.

Wise and virtuous men have thought and reasoned very differently respecting government, but in this they have at length very unanimously agreed, viz., that its powers should be divided into three distinct, independent departments—the executive, legislative and judicial. But how to constitute and balance them in such a manner as best to guard against abuse and fluctuation, and preserve the Constitution from encroachments, are points on which there continues to be a great diversity of opinions, and on which we have all as yet much to learn. The Constitution of the United States has accordingly instituted these three departments, and much pains have been taken so to form and define them as that they may operate as checks one upon the other, and keep each within its proper limits ; it being universally agreed to be of the last importance to a free people, that they who are vested with executive, legislative, and judicial powers should rest satisfied with their respective portions of power, and neither encroach on the provinces of each other, nor suffer themselves to intermeddle with the rights reserved by the Constitution to the people. If, then, so much depends on our rightly improving the before-mentioned opportunities, if the most discerning and enlightened minds may be mistaken relative to theories unconfirmed by practice, if on such difficult questions men may differ in opinion and yet be patriots, and if the merits of our opinions can only be ascertained by experience, let us patiently abide the trial, and unite our endeavours to render it a fair and an impartial one.

These remarks may not appear very pertinent to the present occasion, and yet it will be readily admitted that occasions of promoting good-will, and good-temper, and the progress of useful truths among our fellow-citizens should not be omitted. These motives urge me further to observe, that a variety of local and other circumstances rendered the formation of the judicial department particularly difficult.

We had become a nation. As such we were responsible to others for the observance of the *Laws of Nations;* and as our national concerns were to be regulated by *national laws*, national tribunals became necessary for the interpretation and execution of them both. No tribunals of the like kind and extent had heretofore existed in this country. From such, therefore, no light of experience nor facilities of usage and habit were to be derived. Our jurisprudence varied in almost every State, and was accommodated to local, not general convenience; to partial, not national policy. This convenience and this policy were nevertheless to be regarded and tenderly treated. A judicial controul, general and final, was indispensable; the manner of establishing it with powers neither too extensive nor too limited, rendering it properly independent, and yet properly amenable, involved questions of no little intricacy.

The expediency of carrying justice, as it were, to

not only that punishment be proportionate to guilt, but that all proceedings against persons accused or suspected, should be accompanied by the reflection *that they may be innocent.* Hence, therefore, it is proper that dispassionate and careful inquiry should precede these rigours which justice exacts, and which should always be tempered with as much humanity and benevolence as the nature of such cases may admit. Warm, partial, and precipitate prosecutions, and cruel and abominable executions, such as racks, embowelling, drawing, quartering, burning and the like, are no less impolitic than inhuman; they infuse into the public mind disgust at the barbarous severity of government, and fill it with pity and partiality for the sufferers. On the contrary, when offenders are prosecuted with temper and decency, when they are convicted after impartial trials, and punished in a manner becoming the dignity of public justice to prescribe, the feelings and sentiments of men will be on the side of government; and however disposed they may and ought to be, to regard suffering offenders with compassion, yet that compassion will never be unmixed with a due degree of indignation. We are happy that the genius of our laws is mild, and we have abundant reason to rejoice in possessing one of the best institutions that ever was devised for bringing offenders to justice without endangering the peace and security of the innocent. I mean that of Grand Juries. Greatly does it tend to promote order and good government that in every district there should frequently be assembled a number of the most discreet and respectable citizens in it, who on their oaths are bound to inquire into and present all offences committed against the laws in such districts, and greatly does it tend to the quiet and safety of good and peaceful citizens, that no man can be put in jeopardy for imputed crimes without such previous inquiry and presentment.

The extent of your district, gentlemen, which is commensurate with the State, necessarily extends your duty throughout every county in it, and demands proportionate diligence in your inquiries and circumspection in your presentments. The objects of your inquiry are all offences committed against the laws of the United States in this district, or on the high seas, by persons now in the district. You will recollect that the laws of nations make part of the laws of this and of every other civilized nation. They consist of those rules for regulating the conduct of nations towards each other which, resulting from right reason, receive their obligations from that principle and from general assent and practice. To this head also belong those rules or laws which by agreement become established between particular nations, and of this kind are treaties, conventions, and the like compacts ; as in private life a fair and legal contract between two men cannot be annulled nor altered by either without the consent of the other, so neither can treaties between nations. States and legislatures may repeal their regulating statutes, but they cannot repeal their bargains. Hence it is that treaties fairly made and concluded are perfectly obligatory, and ought to be punctually observed. We are now a nation, and it equally becomes us to perform our duties as to assert our rights. The penal statutes of the United States are few, and principally respect the revenue. The right ordering and management of this important business is very essential to the credit, character, and prosperity of our country. On the citizens at large is placed the burthen of providing for the public exigencies; whoever, therefore, fraudulently withdraws his shoulder from that common burthen necessarily leaves his portion of the weight to be borne by the others, and thereby does injustice not only to the government but to them.

Direct your attention also to the conduct of the national officers, and let not any corruptions, frauds, extortions, or criminal negligences, with which you may find any of them justly chargeable, pass unnoticed. In a word, gentlemen, your province and your duty extend (as has been before observed) to the inquiry and presentment of all offences of every kind committed against the United States in this district or on the high seas by persons in it. If in the performance of your duty you should meet with difficulties, the court will be ready to afford you proper assistance.

It cannot be too strongly impressed on the minds of us all how greatly our individual prosperity depends on our national prosperity, and how greatly our national prosperity depends on a well organized, vigorous government, ruling by wise and equal laws, faithfully executed; nor is such a government unfriendly to liberty—to that liberty which is really inestimable ; on the contrary, nothing but a strong government of laws irresistibly bearing down arbitrary power and licentiousness can defend it against those two formidable enemies. Let it be remembered that civil liberty consists not in a right to every man to do just what he pleases, but it consists in an equal right to all the citizens to have, enjoy, and to do, in peace, security, and without molestation, whatever the equal and constitutional laws of the country admit to be consistent with the public good. It is the duty and the interest, therefore, of all good citizens, in their several stations, to support the laws and the government which thus protect their rights and liberties.

I am persuaded, gentlemen, that you will cheerfully and faithfully perform the task now assigned you, and I forbear, by additional remarks, to detain you longer from it.

REPLY OF NEW YORK JURY TO CHIEF-JUSTICE JAY.

MAY IT PLEASE YOUR HONORS :

The very Excellent Charge given to the Grand Jury of this District by his Honor the Chief Judge of the Federal Court, demands our thanks and particular attention ; and that it may be more influential and impress the mind of our fellow citizens at large beg leave to ask a Copy of it for the press. Your Honors may be assured we shall in our several departments when dismissed exert our influence to promote peace, good order, and a strict regard to the laws of the United States agreeably to the Constitution so lately adopted ; and we trust the judicial department will ever be filled, as it now is, with gentlemen of the first characters for learning, integrity, and ability.

We wish your Honors the Divine presence in all your circuits, and that you may be continually guarded by a good Providence.

BENJ. AUSTIN, Foreman.

May 4ᵗʰ, 1790.

PRESIDENT WASHINGTON TO THE " CHIEF JUSTICE AND ASSOCIATE JUSTICES OF THE SUPREME COURT OF THE UNITED STATES."

UNITED STATES, April 3, 1790.

GENTLEMEN,

I have always been persuaded that the stability and success of the national government, and consequently the happiness of the people of the United States, would depend in a considerable degree on the interpretation and execution of its laws. In my opinion, therefore, it is important that the Judiciary system should not only be independent in its operations, but as perfect as possible in its formation.

As you are about to commence your first circuit, and many things may occur in such an unexplored field, which it would be useful should be known, I think it proper to acquaint you, that it will be agreeable to me to receive such information and remarks on this subject as you shall from time to time judge expedient to communicate.

G. WASHINGTON.

MRS. JAY TO JAY.

FRIDAY, 23d April, 1790.

MY DEAR MR. JAY,

As you have had some disagreeable weather I am impatient to hear whether it has affected your health or not. Peter Munro tells me that in a letter to him you mention having written to me. I have not received your letter. Col. Wadsworth informed me last evening that the influenza was again very prevalent at Hartford. I dread the effect of that disorder more than ever, and sincerely hope you will guard against it as much as possible.

Our little folks are very well. The distance they suppose you to be at present, the still greater distance you are to travel, the impediments likely to intercept your journey and the pleasing idea of your return are the interesting subject of our domestic conversation.[1] A week has elapsed since your departure and the servants have not yet given me occasion for the smallest disatisfaction. To-morrow or Monday I shall pay my father the long intended visit. Last Monday the President went to Long Island to pass a week there. On Wednesday Mrs. Washington called upon me to go with her to wait upon Miss Van Berckel and on Thursday morning agreeable to invitation myself and the little girls took an early breakfast with her and then went with her and her little grandchildren to breakfast at General Morris's, Morrisania. We passed together a very agreeable day and on our return dined with her as she would not take a refusal, after which I came home to dress and she was so polite as to take coffee with me in the evening. I must not omit informing you that the report respecting Judge Bedford and his lady (which doubtless has reached your ear) was altogether groundless. If you see Mrs. Langdon pray thank her for her very polite attention. Governor Langdon was well last evening when I was honored with his company. Adieu! my best beloved! May blessings ever attend you!

SA. JAY.

---

[1] Jay was now absent from New York on his first circuit, his district including New York and New England.

JAY TO MRS. JAY.

MY DEAR SALLY : BOSTON, 6th May, 1790.

As the last post did not bring me a letter from you I conclude that you had gone to Elizabethtown, and had not yet returned. I wrote to you on Monday and on Saturday last. Yours of the 23d of last month is the only one that has reached me.

The business of the court having been finished yesterday I shall have an opportunity of seeing whatever is worthy of notice in and about the place, unless the weather, which is now very disagreeable, should continue so. I had two days ago a pleasant ride to Cambridge over the new bridge, of which you have often heard ; we extended our excursion to some pretty seats not far distant from the College, and among others Mr. Gerry's. On Wednesday next I purpose, on invitation from Judge Cushing and General Lincoln, to visit them. This will take me thirty miles out of my way to Portsmouth, but having time enough and my horses in good order, that circumstance is not very important. Tell Judge Hobart I shall pay particular attention to Hingham, where his ancestors on first coming to this country settled. Mrs. Winthrop made many friendly inquiries about you and the children, and charged me not to omit making her compliments to you. The spring does not appear more forward here than it did at New York when I left you. As yet we have had but very few fine days ; cold easterly winds seem to prevail here. I think our climate a better one.

Adieu, my dear Sally, Yours affectionately,

JOHN JAY.

MRS. JAY TO JAY.

MY DEAR MR. JAY: NEW YORK, May 15th, 1790.

When I wrote you last, William and myself were very poorly, so was likewise Peggy Jay. Thank God! we are all three much better, and will I hope soon be well. The rest of the children are well. Mr. Lewis has recollected that the price Peter offered him was in fact the one he had agreed to take, and so consequently he has received the payment, and that business is settled. A person that has hired a farm adjoining the one of ours at Haverstraw on which old Theel lived, wishes to make a purchase of yours and wants to know the terms he can pay down—200£—and the rest as you may agree.

The President is ill and has been so some days; the family think his illness serious. Dr. Jones has been sent for from Philadelphia and is here now to attend with Bard, Charlton, and McKnight. Judge Hobart called to see me the morning after I received your last favors, and I did not omit telling him what you desired I would. Last evening Mr. King called to see me; he has a little daughter in addition to his flock since you went away. Miss Rebecca Sears is to be married this evening to Mr. Sterrit, a merchant at Baltimore, where I am told he carries her next week. Col. Platt is soon to be married to Miss Aspinwall, the young lady we both admired. Yesterday I rec'd. 50£ from a Mr. Bell, in account of Rutherford for your sister Nancy, and I have just been paying it to Peter Munro for her, which is apropos as he is going to Rye on Monday. The little girls are gone to drink tea with their Cousin Munro, who dines with me to-morrow. We make out very well; no difficulties have yet occurred. Aint you a little fearful of the consequences of leaving me so long sole mistress? Peter Munro paid me 65£ for you which I 've been spending at a great rate. Adieu, my dear Mr. Jay,

Believe me to be sincerely and affectionately yours,

SA. JAY.

Not a single person of Mr. Adams' family have called upon me in your absence.

BENJAMIN VAUGHAN TO JAY.

LONDON, August 4th, 1790.

MY DEAR SIR,

I am much obliged to you for your kind letter, and the sermon which accompanied it, which I should in preference call a discourse, considering its length, matter, and occasion. The letter I carried with me to Paris on account of the hint respecting sheep, and the Duke of Rochefoucauld has retained it, which you will not be displeased at, since in his hands it will do most good. My journey to Paris was partly to see the historical and philosophical fact of the 14th ult., especially as Deputies had assembled from all quarters of France. The spectacle was rather curious, than interesting, owing to the extreme bad management of the procession and ceremony. Notwithstanding the distance was too great for perfect sight and hearing, yet the feelings of every person were sufficiently alive to have admitted of some affecting, as well as sublime scenes, being presented out of the vast materials which offered themselves. Your friend the Marquis de la Fayette (called in public documents the Sieur De la Fayette) stands responsible for the chief of this bad management, by which I perceive that he has essentially lowered himself in the opinion of thinking people, especially the military. In other respects my journey answered sufficiently my views in undertaking it. The people of France seem to me to have thoroughly imbibed the spirit of the revolution, with a few exceptions not worthy of mention. I went by Calais and Arras, and returned by Caen and Cherbourg, and every where I saw signs of unanimity or acquiescence the most complete. The celebration of the 14th in my route home, I found had been universal and enthusiastic, the military combining to outward appearance without exception, and (a certain proportion of the officers allowed for,) with cordiality also. This good will to the revolution was to be expected; but what struck me most was a sort of family-feeling and fraternity which every member of the national guard seemed to have to every other member of it, however strange to him ; and that every man seemed to endeavor to make his private feelings give way to the public interests.

No good man can have witnessed these scenes without being edified, as well as animated. He might sometimes smile, but I think other nations err much more by being short of the truth than the French do by going beyond it. It seems to me that the seed has fallen upon the best soil, all considered, (that is, upon the fittest and most productive) that could be found in Europe ; and I hope it will be a lasting one. I trust our friends in America will not be jealous at hearing, that the French revolution is thought by much the most instructive of any upon record, and as agitating the greatest assemblage of principles respecting human and even domestic society. They had more to do than America, which has led them to aim at every thing. The American revolution was little more than the separation of partnership accounts. When you weed our nonsence out of your laws, and cease to quote an English law authority in your courts, you will make an important addition to your own revolution ; but I fear your lawyers are too powerful to allow of the simplicity and perspicuity called for by common sense. Trade is another crooked plant in your plantation. Religion you have set pretty straight. A few more things well done will create both a love and knowledge of better order, for they will operate as guides to the eye and feelings.—As your people, considering them as persons who have a share in public proceedings, read few books, it is well worth the consideration of the leading persons in America to set on foot better newspapers than those you possess, as well as better magazines ; or which will be much easier, to improve those already established. One of the best newspapers I have seen from your continent was one published somewhere in the woods, to the N. W., if I may judge from some specimens I casually saw of it, consisting in part of exclusively well judged extracts from books. Surely nothing can be more easy than this part of such an undertaking, where there is a good library. Forgive my zeal, which you must allow impartial.

You will expect some politics from me. — France is well disposed to peace, but there are some intriguing spirits who wish to bring on war ; and I was very sorry to hear a person, whom I have before named in this letter, accused as being one. My authority was not a slight one, and the intelligence shocked me so much, that I did not wish to have any conversation with him, when at Paris. I wish he could borrow a little of *your* general's dignity, which would have an astonishing effect just now in France.

We seem here to have little objection to war of any kind ; but I conceive we shall be saved a German war by a pacification between Prussia and Austria, somewhat at the expence of Prussia, who has lately gained a naval victory of some consequence, but which has suffered a subsequent drawback by a smaller victory of the King of Sweden. Spain is yet at issue, but by the inaction of our fleet, you may judge we are not wanting in good hopes of an accommodation. Ireland was becoming restive, but I think matters will settle there for the present, tho' the system of corrupting with money, titles, and places has got to a disagreeable height there, so as to give a wise minister some alarm for its supposed necessity and consequences. A war, I have little doubt, would discover upon the first successes, great dissatisfaction in Ireland, and some in Scotland. Some weak debates have lately occurred in the French national assembly, but they have ended in a very essential object, the giving arms to the nation at the public expence.

I forgot to tell you that Cherbourg is already a safe harbor. How long it will last, how it will be defended, and whether it can easily be entered, are questions of which I am incompetent to the discussion. The breakwater may be finished this year. The forts are scarcely ⅔ finished, and nothing has lately been done in them.

The freedom with which I write will put you in mind of the freedom with which I used to speak, and tell you the cause of it, namely your kindness in favor of it. — I beg my affectionate respects to Mrs. Jay. Mrs. V. joins me in every good wish to you and yours. I am, dear Sir,

Your respectful and affectionate friend and servant,

BENJ. VAUGHAN.

JAY TO MRS. JAY.

BOSTON, 10th November, 1790.

MY DEAR SALLY:

I hope this evening to be favoured with assurances under your hand that you and the children continue well. My cold and consequently the cough occasioned by it have left me. I am happy in being rid of such disagreeable companions.

Governor Bowdoin is to be interred this afternoon. His funeral will strongly mark the estimation in which he was held. Various societies will attend it, etc. To him these attentions will be vain, but to his family pleasing. Posthumous fame is in no other respect valuable than as it may be instrumental to the good of survivors.

I dined two days ago with Mr. Gerry; they have a pretty seat. He will go on to Congress the last of this month; she will remain at home, and both will experience from absence what you and I have often done. Her situation at six miles' distance from Boston will be but solitary, but she has children and domestic employments to amuse and occupy her attention.

I have dined but once at my lodgings, viz., the day I arrived, and am engaged for every day previous to the one on which I shall set out for Exeter—that is, until Monday next. The hospitality and sociability of this place are singular. I remark another circumstance that is pleasing. Almost at every table you find a clergyman. Instead of being a check to the cheerfulness of company, they partake in and promote it. Their characters are in general amiable, and they are respected accordingly.

Be so good as to write a few lines to my brother Peter and let him know that I am well. I hope Nancy does not grow worse; when you see Fady, remember me to him. By this time I suppose the two Peters have returned from Bedford. I should be glad to receive a few lines from them. One of them knows and the other should be apprised that letters by *ordinary conveyances* should contain nothing which in case of publication would produce inconveniences. Between friends slight hints are often intelligible, though not to be understood by others. Young people should early attend to these things; they cannot begin to be prudent too early.

I am, my dear Sally,

Yours very affectionately,

JOHN JAY.

ALEXANDER HAMILTON TO JAY.

MY DEAR SIR,

I enclose you copies of two resolutions which have passed the house of representatives of Virginia. Others had been proposed and disagreed to; but the war was still going on. A spirited remonstrance to Congress is talked of.

This is the first symptom of a spirit which must either be killed or will kill the Constitution of the United States. I send the resolutions to you that it may be considered what ought to be done. Ought not the collective weight of the different parts of the Government to be employed in exploding the principles they contain? This question arises out of a sudden and unfledged thought.

I remain, Dear Sir,

Your Affectionate and Obedient humble Servant,

A. HAMILTON.

" *Resolved*, that so much of the act, entitled an act making provision for the debt of the United States, as limits the right of the United States in their redemption of the public debt is dangerous to the rights and subversive of the interest of the people, and demands the marked disapprobation of the General Assembly.

" *Resolved*, that it is the opinion of this Committee, that so much of the act of Congress, entitled 'an act making provision for the debt of the United States,' as assumes the payment of the state debt is repugnant to the Constitution of the United States, as it goes to the exercise of a power not expressly granted to the general government."

JAY TO PRESIDENT WASHINGTON.

BOSTON, 13th November, 1790.

DEAR SIR:

The act " *to regulate trade and intercourse with the Indian tribes*," passed the last session, directs that the superintendents and persons by them licensed, shall be governed, in all things touching the said trade and intercourse, by such rules and regulations as the President shall prescribe. I was lately asked, Whether any and what arrangements had been made in pursuance of this act? My answer was, that I had not heard, but was persuaded that every thing necessary either had been or would soon be done. As every licensed trader must know what rules and regulations he is to obey and observe, would it be amiss to publish them?

The Constitution gives power to the Congress " to coin money, regulate the value thereof, and of foreign coin ; to provide for the punishment of counterfeiting the securities and current coin of the United States." If the word *current* had been omitted, it might have been doubted whether the Congress could have punished the counterfeiting of foreign coin. Mexican dollars have long been known in our public acts as *current* coin. The 55th section of the act " to provide more effectually for the collection of the duties," etc., enumerates a variety of foreign coins which shall be received for the duties and fees mentioned in it.

The late penal act (as it is generally called) provides punishment for counterfeiting paper, but not coin, foreign or domestic. Whether this omission was accidental or designed, I am uninformed. It appears to me more expedient that this offence, as it respects current coin, should be punished in a uniform manner throughout the nation, rather than be left to State laws and State courts.

The Constitution provides, that " no State shall coin money, nor make any thing but gold or silver coin a *tender* in payment of debts." Must not this gold and silver coin be such only as shall be either struck or made current by the Congress? At present, I do not recollect any act which designates, unless perhaps by implication, what coins shall be a *legal* tender between citizen and citizen.

The Congress have power to establish post roads. This would be nugatory unless it implied a power either to repair these roads themselves, or compel others to do it. The former seems to be the more natural construction. Possibly the turnpike plan might gradually and usefully be introduced.

It appears advisable that the United States should have a fortress near the heads of the western waters; perhaps at, or not very distant from, Fort Pitt, to secure the communication between the western and Atlantic countries, and that the place be such as would cover the building of vessels proper for the navigation of the most important of those waters. Should not West Point, or a better post if it be found on Hudson River, be kept up? An impregnable harbour in the north, and another in the south, seem to me very desirable. Peace is the time to prepare for defence against hostilities.

There is some reason to apprehend that masts and ship-timber will, as cultivation advances, become scarce, unless some measures be taken to prevent their waste, or provide for the preservation of a sufficient fund of both.

Being persuaded that we could undersell other nations in salted provisions, especially beef, porvided none but of the first quality was exported, I am inclined to think the national government should attend to it ; nay, that the whole business of inspecting all such of our exports of every kind as may be thought to require inspection, should be done under their exclusive authority, in a uniform manner. Where State inspection laws are good they might be adopted. If the individual States inspect by different rules, and some of them not at all, the article in question will not go to market with such plain and decided evidence of quality as to merit confidence, especially as various marks under various State laws multiply the means of fraud and imposition ; if only the best commodities in their kind were exported, we should gain in name and price what we might lose at first by diminution of quality.

I think it probable that this letter will find you at Philadelphia ; if not, I presume it will be forwarded by some of your family, but how, or by whom, is uncertain. Much content and good-humour is observable in these States. The acts of Congress are as well respected and observed as could have been expected. The assumption gives general satisfaction here. The deviation from contract respecting interest is censured by some. They say, and not without reason, that the application of surplus revenue to the purchase of stock shows that the measure did not result from necessity.

With the most perfect respect, esteem, and attachment,

I have the honour to be, dear sir,

Your obliged and obedient servant,

JOHN JAY.

PRESIDENT WASHINGTON TO JAY.

[Private.]

My Dear Sir,   Mount Vernon, Nov. 19th, 1790.

The day is near when Congress is to commence its third session ; and on Monday next, nothing intervening to prevent it, I shall set out to meet them at their new residence.

If any thing in the judiciary line, if any thing of a more general nature, proper for me to communicate to that body at the opening of the session, has occurred to you, you would oblige me by submitting them with the freedom and frankness of friendship.

The length and badness of the road from hence to Philadelphia, added to the unsettled weather which may be expected at this season, will more than probable render the term of my arrival at that place uncertain ; but your sentiments, under cover, lodged with Mr. Lear by the first of next month, will be in time to meet me and the communications from the other great departments ; and with such matters as have been handed immediately to myself from other quarters, or which have come under my own observation and contemplation during the recess, will enable me to form the sum of my communications to Congress at the opening of the session.

I shall say nothing of domestic occurrences in this letter, and those of foreign import you would receive at second-hand from hence.   To add assurances of my friendship and regard would not be new ; but with truth I can declare that I am

Your affectionate and humble servant,

GEORGE WASHINGTON.

JAY TO ALEXANDER HAMILTON.

Dear Sir :   Boston, 28th November, 1790.

On returning from Exeter the evening before the last, I had the pleasure of receiving your letter of the 13th instant with the two copies mentioned in it.

Having no apprehension of such measures, what was to be done appeared to me to be a question of some difficulty as well as importance ; to treat them as very important might render them more so than I think they are. The author of " McFingall " could do justice to the subject. The assumption will do its own work ; it will justify itself and not want advocates. Every indecent interference of State assemblies will diminish their influence ; the national government has only to do what is right and, if possible, be silent. If compelled to speak, it should be in few words strongly evinced of temper, dignity, and self-respect. Conversation and desultory paragraphs will do the rest.

Conversing to-day with General Lincoln I find he doubts the expediency of some provision in the proposed act respecting the coasting trade, etc. He seems well informed about these matters. It struck me, and I observed, that his passing a few days at Philadelphia and conversing with you might be useful. I believe he wishes it ; considering the season, he thinks no inconvenience would result from his being absent a little while from his station. If you should think it best to send him leave of absence now, he could immediately set out. I told him I should mention this much to you. I often hear his conduct commended, and I really believe with reason.

I have heard it suggested that a revenue officer should be stationed on the communication with Canada. The facility of introducing valuable goods by that route is obvious. The national government gains ground in these countries, and I hope care will be taken to cherish the national spirit which is prevailing in them. The deviation from contract touching interest does not please very universally.

Yours affectionately,

JOHN JAY.

JOHN ADAMS TO JAY.

PHILADELPHIA, Decr. 20, 1790.

DEAR SIR,

Permit me in this severe season to salute your fireside, and congratulate you on your return from the Northern Circuit.

As the time approaches when we are to expect the pleasure of seeing you at the Supreme Court in Philadelphia, you will give me leave to solicit the honour and the pleasure of your company and that of Mrs. Jay, and whoever else of the family who may accompany you, at Bush Hill, during the time you may have occasion to stay at Philadelphia.

This satisfaction I have here requested as a favour, in hopes that there will be no hesitation or delicacy to prevent you from readily granting it ; but if I should be mistaken in this hope, I shall certainly demand it as a right, because the rights of hospitality are not only sacred but reciprocal.

As you are a Roman the *jus hospitii* will not be disputed by you, and as I wish that I was one, I shall respect it and claim it. We have a handsome and convenient room and chamber, and a decent bed at your service ; and instead of the smallest inconvenience to us, you will confer a real obligation on Mrs. Adams who joins with me in the request to yourself and Mrs. Jay, and on your assured friend

And humble servant,

JOHN ADAMS.

JAY TO PRESIDENT WASHINGTON.

NEW YORK, 13th March, 1791.

DEAR SIR:

Perceiving that you have been pleased to appoint Colonel Smith a supervisor for this district, I conclude that on his acceptance of that place the office of marshal will be conferred on some other person. It is probable that several candidates will offer, and I take the liberty of communicating my sentiments respecting a gentleman who, too delicate to display his own merit, possesses more than falls to the share of many. I mean General Matthew Clarkson. I think him one of the most pure and virtuous men I know. When at Boston, General Lincoln (whose aide he was) spoke to me of him in terms not only of approbation, but affection. During the war he was a firm and active whig, and since the peace a constant friend to national and good government. Few men here, of his standing, enjoy or deserve a greater degree of the esteem and good-will of the citizens than he does, and, in my opinion, he would discharge the duties of that, or any office for which he may be qualified, with propriety and honour.

Be pleased to present my respectful compliments to Mrs. Washington, and permit me to assure you of the perfect respect, esteem, and attachment with which I am, dear sir,

Your obliged and obedient servant,

JOHN JAY.

JOHN ADAMS TO JAY.

DEAR SIR, PHILADELPHIA, January 4th, 1792.

As the week is approaching when you are to be expected at Philadelphia, I take this opportunity to present to you and your lady the compliments of the season, and request the honour and pleasure of your company at our house during your visit to this City. We live in Arch Street at the corner of Fourth Street, where your old bed is ready for you in as good a chamber, and much more conveniently situated for your Attendance on your Court and intercourse with your friends. Mrs. Jay we hope will bear you company, and in this request Mrs. Adams joins with me. The winter is very mild ; Politicks dull, Speculation brisk. As we have little interest in these things we shall have a freer scope for friendship.

I am, my dear Sir, with Sincere Esteem

Yours JOHN ADAMS.

JAY TO J. C. DONGAN.[1]

SIR : NEW YORK, 27th February, 1792.

Accept my thanks for your obliging letter of this morning, which I this moment received.

My answer to the gentleman who applied to me

---

[1] Jay had been nominated, February 16, 1792, for the State Governorship, and the above is in reply to a letter from Mr. Dongan respecting his views on slaveholding in New York. See Jay's "Life of Jay," vol. i., pp. 284–86. Dongan wrote : "As your opponents cannot or dare not impeach your integrity and ability, necessity obliges them to descend to the lowest subterfuges of craft and chicane, to mislead the ignorant and unwary. The part you have taken in the society for emancipating slaves is exaggerated, and painted in lively colors to your disadvantage. It is said that it is your desire to rob every Dutchman of the property he possesses most dear to his heart, his slaves ; that you are not satisfied with doing that, but wish further to oblige their masters to educate the children of those slaves in the best manner, even if unable to educate their own children ; and also that you have procured a bill to be brought into the Legislature this session for the above purpose."

was, that if my fellow-citizens did me the honor to elect me, I would with pleasure serve them ; but that I conceived it would be improper for me to make any efforts to obtain suffrages. They approved of this line of conduct, and in conformity to it I made it a rule neither to begin correspondence nor conversations on the subject. I did presume that the committee here had conveyed this information to some of the most respectable characters in the different counties ; perhaps they considered the publications in the newspapers as sufficient to answer that purpose.

That many election tales will be invented and propagated, and that credulous individuals will be imposed upon by them is not to be doubted.

As to my sentiments and conduct relative to the abolition of slavery, the fact is this :—In my opinion, every man of every color and description has a natural right to freedom, and I shall ever acknowledge myself to be an advocate for the manumission of slaves in such way as may be consistent with the justice due to them, with the justice due to their master, and with the regard due to the actual state of society. These considerations unite in convincing me that the abolition of slavery must necessarily be gradual.

On being honored with the commission I now hold, I retired from the Society to which you allude, and of which I was President, it appearing to me improper for a judge to be a member of such associations. That Society I fear has been misrepresented, for instead of censure they merit applause. To promote by virtuous means the extension of the blessings of liberty, to protect a poor and friendless race of men, their wives and children from the snares and violence of men-stealers, to provide instruction for children who were destitute of the means of education, and who, instead of pernicious, will now become useful members of society—are certainly objects and cares of which no man has reason to be ashamed, and for which no man ought to be censured ; and these are the objects and the cares of that benevolent society.

It will always give me pleasure to manifest the sense I entertain of this mark of your attention, and to assure you of the sentiments of esteem and regard with which I am, sir,

Your most obedient and humble servant,

JOHN JAY.

JAY TO THE PUBLIC.

It having been deemed *expedient* to consider me as the author of certain political papers lately published, I think it proper to declare upon my honour that I am not the author of any political paper that has been published this year ; that I have neither written, dictated, nor seen the manuscripts of any of those which have appeared against Governor Clinton, or any person whatsoever ; and that I do not even know who the writers are, further than that I have heard some of these papers ascribed to one person and some to another. Whoever they may be, they have not been actuated by my advice or desire ; and not being under my direction or control, I cannot be responsible for the pain their publications have given.

JOHN JAY.

JAY TO D. HARTLEY.

NEW YORK, 17th March, 1792.

DEAR SIR :

The impression made upon my heart and memory by the interest you have taken in the prosperity of this country, and by the friendly attentions for which I am indebted to you remain as fresh and strong as ever. Colonel Smith will give you more particular accounts of our public affairs than can be detailed in the limits of a letter. I will only observe in general that we have much reason to be satisfied and thankful. Whether and when your government will, by evacuating the posts, remove that inseparable obstacle to confidence and good humour is a question not a little interesting to both countries ; they wish it may never take place who regard a good understanding between us as an evil.

Mrs. Jay desires me to present her compliments to you ; she brought me a little girl a few weeks ago ; so that I have now five children living. Adieu, my dear Sir,

Yours affectionately,

JOHN JAY.

JAY TO EGBERT BENSON.

NEW YORK, 31st March, 1792.

MY GOOD FRIEND :

I have had the pleasure of seeing Senr. Ciracchi and his model of a monument in honor of the Revolution. The design appears to me to be a noble one, worthy of the attention of the United States and honourable to the taste and talents of the artist. It cannot fail of being interesting to all who contributed to the Revolution and to that glorious triumph of liberty which it exhibited, and which well deserves a magnificent monument. The ancient republics, to whose very imperfections we are sometimes partial, afford precedents.

Why should not the Congress adopt and carry this design into execution ? The expense—for my part I think the expense proper, and therefore confide in the sense and sentiment of the public. If the money was now to be provided, the measure would be *unreasonable* on account of the Indian war. That obstacle will be of short duration. We need not begin the monument this year ; to adopt the plan will cost nothing. The work must necessarily be long on hand, and as the expense will be gradually incurred, it also will be gradually defrayed. The sum annually requisite can be but small compared with the object and with our resources.

Although it would better become the nation than individuals to undertake it, yet provided the nation assume the task, the aid of subscriptions and even State donations might, if necessary, be recurred to.

If you would say it shall be begun as soon as a certain sum is subscribed, there is reason to believe it would be subscribed.

If the ways and means be referred to Colonel Hamilton, he will indicate the most eligible. His official station, information, and talents would render it proper.

The gentleman who formed the design will be the most proper person to execute it; another artist would not feel the same degree of interest in it, nor is it certain that another of equal talents could easily be had. As to his reward—it is a matter which I think should not *at present* be contemplated. Let the work be finished, and *then* make him such an acknowledgment as would become the nation on the one hand and him on the other. I can conceive of no other rule on such occasions, and in relation to such objects.

I confess to you that the effect which this measure would naturally have on the President's feelings is with me an additional inducement. We shall not be reproached for letting him die by an executioner or in chains, or in exile, or in neglect and disgrace, as many Greek and Roman patriots died. On the contrary, we shall be commended throughout all generations for the part we have hitherto acted respecting him. It is only while he lives that we can have the satisfaction of offering fruits of gratitude and affection to his enjoyment; posterity can have only the expensive pleasure of strewing flowers on his grave.

Yours affectionately,

JOHN JAY.

JAY TO MRS. JAY.

NEW HAVEN, 24th April, 1792.

MY DEAR SALLY :

My last to you was written at Bedford, which place I left yesterday and arrived here this evening, in good health. At Norwalk I purchased some seed of the White Mulberry ; you will find a little parcel of it herewith enclosed. Peter may plant some of it in our garden ; if they grow we will send them next spring to Bedford. I have also enclosed some with the letter for my brother Peter, which you will find under the same cover with this, and which be so good as to forward by the boat or other good opportunity. I learn that we shall have much business to do here, there being about forty actions. Judge and Mrs. Cushing also arrived this evening ; they made very friendly inquiries respecting you and the children, and desire to be remembered to you. On the road I saw Mr. Sodersheim ; he called at our house on Sunday last, but as you were gone to Church, did not see you ; it gives me pleasure to find from this that you then were well. He told me Mr. Macomb was in goal, and that certain others had ceased to be rich—how mutable are human affairs ! Mrs. Macomb must be greatly distressed ; your friendly attentions to her would be grateful and proper.

25th April.—Peet went last evening to the post-office, but returned without letters ; this morning yours of the 22d inst. was sent to me, and I thank you for it. Cheerfulness, my dear Sally, is best promoted by frequently reflecting on the reasons we have for being cheerful, and by attention to the health, both of our minds and bodies. I regret the depression you mention, and wish it was in my power forever to banish from your breast every uneasy sensation. My health has been mended by the exercise I have lately had. A gentleman from Philadelphia told me this morning that the plan of *rotation* (as to the circuits) will probably be established by Congress ; perhaps it may not take place, or be of short duration—"Sufficient for the day is the evil thereof."

.   .   .   .

I thank God that you and the children are well ; may you continue so, and be happy. My robe may become useless, and it may not. I am resigned to either event, for no one knows what is best for him. He who governs all makes no mistakes ; and a firm belief of this would save us from many. Mrs. Ridley's silence seems singular, perhaps her letters linger on the way ; she had better write by the post. When I parted with my brother Peter he talked of sending for you ; that is, of sending his horses to put into your carriage. If he should, I wish it may be convenient for Susan to remain with the family during your absence ; one, if not both, of the little girls might go with you. This is fine weather, and I hope your dear little namesake will be the better for it.

I had concluded to send this letter by the packet, but as her arrival at New York may be delayed by contrary winds, I shall send it by the post, and leave the mulberry seed and my letter to Peter to go by the packet. Remind P. Munro of my note to F. Clarkson. I wish no delays or difficulties respecting it may occur.

> I am, my dear Sally,
> Very affectionately yours,
> JOHN JAY.

JAY TO PETER A. JAY.

NEW HAVEN, 25th April, 1792.

MY DEAR SON :

I had flattered myself that a letter from you would have accompanied the one I received from your mama. She will receive two letters from me by the packet which is to carry this; in one of them is enclosed a little white mulberry seed, and I shall also enclose some in this for your Uncle Peter. Plant a few in our garden ; the trees will be but small by the Fall, and we may then carry them to Bedford, where in time they will become ornamental, and perhaps useful. When you visit your uncle you may propose planting some of them in his nursery, or in any other place that he may think more eligible. It always gives me pleasure to see trees which I have reared and planted, and therefore I recommend it to you to do the same. Planting is an innocent and a rational amusement. My Father planted many trees, and I never walk in their shade without deriving additional pleasure from that circumstance ; the time will come when you will probably experience similar emotions.

On my way here I dined yesterday at Lewis's Inn, about three miles west of Stratford on the post road. He told me that several years ago he was grafting apple-trees, and that near them had grown a young walnut-tree. A fancy took him to graft it; he did so, and with an apple graft, it took and flourished, is now alive, and above three inches in diameter. This is singular, and contrary to our modern ideas. If I am not mistaken Columilla mentions something like it. I think he says that any tree may be grafted on any tree; a little experience is worth much theory. If I had leisure I would try many experiments.

I am, my dear Peter,

Your affectionate Father,

JOHN JAY.

ROBERT TROUP TO JAY.

NEW YORK, Sunday, 6th May, 1792.

MY DEAR SIR:

Since my last to you I have received a letter from Mr. Laurence informing me that the two bills I sent him are accepted by Mr. Bell to be paid at the house of Randall, Son, and Stewarts in this City. I have not had any further accounts from Dr. Ramsay.

I have this moment finished reading the different accounts from the Northern parts of the State respecting the election. All our friends express a confidence that you will be successful. The enclosed returns of the election in the Eastern and Western Districts is from Fairlie who is pretty dispassionate upon the present occasion, for he has not been very zealous or active for you from an idea he imbibed in the beginning of the business that you had supplanted his father in law. I therefore rely upon the statement as being pretty near the truth and rather within bounds than otherwise. If, therefore, Clinton does not arrive at Columbia County with a majority of 800 or upwards against you it is more than probable that your election will be safe.

I shall now underneath Fairlies statement proceed to make a statement of the result of the votes in the Southern and Middle Districts. Since writing the above I have added my statement to Fairlie's and the result upon the whole election appears to be a majority of 250 for you. You may rely upon it that my statement is as unfavorable as I possibly could make it. All our friends from Ulster County assure us as well as our friends in Albany that Ulster will yield a majority of upwards 100 for you. Mr. Cantine and Col. Bloom both write that they expect a majority of 500 for you in Dutchess. In Westchester County we do not think from late accounts that our Majority will fall short of 350.

I have also made a very lax allowance for Suffolk, for Orange, and I think, for Richmond.

Upon the whole I am well satisfied that we have succeeded and that you will be carried by a Majority that, under all circumstances, will be deemed honorable to you.—This is also the decided opinion of Yates, Schuyler, Peter Van Schaack, Hobart, Jones, Harison, Duane, Bogart, Hoffman, &c.— In the Northern parts of the State the Clintonians are lowspirited and have done betting. Here some of the leaders are extremely uneasy ; I know that Willet is, from his declarations to me.

I shall continue writing to you and hope my next intelligence will be more agreeable. In the mean time I am with the utmost sincerity

My dear Sir,

Your very affectionate friend

ROBERT TROUP.

ROBERT TROUP TO JAY.

NEW YORK, 20th May, 1792.

My Dear Sir:

I have received several letters from you since you left us and sincerely thank you for the sentiments of friendship which they contain.

Clinton and his worthy adherents (the Livingstons) seem now to be driven to despair. All their hopes of success rest upon setting aside votes for you; their particular object at present is the votes of Otsego County which are pretty unanimous for you and which, from the last information, we have will yield a majority of upwards of 600 for you. The efforts made to prevent the canvassing of these votes by forestalling the judgment of the canvassers upon a mere law quibble are really characteristic of these virtuous protecters of the rights of the people, of the enemies of aristocracy, and the declaimers against ministerial influence. The facts respecting the Otsego votes are briefly these:

In February, 1791, A. B. was appointed Sheriff of that County to hold his office for one year. A short time before the expiration of his year he wrote to the Council of appointment declining a reappointment. About thirty days after the end of his year the council appoint C. D. Sheriff of the County, but the commission is never delivered to him neither does he in any one instance take upon himself the execution of the office. It is said, and I believe with truth, that the reason why C. D. did not take upon himself the office is that he could not obtain the security required by law. In this state of things the old Sheriff continued to act as Sheriff and after the election he received the ballots from the different towns, put them into a box as the law directs, and sent them by a deputy to the Secretary's office. The votes of one of the towns instead of being put into the box were left out of it and sent down under a paper cover. The law requiries that the votes of *every* town shall be put into the box.

Upon this state of facts the Livingstons contend that A. B. was not Sheriff at the time of putting the ballots into the box or afterwards, and consequently that he had no right to send the box to the Secretary's office. They also contend that the votes of one town being left out of the box all the other votes of the County must be lost. After there had been a considerable stir in town about the Ostego votes, Ned Livingston, to my very great surprise, waited upon me with a written case in substance as above, and asked me if I had any objections to giving an opinion upon it. At first I was struck with the indelicacy of the application and of my giving an opinion upon a subject in which my feelings were so much concerned. I replied however that he should have my opinion, and my reason for making this reply was a conviction that their views were corrupt and therefore that it would be right in me to counteract them if I could possibly do it. Before Ned left me he had the modesty in almost plain terms to tell me that I should not meet with any difficulty, he was persuaded, in deciding against the votes, upon both the points raised to me. The moment Ned went away I got down and examined the questions with the closest attention and soon satisfied myself from the books that A. B. was Sheriff at the time of putting the ballots into the box and afterwards, and that he was legally entitled to send the box to the Secretary's office. As to the other question it appeared too absurd to admit of reflection.

I was pressed for my opinion the next morning and I gave it to Ned plumply against him upon both points. The opinion threw the party into consternation. A Cabinet Council of the Governor, the Chancellor, Ned, Brockholst, &c., was immediately called. Soon afterwards Brockholst went about almost like a madman vociferating against the legality of the return of the Otsego votes and roundly asserting that there was not a Lawyer out of this State that would give an opinion that the votes were legally returned.

Since this Brockholst and Ned have been rummaging all the law books in their effects and not a stratagem is to be left unpractised with the canvassers. Hoffman and Brockholst had agreed to state the case and send it to Lewis, of Philadelphia, for his opinion, but when put to the test Brockholst would not agree to a full and fair tale of facts. Hence Hoffman and I have prepared a case to be sent to Lawrence to be laid before Lewis, and I have already transmitted to Lawrence the case as stated by Ned with my opinion and the principles and authorities upon which it is based, with a request that when Lewis is considering the subject he will confer with him. The opinion of an able lawyer in another State, if with us, may be productive of good. Since my opinion has been a subject of conversation, I got King and Benson to come and spend an evening with me that we might examine the Case. We accordingly examined the law together, and they are both clearly with me. So is Mr. Jones, Mr. Harison, and Mr. Hoffman. That the opinion is right I think may be demonstrated as well upon legal grounds as upon principles of public policy. What may finally be the issue of this business it is impossible even to conjecture. Out of the 12 canvassers we have but three friends, Jones, ———, and Roosvelt, and the leaders of the opposite canvassers are prepared for any thing. If a fair canvass takes place we are all very sanguine in our expectations that we shall prevail. Gen. Schuyler was in town a few days ago and was expected again in town last night. He is much elated with our prospects and gives us a much more flattering account of our success in the Western District than I have already communicated to you.

We are all upon deck and keeping a good look out, and if by fraud and violence you should be excluded we are determined to take our stand and make a serious business of it. I wish for your own satisfaction you would look over the election law of this State passed 13 Feb. 1779, in 2 vol. page 27 &c.

The 10th Section declares that the " Sheriff of the respective Counties shall deliver the boxes containing the votes *into the office of the Secretary* and the 11th Section declares that the canvassers shall "*proceed to open the boxes one after the other and the enclosures therein contained respectively and canvass and estimate the votes therein contained.*"

From these clauses it appears to me, and I am not singular in the opinion, that the canvassers cannot inquire whether the boxes were sent to the Secretary's office by a person having competent authority or not.

In reflecting upon the legality of the acts of the old Sheriff of Otsego County it should be remembered that by the words of the Constitution Sheriffs are to be *annually appointed* and that there are no words limiting the office to one year, only during the four years and neither have we any Statue to this effect.

In haste I am, my dear Sir

Your very affectionate friend,

ROBERT TROUP.

ROBERT TROUP TO JAY.

SUNDAY, June 10, 1792.

MY DEAR SIR,

Upon looking over the memorandum you left with me I think I may venture to write you one letter more. This City at present is extremely agitated. The canvassing has proceeded so far as to reduce it to a certainty that you will be elected if the Otsego votes be counted. Albany County yielded you a majority of 734, which has proved decisive. Montgomery, Tioga, Otsego, Ontario, and Clinton Counties remain yet to be canvassed. In Montgomery we expect a majority of between 2 and 300. Ontario will yield a majority of about 100 for Clinton. Tioga will most probably not be canvassed, as the box was delivered by a person deputed by a deputy. All parties allow you the majority if the Otsego votes be received. I suppose from the best information I can get the final majority for you will be about 200 or 250.

As to the Otsego votes the question is extremely doubtful. Some say it is to be determined this day; others that it will be decided in the morning. There has been a great deal of writing upon the subject, and every possible maneuvri'g practised by Clinton and his partners, the Livingstons, to dull (?) the canvassers. Some days ago the Canvassers referred the question respecting the Otsego votes and some question respecting those of Clinton and Tioga Counties to Burr and King for their opinions. This reference was understood by us all as intended to procure a cloak for the Canvassers to cover their villainy in rejecting the votes of Otsego. They knew Burr to be decidedly with them, and that he would give them an opinion to justify their views. Burr and King were conferring together for near two days with a view to fairness (?) as Burr affected to wish.

The quibbles of chicanery he made use of are characteristic of the man. They finally departed, and have given opinions directly opposite to each other. King's is bottomed upon sound legal and political principles; Burr's is a most pitiful one, and will damn his reputation as a lawyer. It is flatly against canvassing the Otsego votes and is grounded upon the British Statutes respecting Sheriffs. A refutation of the principal ground of Burr's opinion is contained in a publication just sent to the Printers. We all consider Burr's opinion as such a shameful prostitution of his talents, and as so decisive a proof of the real infamy of his character, that we are determined to rip him up. We have long been wishing to see him upon paper, and we are now gratified with the most favorable showing he could have made.

After Burr's and King's opinions were received, the canvassers met and discussed the subject for upwards of two hours and then adjourned without coming to a decision. The next day, the lawyers, who are friendly to your interest, met, and we determined to address the public on the subject of the Otsego votes and give a formal opinion upon it as lawyers. The address, with our opinion and names subscribed to it, appeared yesterday. We have taken a bold and decisive part, and one which I think became us as independent citizens. Our address, which is short, concludes with a challenge to come forward with their case and argue the legality of our opinion.

The publishing a fair opinion threw the city into a greater ferment and increased the indignation against the attempt to reject the votes. It threw the Clintonian lawyers also into a ferment; they went about the city to and from the place of canvassing like mad men. The canvassers had early yesterday morning determined to go on with canvassing. They did so, and in canvassing the votes of Clinton's strong town in Montgomery they found a majority of no more than thirty odd for Clinton, instead of between one and two hundred. Upon this discovery, they broke up in confusion and said they were determined to decide the question respecting the Otsego votes before they went further. They adjourned to Corre's to be more private, and after several hours discussion broke up again without deciding the question. In this state the thing remains. It is said that to-day or to-morrow morning the determination will take place. The law required them to finish the business of canvassing on Tuesday next. We have hopes that the canvassers will not, at least that all of them will not, take so desperate a step as to reject the votes and declare Clinton Governor against the known and acknowledged voice of the people. My hopes, however, are not very strong, considering the situation of that infamous party. Jacob Morris is attending the canvassers as a special deputy from the county, and claims of them, as matter of right, that the votes be canvassed. I am persuaded if the votes be rejected the business will become very serious in the State at large. Clinton is now about 500 ahead of you; with the Montgomery, Ontario, and Otsego votes we are confident of success. This is admitted by Clinton's adherents.

I am in the utmost haste and anxiety; our friend Jones is well prepared and reserves himself till the last meeting. He is as firm as a rock. Your friends have done every thing that was right and consistent with their own characters, and regard to yours.

God bless you,

ROBERT TROUP.

MRS. JAY TO JAY.

NEW YORK, 10th June, 1792.

MY DEAR MR. JAY:

On Friday, myself and the children had the pleasure of receiving your kind letters of the last of May and first of June, since which I hope you have received two packets from me, sent to Judge Marchant's care by Captain Peterson and Captain Cahoon. I intended to send this by to-morrow's post, but I have just heard that Captain Peterson is again to sail out Tuesday, so that I think it best to postpone it till then, as I can then send you the papers and give you decisive accounts relative to the election. At present the issue of it is doubtful, rendered so by a quibble. If the suffrages of the people are admitted, they give you a majority of 400 votes, but if the County of Otsego are to lose theirs, Clinton will have the majority of a small number. Yesterday was published in Childs' paper the opinion of eight (?) of the principal lawyers of the city in favor of the return of the votes. I will send you the gazettes that contain the discussions on that question. To-morrow I am informed are to be published the opinions of eight or nine on the other side and to be signed by them. Oh, how is the name of Livingston to be disgraced! Brockholst, Edward, William, S. Maturin, etc., are to be of the number. Those shameless men, blinded by malice, ambition, and interest, have conducted themselves with such indecency during the election, and daily since the canvassing of the votes, as to open the eyes of every one respecting their views in their opposition to you. It is said, and I believe it, that Brockholst and Ned first suggested the doubts on that subject. The canvassers of the votes are eleven, eight of whom are partizans of Clinton, and three are in favor of you. In order, as is supposed, to cloak themselves, they officially asked the opinion of Burr and King. Their opinions have not yet been printed, but I am informed by good authority that King's is decidedly in favor of the old sheriff's being entitled to act until a new sheriff was commissioned to succeed. Mr. Burr (as was supposed) was too sore to be unbiassed ; he has, therefore, delivered an opinion which, like a two-edged sword, cuts both ways, for he declares that there was no sheriff, which, if admitted, destroys the legality of the votes and casts an odium on the Governor for suffering so important an office to be vacant. Should the canvassers be hardy enough to decide against the privileges of the people, and instead of suffering them to *choose* a governor, take upon *themselves* to *give* them one, it will occasion great agitation throughout

the State.   I am satisfied that the sentiments of the people
are with you ; whether you are or are not Governor, it appears that you are the choice of the people.

MONDAY EVENING.

Well, my dear Mr. Jay the Canvassers have taken upon
them to give the people a Governor of *their* election, not
the one the people preferred.   When Governor Clinton
was 108 votes ahead, it was thought dangerous to examine
the vote of Tioga County, it being reduced to a certainty
that that County alone would give you a majority independant of the votes of Otsego.   Another quibble was therefore
invented, and they were likewise set aside.   I am informed
that the Recorder, Isaac Roosevelt, and Mr. Canzwort are
determined to enter their protest, and likewise to publish
the votes of those counties which they think illegally
thrown aside, and which if admitted would have given you
a Majority of a thousand votes.

The dejection, uneasiness and dissatisfaction that prevails, casts the darkest Odium upon our shameless Governor,
while it makes your light shine still brighter than ever.
One of the Clintonians told a gentleman of our acquaintance that he was now convinced of the necessity of a change.
Judge Hobart came last evening to congratulate me on
your triumph ; I told him I really conceived it such.   Peter
Munro is writing to you, and has promised to collect those
papers which are most interesting.   The hand bill enclosed
is Duer's, but I think it best to conceal the author's name.
Those lawyers who had boasted their design of publishing
their opinions against the votes have taken care not to
fulfil their promise.   Since you have so honorably lost
your election, I could acquiesce in it with pleasure did it not
deprive me of the pleasure of seeing you soon and of enjoying your company for a great part of the year ; but I will
not dwell upon one disagreeable circumstance when so
many agreeable ones concur to make me happy.   Oh my
dear Mr. Jay ! what transport does it give me to hear the

praises that are daily bestowed upon you! Much rather would I lose a crown as you have lost the Office contended for, than gain an empire upon the terms Governor Clinton steals into his.

Tuesday Morng.—I find they have not yet announced in the paper the appointment of Governor. I am told that it is intended that it should be accompanied with the protests of Jones, &c. There is such an ferment in the City that it is difficult to say what will be the consequences. I shall leave my letter unsealed until evening; should anything occur in the interval that is interesting you shall be apprised of it. I am sitting in your room to write and at your table and have almost persuaded myself that I am making my communications verbally.

People are running in continually to vent their vexation. Poor Jacob Morris looks quite disconsolate. King says he thinks Clinton as lawfully Governor of Connecticut as of New York but he knows of no redress.

Captain Peterson is ready to sail as soon as the wind changes. I think it best therefore to close this letter and send it. I can again write to-morrow as that is Post day if there is any thing worth writing. We are all well, and had been delighting ourselves with the prospect of seeing you soon. The children, therefore, when they heard of the decision of the canvassers exclaimed, Oh! Mama then we shall not see Papa this great while. My consolation is, that time has wings, and altho' they will appear to me to be clogged, yet they will finally waft you back to us.

Till then my best beloved farewell!

S. JAY.

ROBERT TROUP TO JAY.

NEW YORK, 13th June, 1792.

MY DEAR SIR:

The Clintonian canvassers by fraud and violence have excluded you from the Government. The votes of Otsego, Tioga, and Clinton Counties have been rejected. Those of

Tioga were returned by a deputy's deputy which made their return questionable. Those of Clinton by a deputy appointed by the Sheriff by parol. Both Burr and King were of opinion that a parol deputation was good and there is no doubt that the votes of Clinton were rejected to give a better appearance to those of Otsego. This violent and corrupt procedure has occasioned a great ferment in the City and the people are determined not to let the matter pass over in silence. Our friends amongst the canvassers have protested against the proceedings of the others and their protest will be published to-morrow. If we tamely submit to this flagrant attack upon our rights we deserve to be hewers of wood and drawers of water to the abandoned despots who claim to be our masters.

With the sincerest regard from,
My dear Sir, Yours
ROBERT TROUP.

JAY TO MRS. JAY.

EAST HARTFORD, 18th June, 1792.

MY DEAR SALLY :

About an hour ago I arrived here from Newport, which place I left on Friday last. The last letters which I have received from you are dated the 2d and 4th of this month. The expectations they intimate have not, it seems, been realized. A Hartford paper, which I have just read, mentions the result of the canvass ; after hearing how the Otsego votes were circumstanced, I perceived clearly what the event would be. The reflection that the majority of the Electors were for me is a pleasing one ; that injustice has taken place does not surprise me, and I hope will not affect you very sensibly. The intelligence found me perfectly prepared for it. Having nothing to reproach myself with in relation to this event, it shall neither discompose my temper, nor postpone my sleep. A few years more will put us all in the dust ; and it will then be of more importance to me to have governed *myself* than to have governed the *State.* The weather is very warm ; towards evening I shall go to Hartford, where I hope to find a letter from you. In a letter from Newport I requested you to direct a letter for me there.

Hartford, Monday Evening.—Peet has returned from the office without letters. I fear you did not receive mine from Newport in season.

Tuesday Morning. — I am waiting to have my horses shod, and in expectation that Judge Cushing, who is behind, will be here this morning I have concluded to cross from Bennington to Albany and return from thence by water. A letter directed to me there, if *seasonably* written will probably meet me. My love to all the family.

Yours very affectionately,

JOHN JAY.

LANSINGBURGH COMMITTEE TO JAY.[1]

LANSINGBURGH, June 30, 1792.

SIR :

We beg leave to address you in the simple style of free men, and in the name of the citizens of Lansingburgh, to congratulate you on your arrival at our infant settlement.

---

[1] Jay at this date was on his return home from his eastern circuit which he had just terminated in Vermont. His friends and political adherents received him everywhere with enthusiasm and respect as the legally elected Governor of

Fully impressed with a sense of your patriotism, we embrace this opportunity of expressing our gratitude for your unwearied exertions through the struggles of an oppressive war ; and your eminent services as a statesman and minister at home and abroad.

Our respect for your character, in the dignified office of chief justice of the United States, and our regard for your person, as a man possessing the confidence of the people, give us a most lively hope of shortly embracing you as the chief magistrate of this State : nor can we refrain on this occasion from expressing our sincere regret and resentment at the palpable prostitution of those principles of virtue, patriotism, and duty, which has been displayed by a majority of the canvassing committee, in the wanton violation of our most sacred and inestimable privileges, in arbitrarily disfranchising whole towns and counties of their suffrages.

It was, perhaps, little contemplated, that the constitution of this State, which you had so great a share in framing, should to your prejudice, in the first instance, be in so flagrant a manner violated. However desirous we may be of seeing you fill the office of governor of the State of New-York, we only wish it from the free and fair suffrages of a majority of electors. That majority you have ; and though abuse of power may for a time deprive you and the citizens of their right, we trust the sacred flame of liberty is not so far extinguished in the bosoms of Americans as tamely to submit to wear the shackles of slavery, without at least a struggle to shake them off.

---

the State, whom the party in power had fraudulently debarred from the office. The people of Lansingburgh welcomed him with the above address and on his way down the River further ovations were tendered him, as at Albany, Hudson, and New York. The *New York Advertiser* and Greenleaf's *Journal and Register* for this period indicate the extent and intensity of the election excitement.

JAY'S REPLY TO THE LANSINGBURGH COMMITTEE.

GENTLEMEN :

Permit me to request the favour of you to present to my fellow-citizens of Lansingburgh my sincere acknowledgments for the honour they have done me on this occasion, and be assured that the manner in which you have conveyed their sentiments adds to the satisfaction which they inspire.

Their approbation increases the pleasure with which I reflect on my endeavours to serve the cause of liberty and my country, and that approbation derives additional value from the ardour and firmness which they manifested in it.

The various bounties of Heaven to the people of this State conspire in conferring abundant reasons for harmony and content, and every event is to be regretted that tends to introduce discord and complaint. Circumstanced as I am in relation to the one you mention, I find myself restrained by considerations of delicacy from particular remarks.

The people of the State know the value of their rights, and there is reason to hope that the efforts of every virtuous citizen to assert and secure them will be no less distinguished by temper and moderation, than by constancy and zeal.

In whatever station or situation I may be placed, my attachment to my country will remain unabated, and I shall be happy in every opportunity of evincing my respect and best wishes for the citizens of Lansingburgh.

ALBANY COMMITTEE TO JAY.

SIR:

A Committee of the Citizens of Albany in behalf of themselves and constituents beg leave to pay their respects to you, in your passage thro' this City on your tour of official duty.

With the dignified feelings of independent republicans, we experience real pleasure in acknowledging our obligations to you, for the various services you have rendered this your native State, as well as the States in union, in which you have upon all occasions united exalted abilities with stern integrity.

In thus voluntarily expressing our esteem for your person and character, we have the satisfaction of knowing that we speak the sentiments of a respectable majority of our fellow citizens throughout the State, as at the late Election, it is well known, and generally acknowledged that a majority of many hundred votes would have appeared in your favour for Chief Magistrate, had not a majority of the Committee of Canvassers, by an unwarrantable stretch of power, rejected the votes of several whole Counties, in direct violation of law, justice, precedent, and the most essential principles of our consitution—their object, as it most glaringly appears, being to secure an administration favourable to their views, in opposition to the voice of a majority of the people.

We feel, Sir, for the delicate situation in which you are placed, on this important question; painful must it be to you to see the principles of our State Constitution, which you have had a material agency in framing, so shamefully perverted and abused, and to find yourself the object in which that Constitution, and the laws and liberties of the State have received so daring a stab.

We can only add, that as free and independant citizens, we know no authority but what is derived from the voice

of a majority of the people, and a just and uniform interpretation of their constitution and laws; that we shall
wait with a firm and cool deliberation for Legislative interposition to afford or procure redress. On this we place the
fullest dependance, and could it possibly happen, that we
meet with disappointment, the people must then proceed to
determine, whether a Chief Magistrate is to be elected by
their voice, or by a Committee, the majority of whom were
selected and named by a party; and those who may be the
cause, must then be answerable for the consequences that
may follow.

Be assured, Sir, of our best wishes for your public and
private welfare.

By order of the Committee.

ABRAHAM TEN BROECK,

Chairman.

ALBANY, 2d July, 1792.

JAY'S REPLY TO THE ALBANY COMMITTEE.

GENTLEMEN :

I find it impossible to convey to you adequate ideas
of the impressions which the sentiments expressed in
your address have made upon my heart and mind.
The uninterrupted confidence which my fellow-citizens have reposed in my zeal for the honour and
welfare of our common country is one of the most
pleasing circumstances of my life; and it will never
cease to unite with the still higher considerations of
duty in rendering that zeal permanent and persevering. The approbation of the intelligent, the independent, and the free is valuable because spontaneous
and sincere; and it becomes particularly grateful,

when bestowed in a manner so affectionate by fellow-labourers in the same field. When sentiments and opinions relative to public measures are capable of being ascribed to private and personal considerations, prudence dictates a great degree of delicacy and reserve ; but there are no considerations which ought to restrain me from expressing my ardent wishes that the important question you mention may be brought to a decision with all that mature reflection as well as manly constancy which its connection with the rights of freemen demands ; with all that temper which relf-respect requires ; and with all that regard to conciliation, benevolence, and good neighbourhood which patriotism prescribes.

Accept my warmest thanks, gentlemen, for the particular marks of attention with which you have honoured me ; and be pleased to assure my fellow-citizens of this ancient and respectable city that I most sincerely wish them prosperity.

NEW YORK COMMITTEE TO JAY.[1]

To the Honorable John Jay, Esquire,
    Chief Justice of the United States :

Sir :

Permit us in behalf of ourselves and the very respectable body of our fellow citizens, which we have the honor to represent, to congratulate you upon your safe return to this City from the Eastern Circuit.

---

[1] Jay reached New York July 10th. The *Advertiser* of the 11th reports his reception as follows.

" Yesterday afternoon, the committee appointed at a meeting of the Friends of Liberty, attended by a very great and respectable concourse of citizens, on horse-

The friends of liberty have ever entertained a lively sense of the important services which you have rendered to your country in every situation in which you have been placed. Whether they examine your conduct as a Member of the General Congress at the most trying periods of the late war, and of the Convention which framed the Constitution of this State, or consider your agency in negotiating the treaty which secured to America the blessings of peace, liberty and safety—they find a continued display of abilities and virtue which will hand your name down to remote posterity *as one of the illustrious defenders of the rights of Man.*

It was this sense, Sir, of your public services which induced the independent freeholders of the State to nominate and support you at the last election as a candidate for the office of their Chief Magistrate, and procured you a decided majority of votes. Thus called to enjoy one of the highest honors in the power of a grateful people to bestow, it

back and in carriages, proceeded to Harlem heights where they met Mr. Jay and escorted him into town. When the procession arrived at the two-mile stone, they were received by loud huzzas from a very great number of citizens on foot assembled at that place. As they approached the town, at the head of Chatham street a federal salute was fired and a painting exhibited, on which was written, ' JOHN JAY, GOVERNOR BY THE VOICE OF THE PEOPLE.'

" The procession moved through Queen, Wall, Broad, Beaver streets, and Broadway, to Mr. Jay's house, amidst repeated huzzas and plaudits from his fellow citizens. At his own door he was conducted into his house by the Committee, where he was affectionately received by his family and friends. Before he entered his house, he attempted to say something on the occasion expressive of his feelings, and to make an acknowledgment for the partiality shewn him, but the loud and repeated plaudits of the PEOPLE prevented his being heard.

" In several conspicuous places flags were displayed ; a salute was fired at the Battery, and the bells were rung in all the Churches in the city."

On the 13th the committee of the Friends of Liberty formally congratulated Mr. Jay in the terms of the above address, and on the 19th an " elegant entertainment " was tendered him at the City Tavern by some two hundred citizens. Fifteen toasts were offered at this " feast of freedom and friendship," as described by the *Advertiser*, which closed with one from Jay himself as he retired— " May the people always respect themselves and remember what they owe to posterity." The company then formed in procession and waited upon him to his house.

was not to be expected that you would have been deprived of it by the machinations of a few interested and designing men. In contempt, however, of the sacred voice of the people, in defiance of the Constitution, and in violation of uniform practice and the settled principles of law, we have seen a majority of the canvassing Committee reject the votes of whole Counties for the purpose of excluding you and making way for a Governor of their own choice. This wanton and daring attack upon the invaluable rights of suffrage has excited a serious alarm amongst the electors of the State, and united them in measures to obtain redress. In the pursuit of an object so interesting we shall like freemen act with moderation and order ; but at the same time with zeal and perseverance. Whilst we respect the laws, we respect ourselves and our rights and feel the strongest obligations to assert and maintain them. The cause in which we are engaged being the cause of the people we trust that it cannot fail of success ; but in every event we entreat you to believe that you will retain a distinguished place in our affections, and that we shall embrace every opportunity to manifest the unbounded confidence which we repose in your talents and patriotism.

By order of the Committee,
NICHOLAS CRUGER,
Chairman.

NEW YORK, July 13th, 1792.

JAY'S REPLY TO THE NEW YORK COMMITTEE.

GENTLEMEN :

It is far more pleasing to receive proofs of the confidence and attachment of my native city than it is easy to express the sense which that confidence and that attachment inspire. When I reflect on the sacrifices and efforts in the cause of liberty, which distinguished this State during the late war, my feelings are very sensibly affected by the favourable light in which you regard my conduct during that interesting period. That cause was patronized by Him who gave to men the rights we claimed. He crowned it with success, and made it instrumental to our enjoying a degree of national prosperity unknown to any other people. May it be perpetual ! Such is our Constitution, and such are the means of preserving order and good government, with which we are blessed, that, while our citizens remain virtuous, free, and enlightened, few political evils can occur, for which remedies perfectly effectual, and yet perfectly consistent with general tranquillity, cannot be found and applied.

I derive great satisfaction from the hope and expectation that the event which at present excites so much alarm and anxiety, will give occasion only to such measures as patriotism may direct and justify ; and that the vigilance and wisdom of the people will always afford to their rights that protection for which other countries, less informed, have often too precipitately recurred to violence and commotion.

In questions touching our constitutional privileges, all the citizens are equally interested ; and the social duties call upon us to unite in discussing those questions with candour and temper, in deciding them with circumspection and impartiality, and in maintaining the equal rights of all with constancy and fortitude.

They who do what they have a right to do, give no just cause of offence ; and therefore every consideration of propriety forbids that differences in opinion respecting candidates should suspend or interrupt that mutual good-humour and benevolence which harmonizes society, and softens the asperities incident to human life and human affairs.

By those free and independent electors who have given me their suffrages, I esteem myself honoured ; for the virtuous, who withheld that mark of preference, I retain, and ought to retain, my former respect and good-will. To all I wish prosperity, public and private. Permit me, gentlemen, to assure you and your constituents that, as I value their esteem, and rejoice in their approbation, so it will always be my desire, as well as my duty, to justify as far as possible the sentiments which they entertain of me, and which you, sir, have expressed in terms and in a manner which demand and which receive my warmest acknowledgments.

HENRY MARCHANT[1] TO JAY.

NEWPORT, August 14th, 1792.

RESPECTED SIR,

I presume this will find you returned from Philadelphia and preparing for your Southern Circuit, which we hope may prove an agreeable one. While New England laments the loss the publick may sustain in your quitting your present important federal station, they feel as friends to order,

[1] Judge, United States District Court, Rhode Island.

decency, and the rights of man, a wish, not merely for your success, but the success of constitutional rights ; and would not be happy to find the steady advocates of liberty desert the cause. Example is prevalent ; and in our first setting out we should be cautious how we establish bad precedents. Posterity has a demand upon us—that the laws and constitution we have been blessed with are not handed down to them mangled or in fetters.

The delicate, prudent, and cautious manner, so peculiar to you, in which you answered the addresses of your fellow-citizens, has given great pleasure ; for while it is our duty to contend against the violations of essential rights, it behooves us that we do not by our own conduct establish the violence we contend against. We had better fail—having done all that faithful citizens and guardians of the laws ought to do, than proceed by methods disgraceful to a good cause.

Our country has a claim to the highest exertions of all its sons. I sincerely lament the unhappy dissensions I perceive arising amongst some who are peculiarly bound by every consideration to lay aside *self*, and strive only for the advancement of the peace, honor and happiness of our common country. Let the North and South give up. Let us collect in one center, and making one huge pile of all our self-ambition, jealousies, murmurs, disappointments and discontents, commit them to the flames as a grand sacrifice to the best good of our land, our own peace and honor, and that of millions yet unborn. Let all good men set about this work, and join to set their faces against every opposer to it.

Without flattery, no man is better fitted to take the important lead than yourself. Your opportunities are great, and I know they will be eagerly embraced. Under this consideration I regret the less at your tour to the southward. May success attend you, as do my best wishes at all times and wheresoever you may be. With our respects to Mrs. Jay, I am with all possible esteem and pride, Dear Sir,

Your sincere friend and humble servant,
HENRY MARCHANT.

ALEXANDER HAMILTON TO JAY.

[Private.]

PHILADELPHIA, Sepr. 3rd, 1792.

MY DEAR SIR:

The proceedings at Pittsburgh,[1] which you will find stated in the enclosed paper, and other incidents in the Western parts of this State, announce so determined and persevering a spirit of opposition to the law, as in my opinion to render a vigorous exertion of the powers of government indispensable. I have communicated this opinion to the President and I doubt not his impressions will accord with it. In this case, one point for consideration will be the expediency of the next Circuit Courts noticing the state of things in that quarter, particularly the meeting at Pittsburgh and its proceedings. You will observe an avowed object is to "*obstruct* the *operation* of the law." This is attempted to be qualified by a pretence of doing it by "every legal measure." But "legal measures" "to obstruct the operation of a law" is a contradiction in terms. I therefore entertain no doubt that a high misdemeanour has been committed. The point however is under submission to the Attorney General for his opinion.

There is really, My Dear Sir, a crisis in the affairs of the Country which demands the most mature consideration of its best and wisest friends. I beg you to apply your most

---

[1] With reference to the excise on distilled spirits, which met with vigorous opposition in Western Pennsylvania, and eventually culminated in the "Whiskey Rebellion."

serious thoughts to it, and favour me as soon as possible with the result of your reflections. Perhaps it will not be amiss for you to converse with M͏ʳ· King. His judgment is sound ; he has caution and energy.

Would a proclamation from the President be advisable stating the criminality of such proceedings and warning all persons to abstain from them, as the laws will be strictly enforced against all offenders?

If the plot should thicken and the application of force should appear to be unavoidable, will it be expedient for the President to repair´ in person to the scene of commotion?

These are some of the questions which present themselves. The subject will doubtless open itself in all its aspects to you. With real respect and affectionate attachment,

I remain, Dear Sir,
Your obedient Servant,
ALEXANDER HAMILTON.

JAY TO HENRY MARCHANT.

NEW YORK, 6th September, 1792.

DEAR SIR :

Your solicitude for the honour and welfare of our country is patriotic. If similar sentiments prevailed more generally, there would be less reason for anxiety. But, my good friend, in the present state of society in this country, we must not expect to be entirely exempt from the influence of private passions on public affairs. The people of the United States possess more information than the people of any other country, but they do not in my opinion yet possess throughout a sufficient degree of it. Ignorance and credulity will always be duped and misled by artifice and design ; where all are informed few will be deceived ; and it is only from the number that may be *deceived* that danger or mischief are to be apprehended.

I am, my dear sir,

Your affectionate friend and servant,

JOHN JAY.

JAY TO ALEXANDER HAMILTON.

NEW YORK, 8th September, 1792.

DEAR SIR :

I have conferred with Mr. King upon the subject of your letter of the 3d. inst. We concur in opinion that neither a proclamation nor a *particular* charge by the court to the grand jury would be advisable at present. To us it appears more prudent that the business be opened by the President's speech at the ensuing session of Congress ; their address will manifest the sense of the House, and both together operate more effectually than a proclamation.

No strong declarations should be made unless there be ability and disposition to follow them with strong measures. Admitting both these requisites, it is questionable whether such operations at this moment would not furnish the Anties with materials for deceiving the uninformed part of the community, and in some measure render the operations of government odious. Let all the branches of government move together, and let the chiefs be committed publicly on one or the other side of the question. I perceive symptoms of the crisis you mention ; if managed with discretion and firmness it will weaken its authors. If matters can pass on *sub silentio* until the meeting of Congress, I think all will be well. The public will become informed and the sense of the nation will become manifest ; opposition to that sense will be clogged with apprehensions, and strong measures if necessary will be approved and be supported. If in the meantime such outrage should be committed as to force the attention of government to its dignity, nothing will remain but to obey that necessity in a way that will leave nothing to hazard. Success on such occasions should be certain. Whether this should be done under the President's personal direction must, I think, depend on circumstances at the time, or in other words on the degree of importance which those circumstances combined may evince.

Yours affectionately,

JOHN JAY.

WILLIAM CUSHING [1] TO JAY.

NEWCASTLE (DEL.), Tuesday, Oct. 23^d, 1792.

DEAR SIR :

I have rubbed along as well as I could without you. We had two jury cases at Trenton, and there we took up the matter of invalids—there being no determination upon the

---

[1] Justice, Supreme Court of the United States. He was associated with Jay in his circuits, but was now alone in consequence of the latter's temporary illness. Jay started on his southern circuit, September 17th, but inflammation

subject in that district before, the Judges not having the Statute there last term. Mr. Morris was strong in favor and I was not opposing; so we acted as Commissioners and sent our certificates accordingly (without making any entry in the book about it) to the *Supreme* Secretary of War. At Yorktown [York, Pa.] but one jury cause, which was short. There had been depending about six and twenty actions, but rather than go 90 miles from Phil[a] for trial, the parties had settled about twenty of them; one was tried as aforesaid, and four continued by agreement to next term for trial at Philadelphia. There we had nothing to do with the pension list; the like I suppose will be the case in all places this side the Delaware.

We had a tolerable road to Yorktown, but somewhat cut with waggons a considerable part of the way, but worse on our return by reason of some rains which fell. Some excellent inns on that road. Two indictments were found at Yorktown—one for an insult upon one of the foreign ministers by serving process upon his servant for a debt of about 5 s.; the other for a violent assault of about 50 persons, in disguise, upon an inspector's office in the western part of Pennsylvania.

Mrs. Cushing is with me now on the route to Dover, a fine road south of Philadelphia. I am in strong hopes of the pleasure of seeing you soon, and that your health is fully restored as I heard of your riding abroad sometime ago. I hear of causes to be tried in Maryland, and in Virginia, of above a hundred, which will require both your sedateness and sagacity. At the same time I would not have you risk your health for a thousand of them. I mean [to go] from Easton in Maryland for Kent —— and thence across the Chesapeake, an 8 or 9 mile ferry, to Annapolis;

of the eyes soon obliged him to return to New York, where he remained until early in the following year (1793) before he heard cases at Philadelphia and Richmond.

then to the federal city, perhaps buy a house lot there, and so onward to Richmond.

Mrs. Cushing joins in the most sincere regards to you, Mrs. Jay, and family.

I have the honor to be, with sincere respect and esteem, Sir,

> Your most obedient servant,
> WILLIAM CUSHING.

ALEXANDER HAMILTON TO JAY.

PHILADELPHIA, December 18th, 1792.

MY DEAR SIR:

Your favours of the 26th November and 16th inst. have duly come to hand. I am ashamed that the former has remained so long unacknowledged; though I am persuaded my friends would readily excuse my delinquencies, could they appreciate my situation. 'Tis not the load of proper official business that alone engrosses me, though this would be enough to occupy any man. 'Tis not the èxtra attentions I am obliged to pay to the course of legislative manœuvres, that alone adds to my burthen and perplexity. 'Tis the malicious intrigues to stab me in the dark, against which I am too often obliged to guard myself, that distract and harass me to a point, which, rendering my situation scarcely tolerable, interferes with objects to which friendship and inclination would prompt me.

I have not, however, been unmindful of the subject of your letters. Mr. King will tell you the state the business was in. Nothing material has happened since. The representation will probably produce some effect, though not as great as ought to be expected. Some changes for the better, I trust, will take place.

The success of the vice-president is as great a source of satisfaction, as that of Mr. Clinton would have been of mortification and pain to me. Willingly, however, would I relinquish my share of the command to the anti-federalists, if I thought they were to be trusted. But I have so many proofs of the contrary, as to make me dread the experiment of their preponderance.

Very respectfully and affectionately, dear sir,

Your obedient servant,

A. HAMILTON.

JAY TO ALEXANDER HAMILTON.

NEW YORK, 29th December, 1792.

DEAR SIR:

On my return this evening from Rye, I found your letter of the 18th instant at my house. It is not difficult to perceive that your situation is unpleasant, and it is easy to predict that your enemies will endeavour to render it still more so. The thorns they strew in your way will (if you please) hereafter blossom, and furnish garlands to decorate your administration. Resolve not to be driven from your station, and as your situation must, it seems, be militant, act accordingly. Envy will tell posterity that your difficulties, from the state of *things*, were inconsiderable, compared with the great, growing, and untouched resources of the nation. Your difficulties from *persons* and *party* will, by time, be carried out of sight, unless you prevent it. No other person will possess sufficient facts and details to do full justice to the subject, and I think your reputation points to the expediency of memoirs. You want time, it is true, but few of us know how much time we can find when we set about it.

Had not your letter come from the post-office, I should suspect it had been opened. The wafer looked very much like it. Such letters should be sealed with wax, impressed with your seal.

I rejoice with you in the re-election of Mr. Adams. It has relieved my mind from much inquietude. It is a great point gained; but the unceasing industry and arts of the Anties render perseverance, union, and constant efforts necessary. Adieu, my dear sir.

Yours sincerely,

JOHN JAY.

OPINION OF CHIEF-JUSTICE JAY ON THE SUABILITY OF A STATE. [1]

The question we are now to decide has been accurately stated, viz. : Is a State suable by individual citizens of another State ?

It is said that Georgia refuses to appear and answer to the plaintiff in this action, because she is a *sovereign* State, and therefore not liable to such actions. In order to ascertain the merits of this objection, let us inquire —first, in what sense Georgia is a sovereign State ;

---

[1] The question of the suability of a State by citizens of another State was heard and considered by the Supreme Court at Philadelphia, in February, 1793—the suit having arisen on the claim of two executors in South Carolina to certain confiscated property held by the State of Georgia. Chief-Justice Jay, and Justices Cushing, Wilson, and Blair, were of the opinion that, under the Constitution, the State was suable. Justice Iredell dissented. A summary of the case, which was decided February 18th, appears in Claypole's Philadelphia *Advertiser* for February 20th. The decision excited opposition, not only in Georgia, where the United States Grand Jury presented it as a " grievance," but in Massachusetts, Pennsylvania, and other States ; and in 1798 it was reversed, by the adoption of the Eleventh Amendment to the Constitution. See Dallas' *Reports*, Vol. II., pp. 419–80.

second, whether suability is incompatible with such sovereignty; third, whether the Constitution, to which Georgia is a party, authorizes such an action against her.

Suability and suable are words not in common use, but they concisely and correctly convey the idea annexed to them.

First, in determining the sense in which Georgia is a sovereign State, it may be useful to turn our attention to the political situation we were in prior to the Revolution, and to the political rights which emerged from the Revolution. All the country now possessed by the United States was then a part of the dominions appertaining to the crown of Great Britain. Every acre of land in this country was then held, mediately or immediately, by grants from that crown. All the people of this country were then subjects of the King of Great Britain, and owed allegiance to him, and all the civil authority then existing or exercised here flowed from the head of the *British Empire.* They were in strict sense fellow-subjects, and in a variety of respects one people. When the Revolution commenced, the patriots did not assert that only the same affinity and social connection subsisted between the people of the Colonies which subsisted between the people of Gaul, Britain, and Spain, while Roman provinces,—viz., only that affinity and social connection which result from the mere circumstance of being governed by the same prince. Different ideas prevailed, and gave occasion to the Congress of 1774 and 1775.

The Revolution, or rather the Declaration of Independence, found the people *already* united for
general purposes, and at the same time providing for
their more domestic concerns, by State conventions
and other temporary arrangements. From the crown
of Great Britain the sovereignty of their country
passed to the people of it; and it was then not an
uncommon opinion that the unappropriated lands,
which belonged to that crown, passed not to the
people of the Colony or States within whose limits
they were situated, but to the whole people. On
whatever principles this opinion rested, it did not
give way to the other; and thirteen sovereignties
were considered as emerged from the principles of
the Revolution, combined with local convenience and
considerations. The people, nevertheless, continued
to consider themselves, in a national point of view, as
one people; and they continued, without interruption, to manage their national concerns accordingly.
Afterwards, in the hurry of the war, and in the
warmth of mutual confidence, they made a confederation of the States the basis of a general government.
Experience disappointed the expectations they had
formed from it; and then the people, in their collective and national capacity, established the present
Constitution. It is remarkable that, in establishing
it, the people exercised their own rights and their
own proper sovereignty; and, conscious of the plenti-
tude of it, they declared, with becoming dignity:
"We, the *people* of the *United States*, do ordain and
establish this Constitution." Here we see the people

456 *CORRESPONDENCE AND PUBLIC PAPERS.*

acting as sovereigns of the whole country, and, in the language of sovereignty, establishing a Constitution, by which it was their will that the State governments should be bound, and to which the State constitutions should be made to conform. Every State constitution is a compact made by and between the citizens of a State to govern themselves in a certain manner ; and the Constitution of the *United States* is likewise a compact made by the people of the *United States* to govern themselves as to general objects in a certain manner. By this great compact, however, many prerogatives were transferred to the national government, such as those of making war and peace, contracting alliances, coining money, etc., etc.

If then it be true, that the sovereignty of the nation is in the people of the nation, and the residuary sovereignty of each State in the people of each State, it may be useful to compare these sovereignties with those in *Europe*, that we may thence be enabled to judge, whether all the prerogatives which are allowed to the latter, are so essential to the former. There is reason to suspect that some of the difficulties which embarrass the present question, arise from inattention to differences which subsist between them.

It will be sufficient to observe, briefly, that the sovereignties in Europe, and particularly in England, exist on *feudal* principles. That system considers the *prince* as the *sovereign*, and the people as his subjects; it regards his *person* as the object of allegiance, and excludes the idea of his being on an equal footing with a subject, either in a court of justice or elsewhere. That system contemplates him as being the fountain of honor and authority ; and from his grace and grant derives all franchises, immunities, and privileges ; it is easy to perceive that such a sovereign could not be amenable to a court of justice, or subjected to judicial control and actual constraint. It was of necessity, therefore, that suability became incompatible with such sovereignty. Besides, the prince having all the executive powers, the judgment of the courts would, in fact, be only monitory, not mandatory, to him, and a capacity to be advised is a distinct thing from a capacity to be sued. The same feudal ideas run through all their jurisprudence, and constantly remind us of the distinction between the *prince* and the subject. No such ideas obtain here ; at the Revolution, the sovereignty devolved on the people ; and they are truly the sovereigns of the country, but they are *sovereigns without subjects* (unless the African slaves among us may be so called), and have none to govern but *themselves ;* the citizens of America are equal as fellow-citizens, and as joint tenants in the sovereignty.

From the differences existing between feudal sovereignties and governments founded on compacts, it necessarily follows that their respective prerogatives must differ. Sovereignty is the right to govern ; a nation or state-sovereign is the person or persons in whom that resides. In Europe the sovereignty is generally ascribed to the prince; here it rests with the people; there, the sovereign actually administers the government; here, never in a single instance; our governors are the agents of the people, and at most stand in the same relation to their sovereign, in which the regents in Europe stand to their sovereigns. Their princes have *personal* powers, dignities, and pre-eminences, our rulers have none but *official;* nor do they partake in the sovereignty otherwise, or in any other capacity, than as private citizens.

Second. The second object of inquiry now presents itself, viz., whether suability is compatible with State sovereignty?

Suability, by whom? Not by a subject, for in this country there are none; not an inferior, for all citizens being as to civil rights perfectly equal, there is not, in that respect, one citizen inferior to another. It is agreed that one free citizen may sue another; the obvious dictates of justice and the purposes of society demanding it. It is agreed, that one free citizen may sue any number on whom process can be conveniently executed; nay, in certain cases one citizen may sue forty thousand; for where a corporation is sued, all the members of it are *actually* sued, though not *personally* sued. In this city there are forty odd thousand free citizens, all of whom may be collectively sued by any individual citizen. In the State of Delaware, there are fifty odd thousand free citizens, and what reason can be assigned why a free citizen who has demands against them should not prosecute them? Can the difference between forty odd thousand and fifty odd thousand make any distinction as to right? Is it not as easy, and as convenient to the public and parties, to serve a summons on the Governor and Attorney-General of Delaware, as on the Mayor or other officers of the corporation of Philadelphia? Will it be said, that the fifty odd thousand citizens in Delaware being associated under a State government, stand in a rank so superior to the forty odd thousand of Philadelphia associated under their charter, that although it may become the latter to meet an individual on an equal footing in a court of justice, yet that such procedure would not comport with the dignity of the former? In this land of equal liberty, shall forty odd thousand in one place be compellable to do justice, and yet fifty odd thousand in another place be privileged to do justice only as they may think proper? Such objections would not correspond with the equal rights we claim; with the equality we profess to admire and maintain, and with that popular sovereignty in which every citizen partakes. Grant that the Governor of Delaware holds an office of superior rank to the Mayor of Philadelphia, they are both nevertheless the officers of the people; and however more exalted one may be than the other, yet in the opinion of those who dislike aristocracy, that circumstance cannot be a good reason for impeding the course of justice.

If there be any such incompatibility as is pretended, whence does it arise? In what does it consist?

There is at least one strong, undeniable fact against this incompatibility, and that is this : any one State in the Union may sue another State in this court; that is, all the people of one State may sue all the people of another State. It is plain, then, that a State may be sued, and hence it plainly follows, that suability and State sovereignty are not incompatible. As one State may sue another State in this court, it is plain that no degradation to a State is thought to accompany her appearance in this court. It is not, therefore, to an appearance in this court that the objection points. To what does it point? It points to an appearance at the suit of one or more citizens. But why it should be more incompatible, that all the people of a State should be sued by *one* citizen, than by one hundred thousand, I cannot perceive, the process in both cases being alike ; and the consequences of a judgment alike. Nor can I observe any greater inconveniences in the one case than in the other, except what may arise from the feelings of those who may regard a lesser number in an inferior light. But if any reliance be made on this inferiority as an objection, at least one half its force is done away with by this fact, viz., that it is conceded that a State may appear in this court as plaintiff against a single citizen as defendant ; and the truth is, that the State of Georgia is at this moment prosecuting an action in this court against two citizens of South Carolina.

The only remnant of objection, therefore, that remains is that the State is not bound to appear and answer as a *defendant* at the suit of an individual :

but why it is unreasonable that she should be so bound is hard to conjecture. That rule is said to be a bad one which does not work both ways; the citizens of Georgia are content with a right of suing citizens of other States, but are not content that citizens of other States should have a right to sue them.

Let us now proceed to inquire whether Georgia has not, by being a party to the national compact, consented to be suable by individual citizens of another State. This inquiry naturally leads our attention: 1st. To the design of the Constitution. 2d. To the letter and express declaration in it.

Prior to the date of the Constitution, the people had not any national tribunal to which they could resort for justice; the distribution of justice was then confined to State judicatories, in whose institution and organization the people of the other States had no participation, and over whom they had not the least control. There was then no general court of appellate jurisdiction, by whom the errors of State courts, affecting either the nation at large or the citizens of any other State, could be revised and corrected. Each State was obliged to acquiesce in the measure of justice which another State might yield to her, or to her citizens; and that even in cases where State considerations were not always favourable to the most exact measure. There was danger that from this source animosities would in time result; and as the transition from animosities to hostilities was frequent in the history of independent States, a common tribunal for the termination of controversies became desirable, from motives both of justice and of policy.

Prior also to that period, the United States had, by taking a place among the nations of the earth, become amenable to the laws of nations; and it was their interest as well as their duty to provide that those laws should be respected and obeyed; in their national character and capacity the United States were responsible to foreign nations for the conduct of each State relative to the laws of nations, and the performance of treaties; and there the inexpediency of referring all such questions to State courts, and particularly to the courts of delinquent States, became apparent. While *all* States were bound to protect *each*, and the citizens of *each*, it was highly proper and reasonable that they should be in a capacity not only to cause justice to be done *to* each, and the citizens of each, but also to cause justice to be done *by* each and the citizens of each; and that not by violence and force, but in a stable, sedate, and regular course of judicial procedure.

These were among the evils against which it was proper for the nation, that is, the people of all the United States, to provide by a national judiciary, to be instituted by the whole nation, and to be responsible to the whole nation.

Let us now turn to the Constitution. The people therein declare that their design in establishing it comprehended six objects: 1st. To form a more perfect union. 2d. To establish justice. 3d. To insure domestic tranquillity. 4th. To provide for the com-

to be affected or regulated by the local laws or courts of a part of the nation. 4th. To all cases affecting ambassadors, or other public ministers and consuls; because, as these are officers of foreign nations, whom this nation is bound to protect and treat according to the laws of nations, cases affecting them ought only to be cognizable by national authority. 5th. To all cases of admiralty and maritime jurisdiction; because, as the seas are the joint property of nations, whose rights and privileges relative thereto are regulated by the law of nations and treaties, such cases necessarily belong to national jurisdiction. 6th. To controversies to which the United States shall be a party; because, in cases in which the whole people are interested, it would not be equal or wise to let any one State decide and measure out justice due to others. 7th. To controversies between two or more States; because domestic tranquillity requires that the contention of States should be peaceably terminated by a common judicatory; and because in a free country justice ought not to depend on the *will* of either of the litigants. 8th. To controversies between a State and citizens of another State; because, in case a State (that is, all the citizens of it) has demands against some citizens of another State, it is better that she should prosecute their demands in a national court, than in the court of the State to which those citizens belong; the danger of irritation and criminations arising from apprehensions and suspicions of partiality being thereby obviated. Because, in cases where some citizens of one State have demands against all the citizens of another State, the cause of liberty and the rights of men forbid that the latter should be the sole judges of the justice due to the latter ; and true republican government requires that free and equal citizens should have free, fair, and equal justice. 9th. To controversies between citizens of the same State claiming lands under grants of different States ; because, as the rights of the two States to grant the land are drawn into question, neither of the two States ought to decide the controversy. 10th. To controversies between a State or the citizens thereof ; and foreign states, citizens, or subjects ; because, as every nation is responsible for the conduct of its citizens towards other nations, all questions touching the justice due to foreign nations or people ought to be ascertained by, and depend on, national authority. Even this cursory view of the judicial powers of the United States leaves the mind strongly impressed with the importance of them to the preservation of the tranquillity, the equal sovereignty, and the equal rights of the people.

The question now before us renders it necessary to pay particular attention to that part of the 2d section which extends the judicial power " to controversies between a State and citizens of another State." It is contended that this ought to be construed to reach none of these controversies, excepting those in which a State may be plaintiff. The ordinary rules for construction will easily decide whether those words are to be understood in that limited sense.

This extension of power is remedial, because it is
to settle controversies. It is therefore to be construed liberally. It is politic, wise, and good that not
only the controversies in which a State is plaintiff, but
also those in which a State is defendant, should be
settled ; both cases, therefore, are within the reason
of the remedy, and ought to be so adjudged, unless
the obvious, plain, and literal sense of the words forbid it. If we attend to the *words*, we find them to be
express, positive, free from ambiguity, and without
room for such implied expressions : " The judicial
power of the United States shall extend to controversies between a State and citizens of another State."
If the Constitution really meant to extend these
powers only to those controversies in which a State
might be plaintiff, to the exclusion of those in which
citizens had demands against a State, it is inconceivable that it should have attempted to convey that
meaning in words, not only so incompetent, but also
repugnant to it ; if it meant to exclude a certain class
of these controversies, why were they not expressly
excepted ; on the contrary, not even an intimation of
such intention appears in any part of the Constitution.
It cannot be pretended that where citizens urge and
insist upon demands against a State, which the State
refuses to admit and comply with, that there is no *controversy* between them. If it is a controversy between
them, then it clearly falls not only within the spirit,
but the very words of the Constitution. What is it
to the cause of justice, and how can it affect the definition of the word controversy, whether the demands

which cause the dispute are made by a State against the citizens of another State, or by the latter against the former? When power is thus extended to a controversy, it necessarily, as to all judicial purposes, is also extended to those between whom it subsists.

The exception contended for would contradict and do violence to the great and leading principles of a free and equal national government, one of the objects of which is to ensure justice to all : to the few against the many as well as to the many against the few. It would be strange, indeed, that the joint and equal sovereigns of this country should, in the very Constitution by which they professed to establish justice, so far deviate from the plain path of equality and impartiality as to give to the collective citizens of one State a right of suing individual citizens of another State, and yet deny to those citizens a right of suing them. We find the same general and comprehensive manner of expressing the same ideas in a subsequent clause, in which the Constitution ordains that " in all cases affecting ambassadors, other public ministers and consuls, and those in which a state shall be a party, the Supreme Court shall have original jurisdiction." Did it mean here *party-plaintiff?* If that *only* was meant, it would have been easy to have found words to express it. Words are to be understood in their ordinary and common acceptation, and the word " party" being in common usage applicable to plaintiff and defendant, we cannot limit it to *one* of them in the present case. We find the Legislature of the United States expressing themselves in the like gen-

eral and comprehensive manner; they speak in the
13th section of the Judicial Act of controversies
where a State is a *party*, and as they do not impliedly
or expressly apply that term to either of the litigants
in particular, we are to understand them as speaking
of *both*. In the same section they distinguish the
cases where Ambassadors are plaintiffs from those in
which Ambassadors are defendants, and make different
provisions respecting those cases; and it is not unnatural to suppose that they would in like manner have
distinguished between cases where a State was plaintiff and where a State was defendant, if they had
intended to make any difference between them, or if
they had apprehended that the Constitution had made
any difference between them.

I perceive, and therefore candour urges me to mention, a circumstance which seems to favour the opposite side of the question. It is this: the same section
of the Constitution which extends the judicial power
to controversies "between a State and the citizens of
another State" does also extend that power to controversies to which the United States are a party.
Now it may be said if the word party comprehends
both plaintiff and defendant, it follows that the United
States may be sued by any citizen between whom and
them there may be a controversy. This appears to
me to be fair reasoning; but the same principles of
candour which urge me to mention this objection also
urge me to suggest an important difference between
the two cases. It is this: in all cases of actions
against States or individual citizens, the national

courts are supported in all their legal and constitutional proceedings and judgments by the arm of the executive power of the United States ; but in cases of actions against the United States, there is no power which the courts can call to their aid. From this distinction important conclusions are deducible, and they place the case of a State and the case of the United States in very different points of view.

I wish the state of society was so far improved, and the science of government advanced to such a degree of perfection, as that the whole nation could in the peaceable course of law be compelled to do justice and be sued by individual citizens. Whether that is or is not now the case ought not to be thus collaterally and incidentally decided : I leave it a question.

As this opinion, though deliberately formed, has been hastily reduced to writing between the intervals of the daily adjournments, and while my mind was occupied and wearied with the business of the day, I fear it is less concise and connected than it might otherwise have been. I have made no references to cases, because I know of none that are not distinguishable from this case ; nor does it appear to me to be necessary to show that the sentiments of the best writers on government and the rights of men harmonize with the principles which direct my judgment on the present question. The acts of the former Congresses, and the acts of many of the State conventions are replete with similar ideas ; and to the honor of the United States, it may be observed that, in no other country are subjects of this kind better, if so well, understood. The attention and attachment of the Constitution to the equal rights of the people are discernible in almost every sentence of it; and it is to be regretted that the provision in it which we have been considering, has not in every instance received the approbation and acquiescence which it merits. Georgia has in strong language advocated the cause of republican equality; and there is reason to hope that the people of that State will yet perceive that it would not have been consistent with that equality, to have exempted the body of her citizens from that suability which they are at this moment exercising against citizens of another State.

For my own part, I am convinced that the sense in which I understand and have explained the words "controversies between States and citizens of another State," is the true sense. The extension of the judiciary power of the United States to such controversies, appears to me to be *wise*, because it is *honest* and because it is *useful*. It is *honest* because it provides in doing justice without respect of persons, and by securing individual citizens as well as States in their respective rights, performs the promise which every free government makes to every free citizen, of equal justice and protection. It is *useful* because it is honest, because it leaves not even the most obscure and friendless citizen without means of obtaining justice from a neighboring State; because it obviates occasions of quarrels between States on account of the claims of their respective citizens; because it recognizes and strongly rests on this great moral truth, that justice is the same whether due from one man to a million, or from a million to one man ; because it teaches and greatly appreciates the value of our free, republican, national government, which places all our citizens on an equal footing, and enables each and every of them to obtain justice without any danger of being overborne by the weight and number of their opponents ; and, because it brings into action and enforces this great and glorious principle, that the people are the sovereign of this country, and consequently that fellow-citizens and joint sovereigns cannot be degraded by appearing with each other in their own courts to have their controversies determined. The people have reason to prize and rejoice in such valuable privileges ; and they ought not to forget that nothing but the free course of constitutional law and government can insure the continuance and enjoyment of them.

For the reasons before given, I am clearly of opinion that a State is suable by citizens of another State, but lest I should be understood in a latitude beyond my meaning, I think it necessary to subjoin this caution, viz. : That such suability may nevertheless not extend to all the demands and to every kind of action ; there may be exceptions.   For instance, I am far from being prepared to say that an individual may sue a State on bills of credit issued before the Constitution was established, and which were issued and received on the faith of the State, and at a time when no ideas or expectations of judicial interposition were entertained or contemplated.

ALEXANDER HAMILTON TO JAY.

PHILADELPHIA, April 9, 1793.

DEAR SIR:

When we last conversed together on the subject, we were both of opinion that the minister expected from France should be received.

Subsequent circumstances have perhaps induced an additional embarrassment on this point, and render it advisable to reconsider the opinion generally, and to raise this further question, Whether he ought to be received *absolutely* or with qualifications?

The king has been decapitated. Out of this will arise a regent, acknowledged and supported by the powers of Europe almost universally—in capacity to act, and who may himself send an ambassador to the United States. Should we in such case receive both? If we receive one from the republic and refuse the other, shall we stand on ground perfectly neutral?

If we receive a minister from the republic, shall we be afterward at liberty to say, "We will not decide whether there is a government in France competent to demand from us the performance of the existing treaties"? What the government of France shall be is the very point in *dispute*. Till that is decided, the *applicability* of the treaties is suspended. When that government is *established*, we shall consider whether such changes have been made as to render their continuance incompatible with the interest of the United States. If we shall not have concluded ourselves by any act, I am of opinion that we have at least a right to hold the thing suspended. Till the point in dispute is decided, I doubt whether we could *bona fide* dispute the ultimate obligation of the treaties. Will the unqualified reception of a minister conclude us? If it will, ought we so to conclude ourselves?

Ought we not rather to refuse receiving, or to receive with qualification; declaring that we receive the person as the representative of the government, *in fact*, of the French nation, reserving to ourselves a right to consider the applicability of the treaties to the *actual situation* of the parties?

These are questions which require our utmost wisdom. I would give a great deal for a personal discussion with you. *Imprudent things* have been already done, which render it proportionately important that every succeeding step should be well considered.

With true attachment, I am, dear sir,

Your obedient servant,

A. HAMILTON.

ALEXANDER HAMILTON TO JAY.

PHILADELPHIA, April 9th, 1793.

MY DEAR SIR:

I have already written you by this post. A further question occurs—Would not a proclamation prohibiting our citizens from taking commissions on either side be proper?

Would it be well that it should include a *declaration of neutrality?* If you think the measure prudent, could you draught such a thing as you would deem proper? I wish much you could.

Truly, as ever,

A. HAMILTON.

JAY TO ALEXANDER HAMILTON.

NEW YORK, 11th April, 1793.

DEAR SIR:

Your letters of the 9th instant were this day delivered to me, as I was preparing to go out of town. The subject of them is important. I have not time to judge decidedly on some of the points. The enclosed will show what my present ideas of a proclamation are—it is hastily drawn—it says nothing about treaties—it speaks of neutrality, but avoids the expression, because in this country often associated with others. I shall be at Philadelphia on my way to Richmond. I think it better at present that too little should be said than too much. I would not receive any minister from a regent until he was *regent de facto ;* and therefore I think such intention should be inferable from the proclamation. Let us do everything that may be right to avoid war ; and if, without our fault, we should be involved in it, there will be little room for apprehensions about the issue.

It is happy for us that we have a President who will do nothing rashly, and who regards his own interest as inseparable from the public good.

Yours sincerely,

JOHN JAY.

DRAFT OF PROCLAMATION OF NEUTRALITY, BY JOHN JAY.[1]

Whereas every nation has a right to change and modify their constitution and government in such a manner as they may think most conducive to their welfare and happiness, and whereas a new form of government has taken place and actually exists in France, that event is to be regarded as the act of the nation until that presumption shall be destroyed

[1] See preceding letters. The proclamation as issued by Washington, April 22, 1793, which was more general and condensed than Jay's draft, appears in " Hamilton's Works," " American State Papers," etc.

by fact; and although certain circumstances have attended that revolution, which are greatly to be regretted, yet the United States as a nation have no right to decide on measures which regard only the internal and domestic affairs of others. They who actually administer the government of any nation are by foreign nations to be regarded as its lawful rulers so long as they continue to be recognized and obeyed by the great body of their people.

And whereas royalty has been in fact abolished in France, and a new government does there at present exist and is in actual operation, it is proper that the intercourse between this nation and that should be conducted through the medium of the government in fact, and although the misfortunes, to whatever cause they may be imputed, which the late King of France and others have suffered in the course of that revolution, or which that nation may yet experience, are to be regretted by the friends of humanity, and particularly by the people of America to whom both that king and that nation have done essential services, yet it is no less the duty than the interest of the United States strictly to observe that conduct towards all nations which the laws of nations prescribe.

And whereas war actually exists between France on the one side and Austria, Prussia, Great Britain, and the United Netherlands on the other; and whereas on the one hand we have abundant reason to give thanks unto Almighty God that the United States are not involved in that calamity, so on the other hand it is our duty by a conduct strictly neutral and inoffensive to cultivate and preserve peace, with a firm determination, nevertheless, always to prefer war to injustice and disgrace.

I do therefore most earnestly advise and require the citizens of the United States to be circumspect in their conduct towards all nations and particularly those now at war, to demean themselves in every respect in the manner becoming a nation at peace with all the world, and to unite in rendering thanks to a beneficial Providence for the peace and prosperity we enjoy, and devoutly to entreat the continuance of these invaluable blessings. I do expressly require that the citizens of the United States abstain from acting hostilely against any of the belligerent powers under commissions from either. Such conduct would tend to provoke hostilities against their country, and would in every respect be highly reprehensible; for while the people of all other states abstain from doing injury to any of our people, it would be unjust and wicked in any of our people to do injuries to them.

I do also enjoin all magistrates and others in authority to be watchful and diligent in preventing any aggressions from being committed against foreign nations and their people; and to cause all offenders to be prosecuted and punished in an exemplary manner. I do also recommend it to my fellow-citizens in general to omit such public discussions as may tend not only to cause divisions and parties among ourselves, and thereby impair that union on which our strength depends, but also give unnecessary cause of offence and irritation to foreign powers. And I cannot forbear expressing a wish that our printers may study to be impartial in the representation of facts, and observe much prudence relative to such strictures and animadversions as may render the disposition of foreign governments and rulers unfriendly to the people of the United States.

April 11th, 1793.

PRESIDENT WASHINGTON TO JAY.

PHILA., May 12th, 1793.

DEAR SIR,

Being informed by Col⁰· Hamilton (yesterday) that you propose to commence your Southern tour to-morrow, I take the liberty of enclosing you letters to gentlemen in the only places where I presume you will make any halt.

I have not added one to Governor Lee of Virginia, because I conceive you are well acquainted with him; nor have I done it to Govʳ· Lee of Maryland, because, unless you make a point of it to pass through Annapolis, it is considerably out of the post (and most direct) road.

I wish you (but you must expect the weather to grow warm) a pleasant journey, and safe return to your family and friends—being always, Dear Sir,

Your most Obedient
and Affectionate Servant,
G⁰· WASHINGTON.

JAY TO PRESIDENT WASHINGTON.

PHILADELPHIA, May 12, 1793.

MY DEAR SIR,

I really esteem myself very much obliged and honoured by your kind letter of this day, and those enclosed with it. It is a new mark of that attention to which I am so much indebted and of which I entertain a strong and grateful sense.

With perfect respect, esteem, and attachment, I am dear sir, your obliged and obedient servant,

JOHN JAY.

CHARGE TO GRAND JURY, RICHMOND, VIRGINIA.[1]

It is an observation no less useful than true, that nations and individuals injure their essential interests in proportion as they deviate from order. By order I mean that national regularity which results from attention and obedience to those rules and principles of conduct which reason indicates and which morality and wisdom prescribe. Those rules and principles reach every station and condition in which individuals can be placed, and extend to every possible situation in which nations can find themselves.

Among these rules are comprehended the laws of the land, and that they may be so observed as to produce the regularity and order intended by them, courts of justice were instituted whose business it is to punish offences and to render right to those who suffer wrong.

To inquire into and present those offences is the duty which the law generally imposes upon you, and, as there is a national tribunal having cognizance only of offences against the laws of the United States, your inquiries and presentments are to be confined to offences of that description.

[1] Delivered by the Chief Justice at the opening of the Circuit Court at Richmond, May 22, 1793.

The Constitution, the statutes of Congress, the laws of nations, and treaties constitutionally made compose the laws of the United States.

You will perceive that the object is twofold : To regulate the conduct of the citizens relative to our own nation and people, and relative to foreign nations and their subjects.

To the first class belong those statutes which respect trades, navigation, and finance, and those against forgery and counterfeiting and the other offences enumerated in what is generally called the penal statute ; to particularize and explain each of those would require details which on this occasion would be unnecessary. Among the most important are those which respect the revenue. Their object is to provide for the payment of debts already accrued, and to provide for the *current* and for the *contingent* expenses of the government and nation.

Justice and policy unite in declaring that debts fairly contracted should be honestly paid. On this basis only can public credit be erected and supported ; and they either want wisdom or virtue, or both, who regard fraud and chicane as a justifiable or useful instrument of policy. The man or the nation who eludes the payment of debts ceases to be worthy of further credit, and generally meets with deserts in the entire loss of it, and in the evils resulting from that loss. The current or ordinary expenses of our government are less than those of any other nation. What our extraordinary expenses may be cannot be foreseen and consequently cannot be calculated.

They will depend on events. A war would demand supplies which taxes alone cannot produce and for which recourse must be had to loans. The success of loans will always depend on our credit; and our credit will always be in proportion to our resources, to our integrity, and to our punctuality. All our citizens, therefore, are deeply interested in public credit. It is their duty to unite in preserving and supporting it; and it is your duty, gentlemen, to inquire into and present such violations of the revenue laws as you may find to have been committed within this district. It gives me pleasure to observe that the respect hitherto paid to those laws by our fellow-citizens in general has been exemplary and honourable to their virtue and patriotism. I hope the result of your inquiries will give additional force to this remark.

The present state of affairs requires that the second object of the laws should be attentively regarded. I mean those which regulate our conduct relative to foreign nations.

This head comprises the laws of nations and treaties.

By the laws of nations our conduct relative to other nations is to be regulated both in peace and in war. It is a subject that merits attention and inquiry, and it is much to be wished that it may be more generally studied and understood.

It may be asked who made the laws of nations? The answer is *he* from whose *will* proceed all moral obligations, and which *will* is made known to us by reason or by revelation.

Nations are, in respect to each other, in the same situation as independent individuals in a state of nature.

Suppose twenty families should be cast on an island and after dividing it between them conclude to remain unconnected with each other by any kind of government, would it thence follow that there are no laws to direct their conduct towards one another? Certainly not. Would not the laws of reason and morality direct them to behave to each other with respect, with justice, with benevolence, with good faith—would not those laws direct them to abstain from violence, to abstain from interfering in their respective domestic government and arrangements, to abstain from causing quarrels and dissensions in each other's families? If they made treaties, would they not be bound to observe them? Or if by consent expressed or implied they gave occasion to usages mutually convenient, would not those usages grow into conventional laws? The answer is obvious.

In like manner the nations throughout the world are like so many great families placed by Providence on the earth, who having divided it between them, remain perfectly distinct from and independent of each other. Between them there is no judge but the great Judge of all. They have a perfect right to establish such governments and build such houses as they prefer, and their neighbors have no right to pull down either because not fashioned according to their ideas of perfection; in a word, one has no right to interfere in the affairs of another, but all are bound to behave to each other with respect, with justice, with benevolence, and with good faith.

When two or more of them are at war about objects in which other nations are not interested, the latter are not to interfere except as mediators and friends to peace; but, on the contrary, ought to observe a strict impartiality towards both, abstaining from affording military aid of any kind or giving just cause of offence to either.

The United States are now in this situation relative to the belligerent powers. Strict impartiality is our duty in all cases where prior treaties do not stipulate for favours, and it is no less our interest than our duty to act accordingly. A just war is an evil, but it is not the greatest; oppression and disgrace are greater. War is not to be sought, but it is not to be fled from. Let us do exactly what is just and right, and then remain without fear, but not without care about the consequences. An unjust war is among the greatest of evils; and for this and numerous other reasons—because the blood and misery caused by it must rest on the heads of those who wage it.

I have mentioned respect among the duties which nations owe to each other. This merits attention. Every man owes it to himself to behave to others with civility and good manners; and every nation in like manner is obliged by a due regard to its own dignity and character to behave towards other nations with decorum. Insolence and rudeness will not only *degrade* and *disgrace* nations and individuals but also *expose* them to hostility and insult. It is the duty of both to cultivate peace and good-will and to this nothing is more conducive than justice, benevolence, and good manners. Indiscretions of this kind have given occasion to many wars.

If in this district you should find any persons engaged in fitting out privateers or enlisting men to serve against either of the belligerent powers, and in other respects violating the laws of neutrality, you will present them. Doubtful cases may arise ; on such occasions the attorney-general or the court will afford you the necessary assurance.

But the belligerent powers owe duties to us as well as we to them. They may violate our neutrality and commit offences. If you find any foreigners in this district committing seditious practices, endeavouring to seduce our citizens into acts of hostility, or attempting to withdraw them from the allegiance of the United States, present them. Such men are guilty of high misdemeanour.

A novel doctrine has been propagated and found some advocates even in this enlightened country— viz., that as citizens have a right to expatriate, so they have a right to engage and enlist in the military service of one of the powers at war, provided they at the same time declare that they expatriate. I make no remarks on this ridiculous doctrine—its absurdity is obvious.

Of national violations of our neutrality our government only can take cognizance. Questions of peace and war and reprisals and the like do not belong to courts of justice, nor to individual citizens, nor to associations of any kind, and for this plain reason : because the people of the United States have been pleased to commit them to Congress.

Are we then to punish our citizens for hostile conduct towards such of the belligerent powers as violate our neutrality and do us injustice ? This is a natural question.

There must be order in society or the bonds of it will soon be dissolved. This order consists in every man moving in his own sphere, doing the duties incumbent upon *him*, and not going out of the circle of his own rights and powers to meddle with or officiously supervise those of others.

The great question before mentioned being committed exclusively to Congress, they must be left to deliberate, and their decisions must be conclusive.

We have peace with France, Holland, Great Britain, and others, and in case of certain infractions and aggressions on their part the United States, or the department of the government to which they have delegated that authority, have a right to demand satisfaction, and in case of refusal, to declare war or to direct reprisals, or such other measures as circumstances may dictate. But it does not follow from the existence of such infractions that any other body or person in the United States have authority to do the like.

Such measures involve a variety of political considerations, such, for instance, as these : Is it advisable *immediately* to declare war ? Would it be more prudent first to remonstrate, or demand reparation, or direct reprisals? Are we ready for war? Would it be wise to risk it at this juncture, or postpone running that risk until we can be better prepared for it? These and a variety of similar considerations ought to precede and govern the decision of those who annul violated treaties, order reprisals, or declare war.

The nation must either move together or lose its force. Until war is constitutionally declared, the nation and all its members must observe and preserve peace, and do the duties incident to a state of peace. Such at present is our situation, and in that light, gentlemen, you will regard it. As free citizens we have a right to think and speak our sentiments on this subject, in terms becoming freemen—that is, in terms explicit, plain, and decorous. As judges and grand jurors, the merits of those political questions are without our province. Let us faithfully do the duties assigned to our stations. It is yours to inquire into and present all offences against the laws of the United States committed in the district or on the high seas by persons in it. We have the fullest confidence that you will discharge those duties with diligence and impartiality, and without fear, favour, affection, or respect to persons.

JAY TO MRS. JAY.

My Dear Sally : RICHMOND, 29th May, 1793.

The court is still sitting, and there is no probability of my leaving this place in less than ten days, if so soon. Much business remains to be done, and I cannot conjecture how much time it may take to finish it. One single cause has hitherto employed us, and it will not be finished, I fear, this week.[1] I mention these things to prevent your looking for me at too early a day. . . .

Yours affectionately,

JOHN JAY.

THOMAS JEFFERSON TO CHIEF-JUSTICE JAY AND ASSOCIATE JUSTICES.

PHILADELPHIA, July 18, 1793.

GENTLEMEN :

The war which has taken place among the powers of Europe produces frequent transactions within our ports and limits, on which questions arise of considerable difficulty, and of greater importance to the peace of the United States. These questions depend for their solution on the construction of our treaties, on the laws of nature and nations, and on the laws of the land, and are often presented under circumstances *which do not give a cognisance of them to the tribunals of the country.* Yet their decision is so little analogous to the ordinary functions of the executive, as to occasion much embarrassment and difficulty to them. The President therefore would be much relieved if he found himself free to refer questions of this description to the opinions of the judges of the Supreme Court of the United

---

[1] This doubtless was the case involving the question whether British debts were recoverable in Virginia under the Treaty of 1783, where acts of that State, passed prior to the adoption of the Constitution prohibited their recovery. The judges—Jay, Iredell, and Griffin—held that the debts were obligatory. On one point they disagreed—" whether payments already made into the loan office (by defendants) were not complete bars to the plaintiffs' action for so much as was paid." Jay held for the plaintiffs and his associates for the defendants.

States, whose knowledge of the subject would secure us against errors dangerous to the peace of the United States, and their authority insure the respect of all parties. He has therefore asked the attendance of such of the judges as could be collected in time for the occasion, to know, in the first place, their opinion, whether the public may, with propriety, be availed of their *advice on these questions?* And if they may, to present, for their advice, the abstract questions which have already occurred, or may soon occur, from which they will themselves strike out such as any circumstances might, in their opinion, forbid them to pronounce on. I have the honour to be with sentiments of the most perfect respect, gentlemen,

Your most obedient and humble servant,

THOS. JEFFERSON.

CHIEF-JUSTICE JAY AND ASSOCIATE JUSTICES TO PRESIDENT WASHINGTON.

PHILADELPHIA, 20th July, 1793.

SIR :

We have taken into consideration the letter written to us, by your direction, on the 18th inst., by the Secretary of State. The question, " whether the public may, with propriety, be availed of the advice of the judges on the questions alluded to," appears to us to be of much difficulty as well as importance. As it affects the judicial department, we feel a reluctance to decide it without the advice and participation of our absent brethren.

The occasion which induced our being convened is doubtless urgent ; of the degree of that urgency we cannot judge, and consequently cannot propose that the answer to this question be postponed until the sitting of the Supreme Court. We are not only disposed, but desirous, to promote the welfare of our country in every way that may consist with our official duties. We are pleased, sir, with every opportunity of manifesting our respect for you, and are solicitous to do whatever may be in our power to render your administration as easy and agreeable to yourself as it is to our country. If circumstances should forbid further delay, we will immediately resume the consideration of the question, and decide it.

We have the honour to be, with perfect respect, your most obedient and most humble servants.

CHIEF-JUSTICE JAY AND ASSOCIATE JUSTICES TO
PRESIDENT WASHINGTON.

PHILADELPHIA, 8th August, 1793.

SIR :

We have considered the previous question stated in a letter written by your direction to us by the Secretary of State on the 18th of last month, [regarding] the lines of separation drawn by the Constitution between the three departments of the government. These being in certain respects checks upon each other, and our being judges of a court in the last resort, are considerations which afford strong arguments against the propriety of our extra-judicially deciding the questions alluded to, especially as the power given by the Constitution to the President, of calling on the heads of departments for opinions, seems to have been *purposely* as well as expressly united to the *executive* departments.

We exceedingly regret every event that may cause embarrassment to your administration, but we derive consolation from the reflection that your judgment will discern what is right, and that your usual prudence, decision, and firmness will surmount every obstacle to the preservation of the rights, peace, and dignity of the United States.

We have the honour to be, with perfect respect, sir, your most obedient and most humble servants.

END OF VOLUME III.